In Quest of Livingstone

East Africa

South Atlantic Ocean

Area of Map

Indian Ocean

Sudan

Ethiopia

0   100   200 miles
0   200 kms

Uganda

L. Turkana

L. Albert

Kisangani

Kampala

L. Edward

Kenya

L. Kivu

L. Victoria

• Nairobi

Zaire

Tanzania

• Mombasa

L. Tanganyika

Tabora

Ujiji

• Ipole

Mpanda

Karema — Map 1

Dar es Salaam

Kasanga

L. Rukwa

L. Mweru

Mbala

Mporokoso

Map 2

• Luwingu

L. Malawi

L. Bangweulu

Chitambo's •
Village

Map 3

Malawi

Mozambique

Zambia

Lusaka •

Harare •

Zimbabwe

INDIAN OCEAN

HARVEY
(01786)841202

In Quest of
Livingstone

A Journey to the Four Fountains

Colum Wilson and Aisling Irwin

British Cataloguing in Publication Data
A catalogue record for this book is available from the British Library

ISBN 1-899863-53-2

First published by House of Lochar 1999

Typeset by XL Publishing Services, Tiverton, Devon
Printed in Great Britain by SRP Ltd, Exeter
for House of Lochar, Isle of Colonsay, Argyll PA61 7YR

Dedication

For Juliet and Ernie, and for Joan,
our beloved and long-suffering parents.
And for Cedric, Colum's late father,
who loved adventure
and would have approved, indubitably.

Contents

Maps and Illustrations

Maps provided by Harvey Map Services Ltd.

The photographs are located between pages 50 and 51

Foreword

David Livingstone was, in his own words, 'reduced to a skeleton', when he met H.M. Stanley at Ujiji in late 1871. He was in much better health four months later when Stanley left from Tabora, in present-day Tanzania, to tell the world 'How I Found Livingstone'. What was to be his final journey started from Tabora. Eight months later he and his companions had just reached Chitambo's village in today's Zambia when he died on 1st May 1873. He believed he was on the verge of finding the source of the Nile but in fact had been near the headwaters of the Congo. Livingstone had failed to trace the source of the Nile; he saw no end to the East African slave trade he so abhorred; missions he had sponsored had ended in disaster.

Soon, however, other travellers influenced by him would clarify the sources of the great African rivers. Five weeks after his death the treaty abolishing the East African slave trade was signed and the Zanzibar slave market shut down. Within the next few years many denominations started missions in Central Africa. From these have arisen indigenous Christian churches often linking different traditions. The period of colonial government offered opportunities for development, leaving an infrastructure for the independent self-governing countries which followed. Sadly they have had a troubled history and remain among the poorest countries of the world, crippled by the debts of previous development loans.

I spent some years working in a mission hospital in Zambia in colonial times and thirty years later took part in an expedition which followed my great grandfather's travels after his meeting with Stanley. Despite the great changes in Africa since Livingstone's day the continuity of so many aspects of traditional rural life is quite striking. Although Tanzania and Zambia had been through worse times I could see that much of the infrastructure of colonial days was poorly sustained.

Colum and Aisling, covering much the same route a few years later, pedalled and pushed their heavily laden bicycles, taking two months on their journey from Tabora to the Livingstone Monument. As far as possible they followed Livingstone's route and experienced some of the hazards which he encountered – shortages of food and water, tsetse flies, dusty, rutted tracks through the bush which turned into muddy torrents in the rains. Passing through villages and small towns on foot or bicycle is the way to see rural Africa – these are quite different from the towns to which so many of the people have migrated. As they followed the paths he trod, meeting people whose forebears he could have met, talking with overseas missionaries, local Christians and international aid workers, they read again Livingstone's journal entries and gained greater insight into his life and character.

Biographers have studied Livingstone from many different viewpoints – as a 'hero of missionary heroism', a geographer and scientist, a doctor, an unsuccessful missionary, a great man with flaws of character. How do Africans remember Livingstone 125 years after his death? Does the spirit of Livingstone exist in Africa today? *In Quest of Livingstone* tells the fascinating story of a hard but rewarding journey and the welcome received from people who live and work there – and it explores answers to these questions.

David Livingstone Wilson
Auchterarder
February 1999

About Livingstone

David Livingstone left his heart in Africa. One day in 1873, it was buried by faithful companions beneath a mpundu tree on the shores of a swampy lake. His death was the culmination of an obsessive quest for the source of the Nile, a mystical journey that had taken the old man through drought, near-starvation and, finally, into the marshes which border Lake Bangweulu in the depths of today's Zambia.

Livingstone had been seeking the elusive Four Fountains, the springs reputed by ancient philosophers to be the origin of the sacred river. During his last journey, the facets of his personality were laid bare with stark clarity: his solitary spirit, his unparalleled stoicism, his near-mystical faith, and the delusion which drove him on when another man would have turned back.

Saint to some, madman to others, Livingstone embodied much that defined the Victorian age. In Africa, where he spent most of his adult life, he evangelised and fought against the slave trade, and he recorded in detail the minutiae of God's natural world. He also indulged his interest in exploration and geography. These were fields in which his ambition knew no limits, even to the extent that it made him careless with other lives.

Born in 1813 into the industrial world of the cotton mills of Blantyre, near Glasgow, Livingstone had a harsh childhood. Through sheer determination and hard work he escaped his grim background and by the age of twenty-eight he was a medical missionary in Africa. He spent most of the ensuing twenty-three years there, engaged in exploits which brought him extraordinary fame – and which also plunged him into ignominy.

During his first sixteen-year posting as a missionary, his evangelical work was much publicised at home but actually had little effect in southern Africa. The feat for which he will be remembered was the crossing he made of the unknown continent from coast to coast, walking almost the entire course of the Zambezi river. He returned with stories of fertile uplands ripe for colonisation by a benevolent British people. Capitalising on a confident trading and missionary agenda, Livingstone returned to Africa a second time, at the head of an expedition whose purpose was to establish the Zambezi as a wide and navigable waterway into the interior.

The Zambezi expedition was a disaster. It was confronted by insuperable rapids, and his party disintegrated under his surly leadership. Before, Livingstone had found fame and acclamation in Britain. Now he returned home to notoriety and silence. Nevertheless, his exploits had caught the imagination of the British public by revealing that Africa was not the barren, uninhabitable place it was thought to be. He had drawn the attention of an avaricious world to a continent of massive, untapped potential. Imperialists of the next generation would invoke his name as they descended on Africa with motives both sacred and profane.

When Livingstone returned to Africa for the third and last time, his purpose was to document the slave trade and to search for the source of the Nile. After six years scouring the interior, the ailing fifty-eight-year-old might have perished had he not been found by a brash young journalist, in the celebrated meeting in Ujiji in 1871.

When Stanley left him, the explorer melted back into his beloved continent, never to be seen again by his compatriots. The eight-month journey he then began is one of the least-known episodes of Livingstone's life. It was a journey characterised by unprecedented suffering and self-discovery. There could not have been a more apt conclusion to the life of a man who was prepared to stretch the bounds of endurance for the sake of a dream.

Acknowledgements

There are many people, Tanzanian and Zambian, without whom our journey would have been difficult, if not impossible. We thank them for their help, and for the concern that they showed for our safety. Keith and Isobel Lilley bolstered us in numerous ways before our journey and retrieved us afterwards, thin and exhausted, in Dar es Salaam.

We would like to acknowledge the support we received with our research from the David Livingstone Centre in Blantyre, from the Royal Geographical Society in London, and from the Map Office in Dar es Salaam. Based on his interest in his ancestor, and on his own expeditions in East Africa, Dr David Livingstone Wilson was able to give us invaluable advice, for which we are very grateful.

Finally, thanks to our friends Michael Pockley, Mark Rogers, Claire Sanders-Smith, Vittoria D'Alessio, and Martin and Sophie Pearse for their useful comments and warm support.

Notes on the Text

For reasons of authenticity, Livingstone's journal entries have been left unaltered. The blanks which he left and which he intended to fill in later have been preserved, and his grammar and spelling have not been touched. His spellings of place names are often inconsistent – they are simply renditions of what he had heard. In many cases, his spellings differ from the modern spellings, although they remain easily recognisable. A full list of his spellings and today's equivalents can be found in the Appendix.

The names of most of the people we encountered have been changed and the locations and timings of several events have been altered.

1

London
by Aisling

So great was his fame amongst all classes of the British people, so powerful his influence on public opinion, and so far-reaching the effect of what he said and did on the destiny of Africa that he must be ranked among the greatest of the great Victorians.
Reginald Coupland, Professor of Colonial History at Oxford University, 1945.

'THERE is no such thing as a natural death.' The chief scowled. He was old. The hand that held the staff was quivering a little.

The interpreter continued: 'My father respectfully tells his guests that Dr Livingstone must have died from some other cause. There is no such thing as a natural death.'

Colum and I looked at each other. We thought we knew the story well. All contemporary reports and expert opinion said that Livingstone bled to death as a result of dysentery and piles, aggravated by atrocious hardship.

'May we suggest that the cold and the wet killed Livingstone?' I asked.

The young man translated. The chief tutted impatiently and shook his head. His withered courtiers murmured behind cupped hands.

'The chief says the cold and the wet may have helped him to die, but these were not the causes...' The interpreter paused, and then continued in a conciliatory tone: 'You see, the chief's grandfather met Dr Livingstone, so the chief knows. Dr Livingstone's body was feeble and his hair was grey. But he was sick... here.' The interpreter laid his hand across his left breast.

'In his chest?'

'No... no. In his heart...'

'In his heart?'

'Yes. There was something else. Something else made him die.' The son fell quiet, glancing apprehensively at the chief who regarded us with small, bright eyes.

'Something that was not natural... something that forced him to his death. You see, in Africa there is no such thing as a natural death....'

*   *   *

I first heard of Dr Livingstone when I was nine years old. Cross-legged on the cold linoleum at Sunday school I listened to the story of the missionary who roamed Africa, a land so overgrown that its tendrils dangled in the oceans. Dr Livingstone delivered slaves from their chains and saved the pagans from hellfire. He also cared for the jungle animals – or perhaps that was Dr Dolittle.

A decade later I absorbed my generation's embarrassment about its imperial past. I discovered that Dr Livingstone had only converted one African to Christianity, a chief who later lapsed. I learned that he drove his wife to alcohol and neglected his children. At first I was indignant, then uninterested – and then I forgot about him.

Ten years after that I married a man who wished he was a nineteenth-century explorer.

Colum claimed there were virtues to be found in Victorian men: physical bravery, single-mindedness, often moral courage. His admiration was unquestioning but then so was my cynicism.

Colum went to East Africa to work for a development charity, sleeping outside with only the stars for a blanket. Before he left we opened our atlas to search for Tabora, the town in Tanzania where his charity was based. It lay east of the Great Lakes in a bare region, shaded with the fierce orange that denotes the remote uplands of central East Africa. It was 950 kilometres from the coast and the brave spine of a colonial railway ran through it on its journey even farther west to Lake Tanganyika.

Tabora was where Livingstone had lived for a time, 125 years before. He was fifty-nine and, he wrote, '*very old and shaky… cheeks fallen in… the mouth almost toothless*'.

It was from near Tabora that the old man one day began a long journey to the south in search of the answer to the great riddle of Africa, a puzzle that had haunted men and women for millennia. He was hunting for the source of the Nile. Livingstone was sure that he would find the Nile's origins, for his inspiration came not just from geography but from God and from the testimonies of the Ancients. But he failed in his quest.

He sought the Nile for eight months. He edged around mountains, waded through swamps, suffered in the heat and then suffered worse in the rains. He grew weaker and weaker and, finally, he began to bleed to death. He died on the shores of a swampy lake where they buried his heart, under a mpundu tree.

We formed a plan. When Colum finished his work we would pursue Livingstone from Tabora to where he died. We would recreate his last journey, bring his writings to life, search for his spirit amongst the mud villages and in the wilderness. A hundred and twenty five years after he had trodden there, we would look for his footprints.

Colum hurried to the Royal Geographical Society in London, the wood-panelled shrine to explorers' victories over the natural world. In the holy silence of its map room he found a yellowing chart, dated 1874, drawn up from measurements gleaned from Livingstone's notes after his death.

At home we unfolded new maps of East Africa. A spill of modern colours, they outshone the single, black and white photocopy from the Royal Geographical Society. But it was that chart which gripped us. We followed its sketchy markings, defiant threads of knowledge on a background of pure, ignorant whiteness. Dribbles of information spread from the line that marked Livingstone's route. Rivers he had crossed extended tiny creepers to each side but soon expired just as his knowledge of them did. Contours suffered a similar fate. Any feature that fell outside Livingstone's narrow beam had been non-existent to the geographers back home.

Livingstone travelled south-west from Tabora. We would follow him along dirt tracks and paths until we reached the shores of Lake Tanganyika. There, we would turn south with him, clinging to the shoreline until we reached the lake's tip in northern Zambia. Livingstone then turned west before striking south towards Lake Bangweulu. As his path became circuitous and unclear, we would trace his route through the swamplands. It had taken Livingstone more than eight months, a journey of a thousand kilometres.

Even today large-scale maps of Tanzania and Zambia can be hard to find. For Zambia we had to rely on black and white copies of maps published in the 1960s some of which seemed to be hand-drawn. I lingered over one which portrayed a region somewhere north-west of Lake Bangweulu where the old man died. While I could visualise fishing villages, or Lake Tanganyika, or mountains smothered in scrubby jungle coverings, my imagination stalled at those empty flatlands where Livingstone wrote in his journal of the ethereal call of the fish eagle. There were hardly any markings on the whole expanse of that single map, just a grid imposed on nothing. The gasping loneliness of the place was captured in a single dotted line which began from nothing about an inch from the top of the map, wandered south for thirty kilometres and then vanished.

In the mid-nineteenth century the centre of Africa was as much an emptiness on European maps as it had been in the days of Ancient Greece. When Livingstone entered the region, and discovered that the mythical barren loneliness was in reality vibrant with rivers, trees, animals and people, it was as if a man had been put into space. When he died decades later he was a hero. Crowds gathered in Southampton before dawn to watch his coffin arrive from Africa on the deck of a steamship. Twenty-one gun salutes crackled through the air.

Such popularity arose from the richness of Livingstone's character. He was the natural historian, the geologist, the geographer, the explorer, the missionary, the campaigner against slavery, the working class man who mingled with the English and Scottish establishment.

But he was more than this. He moulded his ideas and interests into a mission, a manifesto for Africa. Generations of missionaries, traders and warmongers would later justify their descent on Africa with the invocation of his name. He was their icon because he had articulated a programme for the economic invasion of Africa based on a foundation of Christian ethics, and on the belief that exporting British values and culture to Africa was a moral duty.

They buried his body in Westminster Abbey in an exalted position at the centre of the nave. You can read its polished brass lettering if you peer through the persistent shuffle of tourists' feet:

> *Brought by Faithful Hands over land and sea here rests David Livingstone*
>   *Missionary, Traveller, Philanthropist*
>   *Born 19th March 1813*
>   *Died 1st May 1873 at Chitambo's village, Ulala*
>   *For 30 years his life was spent in an unwearied effort to evangelise the native races, to explore the undiscovered secrets, to abolish the desolating slave trade of Central Africa. Where with his last words he wrote: 'All I can add in my solitude is may heaven's rich blessing come down on every one, American, English or Turk, who will help to heal this open sore of the world.'*

No one could have devised a more symbolic manner of death for Livingstone. He died in the heart of the continent to which he had dedicated his life, far from any other white man – just as he had always preferred to be. He died in action, at the boundary of human endurance, driven as always by obsession. He died, so they say, in an attitude of prayer.

*   *   *

A few weeks before Colum left for Tanzania we visited Blantyre, the village in Lanarkshire where Livingstone lived as a boy, and where there is now a museum devoted to him. It occupies the old tenement in which he grew up, sharing a single room with his parents and four siblings. Once it was a rotten place where he endured the toughest of childhoods, working in the local cotton mill. Now Blantyre is just outside Glasgow and the museum is its jewel. The tenement's whitewashed walls sparkle in the cold Scottish sunlight. Its dimmed interiors have become a shrine to Livingstone's life, adorned with curiosities, from the microscope with which he made his prolific studies of nature to a wooden yoke which he is said to have removed from the neck of a slave.

Yet there is a sense of unease in Blantyre. The neat old lady in the museum gift shop put Colum's change into his cupped palm. She hesitated, her fingers touching his, and the creases of her powdery face tightened a little: 'You will treat him nicely in your book won't you?' she asked, her kind eyes as intense as watery eyes can be.

High on a bookstand behind her a brooding image of Livingstone glowered down from the cover of a revisionist biography written by Tim Jeal in the 1970s. The book, meticulously researched, tears Livingstone apart, before putting him back together as a flawed, if brilliant, individual. Blantyre's luminary is accused of a grievous negligence in Africa which led to the deaths of several young missionaries and their families. He is charged with an insane and irresponsible over-optimism which drew a bishop to his death in the Shire Highlands of East Africa. He is reproached for his indifference to the sufferings of his fellow European travellers, including his wife and children. Even the death of Livingstone's baby is revealed to be the result of his callous lack of care of his pregnant wife. Worst of all, the author accuses Livingstone of emerging from these disasters in a manner that was calculated to fulfil a single end – the protection of his own reputation in Britain.

In a back room at the David Livingstone Centre we stared at three small, leather-bound books in which Livingstone recorded his last journey. They had survived months in Livingstone's tin box, they had bobbed around in leaking canoes and been lifted high above the heads of porters crossing numerous rivers: they had been beside him when he died. I edged the first one open to reveal crabbed handwriting which grew more spidery with weakness. Little phrases caught my eye. I already knew them well from the uniform typeface of the published version, but reading them again now, in the writer's own hand, transformed his prose into a vivid human experience.

We were searching for the passages that Livingstone's editor, the anti-slavery campaigner Horace Waller, had thought it prudent to omit when he published the journals in 1874. Curiously, when Livingstone mentioned that he was '*ill with bowels*', Waller had excised the biological term and replaced it with 'old complaint'. Waller's principal omissions, however, were Livingstone's obsessive rantings – against the Foreign Office, against his old friends, against rival explorers he believed were also hunting for the Nile, and against the miscellany of humankind who had offended him during his life, some of them decades before. They were bitter passages, the product of a mind that had turned in on itself.

Already our study of the man had evoked in us emotions ranging from adoration to loathing. Wherever we turned, a different image gazed back at us – saint, tyrant, visionary, egotist. It was not, by any means, a whole picture that we saw. It was more as if we had thrown an oblique light on his character, picking out some features brightly, while leaving much more in shadow. It was not until we followed his footsteps and, intimately, each entry in the diary he kept until his death, that we found the kernel of the man – and felt we could understand him.

*   *   *

As we tried to plot the route on modern maps it seemed as if the African bush had sprung back over Livingstone's path. He measured and recorded his position most days despite fatigue and hunger. Yet somehow Africa refused to be trapped on paper.

Livingstone recorded the names of the chiefs he met and of the villages through which he passed. But villages of mud and straw slip easily away, or shift with the rains, with the fecundity of the soil, with tribal allegiances or with the desecration of war. Near Lake Bangweulu he describes a village of just two huts, perched on an ant hill to escape the encroaching swamp and mud of the rainy season. Within months of his passing the 'village' would have dissolved into the water.

Africa is fickle. She can alter her appearance with the seasons and suddenly travellers are lost. With a blast of rain she floods a lake so that its islands vanish and it is twice its former size. She scorches the life out of the soil and starves the traveller, who wanders distracted until judgement ebbs away. Africa has a thousand ways of undermining the records. Once, with a small earthquake, she jarred Livingstone's precious chronometer and, as a result, his longitudes were wrong. And so she sends the traveller home with records awry: in places we will never know exactly where Livingstone trod.

We discovered these exasperating problems in the Royal Geographical Society during days spent trying to trace Livingstone's route. Even fifty years after his death, when geographers produced the first gazetteer of East Africa, only a handful of the 130 villages he mentioned still existed.

But eventually we found a landmark that is etched more permanently onto Africa – her rivers. They are described in abundance in Livingstone's journals because his men and livestock had often confronted them. His two closest companions, Suzi and Chuma, carried their failing leader on their shoulders through the rivers when he was weak and losing blood but, despite his illness, he noted them all: '*Eight yards wide and thigh deep... 100 yards wide and waist deep... 300 yards wide and thigh deep... 2000 feet broad and the main stream came up to Suzi's mouth*'. Many of them are smaller now but their names remain the same and so, by working out the order in which he encountered them, we were able to identify a corridor through which Livingstone must have travelled. For much of the time we would tread exactly on his path. Where the route was hazy, we would never be more than twenty-five kilometres away.

The remaining question was how we should travel – what would best accompany the slow trudging of an old man who had with him sixty native porters, a basic supply of food and medicine, and a few cows and donkeys? To walk was out of the question – the water sources have dwindled since Livingstone's day and are now too far apart for anyone to pursue his exact route on foot. And we did not relish bringing pack animals to die among the tsetse in the first few weeks, as Livingstone's did.

Authenticity was all-important; but it was a word that had a hundred shades of meaning. For me authenticity lay in searching the same landscape through which Livingstone walked in order to understand his legacy, but for Colum the concept was more precise. For him authenticity lay in the geographical and physical challenge of discovering and pursuing Livingstone's route with the greatest possible precision. To do this we had to be free to pass into the depths of the land, not knowing when we would return to a road.

Bicycles were the answer: they would be our pack-animals. We could carry them, push them, haul them over rivers and up mountains – they would carry more water than we could ever carry alone. On remote footpaths they would speed us between water sources, opening routes to us that would otherwise be closed.

There was only one obstacle that could not be tackled by bicycle. Strangely, it was a rare stretch of track rather than a mountain or swamp. It looked on the map like a four-day cycle ride with only one water source along the way, at a place marked 'Koga'. It would not be possible to carry enough liquid. Reluctantly we predicted that we might be forced to accept a lift along the Koga track – but the rest of the journey we would do ourselves.

Colum left for Tanzania. Later in the year I joined him in Dar es Salaam, on the shores of the Indian Ocean.

2

To Tabora by Train

by Aisling

*I beg to direct your attention to Africa. I know that in a few years I shall
be cut off in that country, which is now open; do not let it be shut again.*
David Livingstone, in a lecture to Cambridge University, 1857

WITHIN the peeling colonial buildings of Dar es Salaam railway station
you can buy a ticket for one of the great train journeys of the world. Three
times a week the battered carriages slither westwards into the bush. They
halt 1,300 kilometres later at Kigoma station, their over-heated occupants
having been scattered among the villages of the flatlands along the way.

I stood bewildered at the station's single platform on an island of boxes
and cases while Colum sorted out paperwork with the '*steshenmasta*'. Colum
had darted easily into the confusion, inured by months of experience in
Tanzania. In contrast I watched, dazed, as the kaleidoscopic population
drifted towards the train. It was a long walk. Far away, where the platform
finished, the train waited, inexplicably, in the wilderness.

Humanity eddied past me, a stream around a lonely rock. Some
passengers were spotless townies off to visit rural families. Others were
villagers returning from a big trip to the capital with mysterious packages
and tales of the city for their wide-eyed relatives. Women slapped the
ground with heavy, flip-flopped feet, bags sitting easily on their heads and
inert babies bound to their backs by cloths pulled so tightly that it was a
wonder they could breathe. Often the women would pause to rest on their
way, gathering their big wraps and knotting them with new firmness around
their waists.

Barefoot boys spilled around the adults, their eager, chestnut faces
focused in tight concentration. They were working. They called at the
throng to buy their white sliced bread; their boiled eggs; their bottles of
Glacier water 'produced under strict supervision and in most hygienic
environment'; and bottles of the most honestly named soft drink in the
world – 'Chemi-Cola'.

With a screech the train began a complicated shunting in and out of the station to pick up carriages. Those who had not scrambled onto it while it was in the wilderness turned wearily to follow it back. During one of the train's sojourns at the platform Colum emerged from the crowd and we boarded, hauled our luggage out of the rabble and into our cabin and locked the door. At exactly 6pm the train creaked out of the capital. Corrugated slums became surburban concrete houses, which gave way in turn to huts of mud and straw. We were clattering at fifty kilometres an hour into Africa. Tree branches loaded with huge hollow seeds dangled briefly through the window and exotic vegetation clawed at the flanks of the train. Occasionally I glimpsed a small path with a solitary mudbrick hut at the end.

Sometimes the horn would sound announcing our imminent arrival at a village. With a grinding of brakes and a jolt we would halt at a sprinkling of huts, hens and children. Boys and girls would crowd under the high windows thrusting up coconuts, mugfuls of water and earthenware pots. Old women with cavernous faces worked their way down the trackside pleading for alms, while boys led tottering blind men and shouted for money on their behalf. I would step back into the shadow of the carriage, afraid of attracting the attention of these desperate old folk. For the few minutes granted them by the train driver the villagers would frantically sell or beg. Then the great horn would sound again, and the train would heave itself away, leaving the storm to subside until next time.

Gradually the trees became silhouettes against a cobalt sky. Pinprick stars appeared. We clattered on westwards towards a shred of red cloud that marked where the sun had set, and at last we retired in the warm darkness to our bunk-beds. From time to time through the night the train stopped. Then, to the murmur of night-time voices, I would crawl to the window to witness a lone building, and an unknown name painted on a wall.

Morning was a fleeting coolness. We had awoken to find that the landscape had become flat and dead – scrawny bush sometimes interrupted by wide, dry river beds pock-marked with muddy holes dug by women in search of water. Men on bicycles paused to watch us trundle past. Once there was a cloud of earth kicked up by a herd of bony cattle which looked as if they were on their way back to the dust from which they came.

This African world had hardly changed since Livingstone's day. But the European world from which we came had moved on – we entered Africa with more security than he had ever known. We could purify water. Livingstone drank fetid brews that sickened and ultimately helped to kill him: '*I have drunk water swarming with insects, thick with mud and putrid with rhinoceros urine and buffaloes' dung, and no stinted draughts of it either.*' Against the malevolent mosquito we had sprays, creams, coverings, nettings and tablets. Livingstone knew nothing of bacteria or insect-borne diseases. He had a medical education that was a hindrance, based on theories that illness was caused by excessive heat or by inflammation of the veins.

The London Missionary Society had equipped him with Latin, Greek, Hebrew and Theology as evangelising tools. They were disciplines which were also spectacularly useless for the missionary life he had chosen. The only skills that would be of use to him had developed long before, during his childhood in the sapping heat of the cotton mills of Blantyre. Those early experiences had exposed in him an extraordinary self-discipline and fearful powers of endurance.

Morning evaporated and our cabin grew hot. A fan whirred but there was little new air for it to circulate. The many tasks we had planned for the train journey seemed increasingly onerous and I collapsed back into a corner, watched the dry land for a little, and imagined how Livingstone must have felt when he first saw Africa.

He left Britain at the end of 1840, aged twenty-seven, bound for a missionary posting in Kuruman, a 950-kilometre journey by ox wagon from Cape Town. He had been sent to build a new evangelising station and to remain there, perhaps forever, ministering to the local people.

But soon after he arrived in Africa he realised the truth about the African missions: the stories he had been told of mass conversions to Christianity were propaganda put out by the Society in order to raise funds. Even in Kuruman, where the distinguished preacher Robert Moffat had lived for twenty years, only two Africans were won to Christianity each year – and each year one African was lost again.

A second revelation came more slowly. With a relativism more characteristic of a later generation he admired the Africans and understood their resistance to Christianity. '*Africans are not by any means unreasonable,*' he was later to write. '*I think unreasonableness is more a hereditary disease in Europe than in this land.*'

His attitude was typical of the broad-mindedness he consistently showed towards the local people. It was a generosity of heart that allowed him to excuse in them all manner of misdemeanours. When travelling, Livingstone showed extraordinary tolerance towards African porters who mistreated his pack animals. Later, when most of his porters abandoned him at one of his bleakest hours, he showed even greater forbearance. '*I did not blame them very severely in my own mind,*' he wrote. '*They were tired of tramping, and so verily am I... Consciousness of my own defects makes me lenient.*'

He also grasped more acutely than others that the Africans had social systems which fitted the exigencies of tribal life. He realised, however, that those systems were inimical to Christianity. Despite his cultural empathy

Livingstone was foremost a religious absolutist. His insight showed him that local cultures would have to be destroyed if Christianity was to succeed.

This first venture into Africa was to last sixteen years, and during the first few of them Livingstone was torn by a conflict between duty and desire. His contract committed him to the dull and generally futile job of static preaching, which, he increasingly saw, would mean a life of tedious insignificance. On the other hand he harboured a growing passion to explore Africa. Exploration was adventure, the potential of Africa lay in new discoveries. And there were other reasons why he wanted to set out on his own. He had become a quarrelsome man. A loner's life in the unexplored interior would suit both his talents and his flaws.

Ultimately Livingstone found a way to combine his passion and his duty by creating for himself a new role. He would be a missionary prospector, an advance party searching for suitable places where those who followed could work. *'I would never build on another man's foundation,'* he wrote. *'I shall preach the Gospel beyond every other man's line of things.'* The idea was to infuse his life's work.

He spent the rest of those sixteen years pestering at the northern fringes of British knowledge of southern Africa, justifying his efforts with the vague idea that he was searching for healthy lands where missions could be founded. His journeys were studded with evangelical failures – tribes people howled with laughter at his psalm-singing, and once, he mistakenly preached the word of 'rain' rather than the word of 'God'. These setbacks only served to drive him farther north.

At last, in a glorious finale that was to bring him eternal fame, he achieved a feat never before accomplished by a European. Enduring drought, disease, and hostile natives, and stumbling amongst the bloodshed and terror of slave-raiding, he crossed the Dark Continent from west to east. In doing so he walked almost the entire course of the Zambezi river.

He returned to Britain a famous man, 'a truly apostolic preacher of Christian truth', according to one newspaper which continued: 'Seldom have savage nations met with the representative of English Civilisation in such a shape... Europe had always heard that the central regions of southern Africa were burning solitudes, bleak and barren, heated by poisonous winds, infested by snakes and only roamed over by a few scattered tribes of untameable barbarians. But Dr Livingstone found himself in a high country, full of fruit trees, abounding in shade, watered by a perfect network of rivers.'

Livingstone's visionary powers were at their height and he used his new fame to gather support for an ambitious manifesto for Africa. The magnificent river he had followed – the Zambezi – was at the core of his dream. He perceived it to be a wide and navigable waterway stretching far into Africa's interior, a river that one day would bustle with British merchants trading for ivory, gold and other raw materials. British colonists would settle on healthy uplands surrounding the river. Britain would prosper, and the colonists would benefit Africa '*as members of a superior race and servants of a Government that desires to elevate the more degraded portions of the human family.*'

Livingstone believed that philanthropic British businessmen had nothing less than a divine obligation to annex parts of Africa and improve it through Commerce and Christianity, a popular Victorian formula. Commerce would undermine tribal organisation, creating the social confusion necessary to plant the seeds of the religion. *Legitimate* commerce, as he called it, would also remove another bitter obstacle to missionary success: the slave trade. The tribes with which Livingstone had mixed were all involved, raiding subservient tribes to maintain a supply of human merchandise for the Arabs. Livingstone argued that the pervasive grip of the slave trade would weaken only in the face of other, equally lucrative commerce.

With these missionary and trading agendas he won the confidence of his British audiences and soon he had organised a new expedition. On this, his second journey to Africa, he was to travel to the mouth of the Zambezi and see how far he could ascend it by boat.

But on the Zambezi expedition, Livingstone was plunged into disaster by the very characteristics which had driven him to the pinnacle of his career. He had been optimistic to the point of fantasy about what could be achieved. In reality the Zambezi was a treacherous waterway and the surrounding lands were infested with disease. The local people were so brutalised by slave raiding that peaceful trading or missionary work were out of the question. Yet, even when the futility had become obvious to the other members of Livingstone's party, he still refused to face the truth himself.

As morale drained away and as fever killed several of his party, the expedition gradually disintegrated under Livingstone's brooding leadership. When he returned to Britain it was to silence and disgrace. The child of the satanic mills had scaled the mountain of heroism and marched on down the other side into notoriety.

Africa the seductress, beckoning the credulous white man to his salvation – or to his doom. I opened the train window as far as I could and watched the long maroon body slide round a low escarpment. Below, the land stretched away, empty, bleached and flat. The only relief to the eye came from scrubby patches of greenery on the grey earth and, once, from a lone man standing in the blankness watching us.

A cluster of abandoned corrugated iron huts appeared, a gleaming railway work camp designed, apparently, to be as unbearably hot as possible. We were in a similar hut – our cabin was a small cupboard in an iron box on wheels. My final action that afternoon was to reach up and switch off the fan which had blasted us with heat until we were nauseous. Colum's bicycle maintenance manual fell to the floor, his head sank towards his chest. After nineteen hours the magic of Africa had gone. Beyond the window the sun clung to the height of the sky and poured its white heat onto a land where there were no shadows – just the low trees, coarse grass, and scrawny profusion of tangled plants that is the African bush. Nothing delicate could survive in such a country: could Livingstone's spirit, indomitable though it was, have left its trace?

The Zambezi expedition altered him forever. Physically he was weakened by malaria, dysentery and haemorrhoids – swollen anal veins that would bleed at the smallest provocation. Emotionally he was battered too. He had more than the deaths of his compatriots on his conscience – his unhappy and alcoholic wife had also died on the Zambezi expedition. Her death left him penitent: '*There are many regrets that will follow me to my dying day*,' he wrote to his mother. Later he also wrote remorseful letters to his children.

Yet in spite of all these setbacks, he left for Africa again in 1865 – where else could he go? '*I don't know whether I am to go on the shelf or not*,' he wrote to his brother, Charles. '*If I do, I make Africa the shelf.*' Africa was his theatre. It was where he had become 'amongst the greatest of the great' as well as where he had fallen from grace. The means of his resurrection lay only in Africa and, Livingstone began to believe, it lay at the continent's heart. He determined to win back his reputation as Britain's supreme explorer by finding the answer to the greatest geographical riddle of Africa – the source of that ancient river, the Nile.

Livingstone believed he was the only man who knew where the Nile arose, and he began to think that with the discovery of that spring would come an abundance of good. He would be fêted again, above other explorers such as Baker, and Burton and Speke, who argued so acrimoniously about the Nile's source. He would prove that Biblical references to the Nile were true, and in doing so he would strengthen the acceptance of God's word.

Another journey into the interior would also push forward his moral programme for Africa. Livingstone's plans had been severely damaged and he had wearily concluded that Christianity and Commerce could not take root in Africa until the ruthless and bloody traffic in humans had been banished altogether. He now knew that the Arab slaving caravans penetrated deep into East Africa. Every year twenty thousand men, women and children, pinned in slaving forks, emerged at the coast. They were destined for the slave market on the island of Zanzibar, off the East African coast.

If Livingstone could gather evidence of these atrocities, he might persuade the government to pressurise the Zanzibar Sultan to put an end to the trade. Then the real work could begin. So Livingstone wove his passions together and argued that the heart of the Arab slave trade lay exactly where a journey to the Nile's source would take him. '*The Nile sources,*' he said, '*are valuable only as a means of enabling me to open my mouth with power among men.*'

His third and final trek through Africa was to last seven years. He had set off in exhilaration but soon his troubles began. The last journey was to be one of almost unmitigated suffering.

Livingstone landed on the east coast of Africa at the River Ruvuma, which marks what is today the border between Tanzania and Mozambique. He spent the next five years journeying with increasing frustration amongst the rivers and lakes of the central African watershed. His porters absconded; he lost his medicine chest; slave-raiding was rife and severely restricted his mobility and his procurement of food. Livingstone's stores ebbed away so that he became destitute and, at times, dangerously ill. He bled profusely from his haemorrhoids.

Finally Livingstone accepted help from the very Arabs whose activities he so detested. It was a questionable move, but the truth was that without their help he was impotent. Travelling for a while with their well-supplied caravans he could both pursue his geographical interests and witness the slave trade, writing some of his most moving dispatches:

'*The strangest disease I have seen in this country seems really to be broken-heartedness,*' he wrote, '*and it attacks free men who have been captured and made slaves.*' The afflicted, he said, '*ascribed their only pain to the heart, and placed the hand correctly on the spot.*'

It was at this time, in a peaceful market town west of Lake Tanganyika, that Livingstone had perhaps the most momentous experience of his life. He witnessed a massacre so gratuitous and so bloody that his reports nudged the wavering British government into taking action that led to the closure of the Zanzibar slave market the following year. Livingstone never lived to hear of this, his greatest achievement.

Only one white man ever saw Livingstone again after he disappeared into Africa in 1866. Henry Morton Stanley, the explorer and journalist, discovered him, penniless and weak, in Ujiji, a village on the eastern shores of Lake Tanganyika. Stanley nursed Livingstone back to relative health and tried to persuade him to return to Britain with him, but Livingstone refused. He had to go on; he had to find the source of the Nile.

Perhaps the ailing fifty-nine-year-old perceived his life to have been a failure: he had made no Christian converts; built no highway into the interior; struck no significant blows against the slave trade as far as he knew. He had even failed as a husband and as a father. But ahead lay the possibility of geographical and moral success – and rehabilitation in his homeland.

Stanley promised to send Livingstone supplies. Then he left him. Livingstone lived for a while amongst the Arabs in Unyanyembe near Tabora and then melted back into Africa, never to be seen by white men again.

One of the principal arteries of the slave trade was almost exactly the route we were following in the train. One hundred and twenty-five years earlier this journey would have been undertaken in a large convoy for fear of attack. Bearers would have tramped for weeks through the heat, losing some of their group to malaria along the way. Cholera would have jumped across from Zanzibar and chased its victims along the slave routes.

Now, in the comfort of a first class cabin on this twentieth-century machine, the trip was as easy as a long journey in East Africa could be. Yet it had left me exhausted and I realised I was soft; I could never emulate the valour of Livingstone. I foresaw that over the next few months there would be no energy for thought or for questions. Colum – physically strong, used to Africa – would drive our expedition onwards while I would be an encumbrance, as obstinate as a donkey and as drained as a dog panting in the shade.

Log Book Extract

DAY 0 – Monday 24th November

FINAL DAY OF PREPARATION IN TABORA
   Staying in cheap hotel.

DISTANCE CYCLED : None

BICYCLES: Fine tuning of brakes. Familiarisation with rear wheel
   sprocket, gear shift mechanism. Packing of spare parts and toolkit.

WEATHER: Heavy rain pm is ominous.

HEALTH: Aisling a bit sick, probably due to the heat and change in
   diet. No temperature.

EQUIPMENT: Final check on equipment list and purchase of sundry
   items including an aluminium pan, two mugs, assorted nuts, bolts and
   jubilee clips, a machete and cooker fuel. In some doubt about
   whether to take sleeping bags. In the end, we decided to take one
   only, with two thin foam mattresses.

   Trial run with the specially-made water filtration bags was not
   successful: it took all night to filter half a litre as the canvas is too
   thick. We will have to rely on iodine, chlorine tablets and the filter
   pump. Testing of cooker, water filter pump. Minor damage sustained
   to both.

EXPENDITURE: 6,500 Tanzanian Shillings (TSh) on last bits of
   equipment. (EXCHANGE RATE: £1 = Tsh1,000 approximately)

COMMENT: Broad planning of Phase 1, which will take us from here
   to Mpanda across Livingstone's 'Flat Forest'. It should take us 13
   days, including 4 rest days. Detailed planning of first three days'
   journey. We estimate that we can carry sufficient food for two days,
   or three days at a push, although Colum says that water is going to
   be the problem in Phase 1. Wrote letter to British Embassy in Dar
   with finalised route.

   Some difficulty deciding on where to store our money and
   travellers' cheques. In the end, we have divided it between our
   bicycle frames (in the handlebars), in secret pockets sewn into the
   inside of our shirts, in the hem of Colum's tee-shirt and in our boots
   in tough plastic bags.

   Packing of equipment into panniers: a very tight fit. We are taking
   a tin of cocoa and a small tin of cheese as special luxuries.

Note:
   mzungu (Swahili) = foreigner (plural *wazungu*)
   hoteli = restaurant

LIVINGSTONE: Making final preparations. Livingstone left a case of
   powdered milk behind – something which he was later to regret. We
   made sure ours went in.

3

From Tabora to Ipole
by Colum

Geographers on Afric Maps
With savage Pictures fill their Gaps
O'er uninhabitable Downs
Place Elephants for want of Towns.
Jonathan Swift

THROUGH June, July and August 1872, Livingstone waited at Tabora and fretted. Stanley had left for the coast in May, promising to despatch men and equipment from there to allow Livingstone to continue his explorations. But for Livingstone, who believed he had the source of the Nile so nearly in his grasp, time passed painfully slowly. *'Weary waiting this, and the best time for travelling passes over unused... I can think of nothing but "when will these men come?". Sixty days was the period named, now it is eighty-four.'*

At last, on 9th August, he was able to write: *'I do most devoutly thank the Lord for His goodness in bringing my men near to this... how thankful I am I cannot express.'* And within a few days he was making final preparations. In the words of his publisher Horace Waller: '... all is pounding, packing, bargaining, weighing and disputing among the porters.'

The scribbled lists in Livingstone's notebooks reflect the formidable logistics behind an African expedition. The bulk of his luggage was calico, beads and brass wire for bartering with tribesmen. In addition, there were assorted cases of pots and pans, and boxes of the foodstuffs unobtainable in the interior – wheat flour, coffee, tea and sugar. His party also carried string, a toolbox, a case of candles, and a medical kit. Livingstone's personal possessions included his tent – with tar for its re-waterproofing, a bed, and two tin boxes which held his precious notes. His sextant and chronometers were packed separately. He divided the pile of equipment into equal loads of fifty pounds, and distributed them among the fifty-seven members of his party.

*　　*　　*

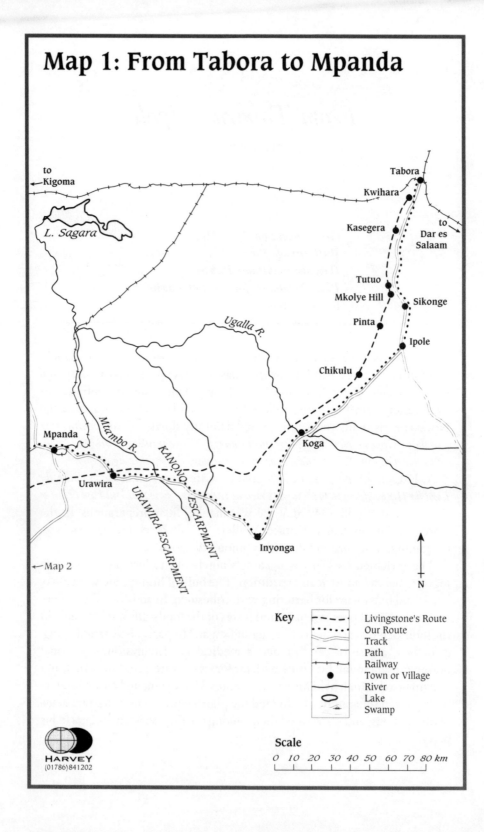

Map 1: From Tabora to Mpanda

to
Kigoma

L. Sagara

Tabora
Kwihara

Kasegera

to
Dar es
Salaam

Tutuo
Mkolye Hill   Sikonge

Pinta

Ugalla R.   Ipole

Chikulu

Mpanda

Mtambo R.

KANONO ESCARPMENT   Koga

Urawira

URAWIRA ESCARPMENT

←Map 2

Inyonga

N

Key

- – – – – Livingstone's Route
- • • • • • Our Route
- ——— Track
- – – – Path
- —+—+— Railway
- ● Town or Village
- River
- Lake
- Swamp

Scale

0 10 20 30 40 50 60 70 80 km

HARVEY
(01786)841202

In a Tabora hotel room with a dusty concrete floor, we organised and reorganised our expedition equipment. Helplessly, I watched as our pile of luggage grew. Even with dollar bills and Tanzanian shillings in place of Livingstone's bulky trading goods, it was difficult to see how we were going to fit everything into four large bicycle panniers.

For a start, there was our medical kit – it would take up almost a full pannier on its own. Then there were the books we considered indispensable – Livingstone's journal and our logbook, history books and a Swahili dictionary. We also had to find room for twenty-eight assorted maps. Scattered around were spare clothing, the tent, pegs and poles. The intervening spaces were cluttered with oddments which were of negligible size, but altogether of substantial bulk – the camera film, the flyspray, our spare socks, fifty-two spare batteries, toothbrushes, sunglasses, torches, short-wave radio and a hip-flask. Now, somehow, we had to impose order on this confusion, breathe life and coherency into the expedition.

Our bicycles were a particular source of apprehension to me. Like Livingstone's donkeys, they were to be loaded up, ridden and cajoled through rough terrain. When they became worn down by the journey, we would have to nurse them until they recovered. But whereas Livingstone had a comfortable familiarity with donkeys, I felt in awe of our new bicycles, so shiny and beautiful. They came with a daunting array of tools, whose carefully machined heads with elaborately splayed tines were like the blooms of magnificent metal flowers, laden with the heavy bouquet of lubricant.

During that final week of preparation in Tabora, I laboured late into each night over the manual, learning to disassemble and reassemble the various bicycle parts. One evening I was finally defeated by a recalcitrant nut at the mechanical heart of Aisling's machine. Downcast, I wheeled the bicycle through the dark streets to a dim workshop in the ramshackle market. There, by the light of a guttering oil-lamp, an oil-streaked man beat the bicycle with a hammer, and the nut miraculously yielded.

'To where?' he asked, as he wiped his hands on his ragged shirt.

'To Zambia,' I replied. 'We'll go south through the Ugalla River Game Reserve.'

'Ugalla?'

'Yes.'

He tutted, and spoke rapidly in Swahili to an old man heaped like a crumpled blanket on an oil drum. There was a barrage of tutting. 'Many bad men...'. I turned to go.

'... and maybe lions,' he added.

The next morning, reflecting that Livingstone's men had been armed with rifles and copious ammunition, I bought a machete. It had a scabbard made from an old inner tube and looked very like a letter-knife my father had owned, except that its blade was a foot and a half long.

As I returned from the market, the rain began. Fierce stuff, it thrummed on the dusty ground around me and formed rivulets down the road. With cold uneasiness, I remembered that Livingstone's equipment for dealing with the rain had included a small, segmental boat and paddles. We were bringing nothing but waterproof ground-sheets. The rainstorm was a turning point. With startling clarity I saw the enormity of our undertaking. To succeed in following Livingstone to his grave would depend on a long string of triumphs over broken bicycles, swollen rivers, pathless mountains and endless swamps. How could we possibly triumph over such odds? Now, as I walked back to the hotel in the downpour, our preparations seemed naïve: we were children playing at a grown-ups' game.

In our room, Aisling eyed the machete uncertainly: 'What's that for?'

'Well... you never know...,' I said as I strapped it to the bicycle frame, where it immediately looked incongruous. It was just a precaution, I told myself, against the unexpected.

*   *   *

Livingstone was confident that he knew exactly what to expect on his journey. He was a seasoned traveller and was never happier than when on the tramp. Just a few years before he had written:

The mere animal pleasure of travelling in wild unexplored country is very great. When on lands of a couple of thousand feet elevation, brisk exercise imparts elasticity to the muscles, fresh and healthy blood circulates through the brain, the mind works well, the eye is clear, the step is firm... the mind is made more self-reliant... Africa is a wonderful country for appetite... no one can truly experience the charm of repose unless he has undergone severe exertion.

Now, in his last days in Tabora, he was again relishing the thought of departure. He was not to know that the events of the next nine months would make his eulogy on African travel seem like a cruel joke.

*   *   *

Aisling was hunched in a corner, her arms clasped around her knees. Her face was pale and tear-stained. Like a frightened rabbit, she watched as I closed the door softly behind me. I picked my way across the floor and stopped in front of her.

'I can't do it.' Her voice was flat.

My eyes slid away from her face down to the floor where mechanical detritus lay strewn about her. I recognised the bevelled arm of brake callipers, and the springs that normally lay coiled up inside the brake-housing like small, silver snail-shells. I looked back to her face, but her head was bowed. 'I don't care. I can't do it.'

She was rocking to and fro. Gently, I took the pliers from her hand. When she spoke again, her voice still echoed with tears: 'How can anyone be expected to adjust something in three directions at once? It's impossible. Impossible.'

It was to have been her job. Aisling was going to look after the brakes on each bicycle. But over the last few days, try as she might, the self-assured city girl had been unable to master them. And now the strain had started to show.

There were other tearful exchanges in those final days of preparation, and abrasive words. It was just a fortnight since Aisling had left London, and she needed more time than we could afford to adjust to a life to which I had become inured during several months. One afternoon, we fought in low angry voices over a bottle of shampoo. It was not in the spirit of Livingstone, so it should not come with us, I said. Then I left the room to escape the taut silence. When I returned, Aisling fixed me with cold, hard eyes and then started reading aloud:

'7 March, 1873. The donkey had to be tied down in the boat, and he came in stiff and sore. We had him shampooed all over.' She snapped Livingstone's journal shut. When she spoke again, her voice was icy. 'So I think you'll agree that it is reasonable for me to bring my shampoo.'

*   *   *

Extract from Aisling's journal: Saturday 23rd November

Today Colum took out our new water filter, a state-of-the-art, ceramic affair that can remove every contaminant but viruses. He dropped it and it cracked.

'Don't worry,' he said. 'I've got glue. I'll stick it back together.'

He began to investigate our new cooker instead. It's a small, powerful thing which scares me because of the high pressure to which the fuel has to be pumped. Colum dropped it and it cracked. 'Don't worry...' he began.

'… we've got glue, we can stick it back together,' I chorused. But I'm upset. These pieces of equipment are the thoroughbreds of the camping equipment world. They are the inventions of industries that have long ago left behind the basic principles of robustness and versatility. If we break or lose any of the tiny elements of the filter or the cooker they will instantly be useless. Our bicycles are hypersensitive machines as well, designed with a million new and sophisticated ways of breaking down. The Tanzanian bone-shakers, in contrast, look indestructible. They are great, majestic, black and silver machines with shiny bells, the simplest bicycles possible. Their owners covet our bicycles and I look longingly at theirs.

*   *   *

It was the day before we were due to leave, and I was standing outside the hotel at the edge of the dusty track. My impromptu audience looked at me uncomprehendingly: something was being lost in translation. I tried again: 'Look, there are twenty-four birds circling the earth, you see, and this machine talks to them and that's how we find our way.'

I looked down at the global positioning system nestling in the palm of my hand, not much bigger than a pack of cards. The instruction manual had told me to calibrate it before setting out, and now the screen was full of electronic doodlings as the short, stumpy aerial collected data from orbiting satellites. And that was where my translation problem lay. In Swahili, *ndege* means 'satellite'; it also means 'bird'.

As I flipped away the aerial, I saw one boy glance doubtfully at some large black crows scavenging on a smouldering pile of rubbish. Again, our incongruity needled me: was Africa really to be no more for us than a playground? For Livingstone it had been different. He was not a man sensitised by the doubts of our late twentieth-century generation. All at once, I envied Livingstone. I envied him his simplicity of vision, but above all, I envied him his conviction.

That afternoon we moved to Kwihara, just outside Tabora, where a sleepy village nestles around a replica of Livingstone's ochre-painted house. We pitched our tent on the low front veranda. We were on gently rising ground amongst trees that rose like pillars supporting the roof of a cathedral. All the long hot afternoon we rested in the drowsy stillness, and listened to the silence amongst the trees.

The light turned from white to gold and then to soft yellow. Night came fast, and with unexpected pleasure we cooked and ate our dinner. Then there rose the largest moon I had ever seen, and the forest floor was latticed with heavy light. My mind drifted back to Livingstone. Was he restless the night before he set out? Did he feel any foreboding? Or was he fortified by the obsession which he was to nurse in his heart like a small hot flame until his death?

*   *   *

In 1872 Livingstone was totally absorbed by his quest for the origins of the Nile. The riddle of the river's source had recently resurfaced in Victorian consciousness as a result of the vitriolic public debate raging between the veteran explorers Burton and Speke.

In 1858 Speke had been the first white man to lay eyes on Lake Victoria and, on his return to Britain, had confidently announced that this was the answer to the riddle of the Nile. Burton, piqued at having missed out on the 'discovery' of the source, argued that while Lake Victoria did feed the Nile, it was probably not its true source. He was quick to point out that there was another lake that drained into the Nile – the recently discovered Lake Albert. If that lake had any tributaries they could also be considered to be origins of the Nile.

Livingstone had listened to the debate with great interest and had quietly evolved a theory of his own. When the president of the Royal Geographical Society asked him to establish the truth once and for all, he was only too pleased to have the chance to test his ideas. Livingstone broadly agreed with Burton but went further, suggesting that other central African lakes farther south might also contribute to the Nile. On his return to Africa for the final time in 1866, this was the theory that Livingstone set out to test. However, during his explorations in 1871, he was dismayed to discover that Lake Tanganyika was not linked to the lakes farther north. To support his theory about the central African lakes as the origin of the Nile, he now had to look farther afield.

Some years before, on hearing the rumour of a vast watercourse far to the west of Tanganyika, Livingstone had pushed deep into the interior, and had finally stood on the banks of a mighty river which the locals called the Lualaba. It flowed north. This now became the focus of his attention, and the years of speculation gradually crystallised into certainty in his mind: this hitherto undiscovered line of drainage was none other than the upper reaches of the Nile. Now it was just a question of intercepting his river in its infancy, somewhere far to the south, where, in 1868, he had discovered Lake Bangweulu. He was now convinced that if this marshy lake did not actually spawn the Nile, it was, at the very least, intimately connected with the origins of that great river.

*   *   *

It was 6am on the first day of our journey. The sun had just risen. I watched Aisling free-wheel down the track from Livingstone's house. Soon she was no more than a small figure in the mist that lapped around the grey silhouettes of the trees.

Livingstone set out on the afternoon of 23rd August 1872. The journey that was to culminate in his death was to contribute nothing to the debate about the river's source because Livingstone's assumption about the Lualaba was wrong. That river is in fact the main tributary of the upper Congo and has nothing whatsoever to do with the Nile. At a point some 1,500 kilometres north of where Livingstone died, a river spilled out of Lake Victoria at the Ripon Falls. It was there that the Nile had its beginnings; history was to credit Speke with its discovery after all.

I mounted my bicycle and set off. Cold night smells still hung in the air, and blur-edged shadows slanted across the forest floor. I had expected to feel elated, but all I felt was the weight of the silence that lingered at Kwihara. It was as if this place was in timeless mourning for an explorer's bravado brought to nought, for the ultimate fallibility of a worn-out old man.

Soon, sunrise gave way to breathless morning heat, and still the silence clung to us. There was no sound but our own laboured breathing, no breeze to stir the brittle leaves. Before long, the sun was high, reducing shadows to small dark stains on ground the colour of dry ash.

Livingstone spent one of his first nights at the small village of Kasakera. The arrival of his party of fifty-seven must have created a stir – our arrival caused nothing more than a ripple in the bright stillness. An old woman hobbled out and squatted beneath a tree by a pile of mangoes, and a youth sold us small leathery fish that smelled of smoke and gleamed like fragments of sky. From another man we bought packets of stale biscuits. We sat in a small patch of shade.

'How far to go?' Aisling's voice was plaintive. We had only been cycling for two hours. I brought out the map.

'Forty kilometres.' I avoided looking at her. Out of the corner of my eye I saw her head sag, as if she was wilting in the heat.

One afternoon shortly after I arrived in Africa I had written to Aisling hoping to open her eyes to the intensity of the heat, to tell her how it drags at the limbs and licks them with sweat. Perhaps it had been a crisp, autumnal, London afternoon when she had read my letter. Perhaps it had reminded her, in a theoretical way, to expect uncomfortable warmth in Africa. But now, stranded on an island of shade in a white sea of heat, I realised that nothing could have prepared her for this. I folded the map away, and winced as the sweat stung my sunburnt neck.

'Come on,' I said softly. Without a word, she got to her feet, and once more we plunged into the sunlight.

Later our dusty track became thick white sand and we reached a gentle hill. Before long we were both pushing our heavily loaded bicycles. At the crest of the hill, I looked round and found that I was alone. Aisling was a small figure crumpled at the side of the track. I could see the heavy trench that she had forced through the sand, and the equipment which was scattered widely around her like the debris from a small explosion. Slowly I retraced my steps.

'I can't go on. I can't do any more like this.' Her voice was uneven, and she held her head in her hands; their reddened backs were glistening with sweat. Piece by piece I started to collect her discarded kit, wondering at the brief, savage rage that she had vented on her bicycle and its load.

At last I sat down beside her and we looked out at the bleached rim of the horizon, where the forest finally merged with the sky.

'We have to go on. We have to reach water.' The afternoon stretched on and we crawled along the sandy track like ants. Soon our water was finished and we became dizzy, the silence ringing in our ears. When the heat abated a little we stopped and slumped beneath a spreading tree.

'Reached Mayole village in two hours and rested; S [south] *and by W* [west]. *Water is scarce in front. Through forest to a marshy-looking piece of water, where we camp, after a march of one and a half hours; still S by W.'*

On modern maps, Livingstone's Mayole has given its name to Mkolye Hill. Today, the village of Tutuo stands nearby – an untidy scattering of mud buildings around a decaying marketplace. Light-headed, I wandered amongst the huts in search of water.

*   *   *

That night, an Arab shopkeeper insisted that we stay with his family. His house had concrete walls and a tin roof – it was the most substantial house in the village. Gratefully, we drank hot sweet tea made from milk laced with cardamom and ate chicken with rice and boiled banana. He would accept no payment. Later, our host and his family sat round the walls of the small enclosed courtyard and watched as we clumsily stripped the bicycles.

Later, we were shown to a room with a wide, comfortable bed. In the darkness I lay awake watching the silhouette of a palm tree against the blue velvet sky. I knew from her breathing that Aisling was also awake, but she was unusually quiet. I did not feel inclined to talk either: it seemed as if the bleakness which had fallen over us in Tabora was shadowing us still.

We had known that we could expect hardship: all the commentators agreed that one of the most remarkable aspects of Livingstone's last journey was the heat, the thirst and the hunger that the explorer had endured. His suffering was established as a comfortable, undisputed fact, an element to be manipulated by academics and woven by storytellers into the fabric of myth.

Everyone knew about Livingstone and hardship, and that made it easy to forget about the messy, unglamorous reality. I had run our adventure past the window of my imagination many times, as if it were an old silent movie. But imagination is a fickle thing which allows you to see but not to experience, to watch but not to feel. Now, after just one day, Aisling's vivacity had been reduced to sweaty sullenness and I felt subdued. The next day, the next week, the next month had all become too hard to contemplate.

Livingstone was not troubled by such foreboding. The inspiration for his expedition filled his entire mind and gave him an intensity which I could sense, but which I did not yet understand.

For Livingstone, the first weeks of his journey barely merited comment. Where I was unsettled by the mournful bird cries sliding from eerie falsetto to heart-beat base before dwindling into the forest silence, Livingstone was encountering nothing new. His journal was a business-like catalogue of distances and directions, a log-book where he recorded tersely: '*Trees present a dry, wintry aspect... Level forest without water.*' For us, pale shadows of Livingstone trailing along in his wake, his abruptness made him an uneasy travelling companion.

*   *   *

For some days beyond Tutuo it was difficult to know exactly where Livingstone went, as the small settlements that he had found deep in the forest no longer exist. Pinta and Chikulu were villages that had been born, had lived briefly for a blink of the sun's gaze, and had crumbled back into the dry forest floor. Now, all our map showed were some dots, with the inscription 'Bee-Keepers' Dwellings (Temporary)'.

'Yes, there is still a path that way,' our Arab host told us. 'But no one ever uses it. Too much sand. Very dry. Many wadudu.' *Wadudu* is an ambiguous word. It means pests – anything from a tsetse fly to a ferocious buffalo. I nodded.

'There is nothing on that path. No water, no people. Nothing.'

I was starting to get the message. To follow that route would be madness.

'You must instead go left at the junction. Sometimes, a vehicle will pass that way, and they can give you help... if you need it. Beyond Ipole, you will have to take the bus anyway. No one ever gets through the forest on bicycles.'

We followed the Arab's directions, and in the early afternoon we came to Sikonge, a village shaded by palm trees in the bowl of a low valley. At a hand-pump we drew bright, cold water from a well and drank deeply, gratefully soaking our shirts and hats. Then back to the hot, empty track, and soon the water bursting from the handpump like a cascade of diamonds was no more than a fading memory.

From time to time, a pannier would detach itself from my bicycle and lodge in a bank of sand. Then, as I trudged back to recover it, I felt that modern paraphernalia seemed to be nothing more than a bulky encumbrance. Livingstone took great pride in carrying with him '*no nick-nacks advertised as indispensable for travellers*'. By the standards of the time, his was an extremely lightly equipped expedition. On a comparable venture in 1858, Grant and Speke had an equipment list that included, amongst other things, four iron stools, four packs of cards, twelve pocket handkerchiefs and a large spring balance, all items which Livingstone would undoubtedly have dismissed as 'nick-nacks'. By contrast his expedition carried barely enough to ensure its viability. His beads and calico would buy him food and safe passage for some months, and his assorted provisions and ten head of cattle would stave off starvation for a short time, but the meagreness of his supplies left little contingency for disaster.

Two days after his party marched out of Kwihara, Livingstone wrote: '... *lost a cow out of ten head. Sent back five men to look... Cow not found...*'. Four days later, he recorded that he '... *lost all the cows yesterday... They were found a long way off, and one cow missing*'. If Livingstone perceived the losses as a major setback, there was no indication of it in his journal. When I had read and re-read it before we set out I had seen his phlegmatic reaction to the losses as another example of his stoicism.

But now, as his cattle disappeared into the dry wilderness around us, the event cast Livingstone in a different light, and I began reflecting that it is a thin line between personal stoicism and foolhardiness. Perhaps other leaders, mindful of the long-term welfare of their party, would have turned back to collect new cattle.

My musings were interrupted by Aisling. 'Colum, stop. Something's leaking...'

I quickly dismounted and laid the bicycle down on the sand. With dread tightening my throat, I plunged my hand into the hard-packed chaos inside the pannier. Oil. Oil everywhere. Everything was coated with its silky warmness. When the pannier had fallen, it had crushed the flimsy container and the lubricant for all our moving parts had drained away.

This was a disaster. I imagined the obituary to our expedition. 'On the second day, their oil leaked. Then on the third day, their bikes seized.' Was our expedition to end as ignominiously as this?

Yet even though we had only been travelling for two days, I could not even contemplate retracing our steps.

'*She was our best milker…*' Livingstone had written, and had then pressed on, without so much as a backward glance.

4

In Ipole
by Colum

WE ARRIVED at Ipole in the middle of the afternoon. A thick somnolence held everything immobile. In the shade of tall mango trees silent women sat behind market stalls and watched, like lizards. At the heart of the village was a wide open space of dazzling white. It was lined with broken mud houses and scant structures with tattered palm-leaf roofs – skeletal shorthand for shelter from the unrelenting sun.

At one end of the open space a grotesque figure stood in the full glare, watching us. We drew near, fixed by its empty gaze, until finally we faltered to a halt. The deep, lifeless eye sockets regarded us steadily. The shattered buffalo skull, thrust onto a jagged timber post, marked the point where the track divided. Ipole is strung down the side of an imperceptible ridge, and the track we were to follow stood out below the village, a livid, ragged-edged cut that ran perfectly straight across the forest, until it lost itself in the haze of the horizon.

Beyond Ipole, there would be more emptiness. From edge to edge, the map was stippled with the stylised miniature of a leafy tree, representing 'woodland' in the key. The trees repeated with the comfortable predictability of a pattern on children's wallpaper. Hesitant contours meandered amongst them like an illicit childish scribble in brown crayon.

For numberless miles around Ipole the hard sunlight had bleached colour from brittle leaves, and had twisted grey trunks into tortured shapes. There were no smells, only the dry taste of wood ash. And there was silence, broken from time to time by the hum of an unseen swarm of insects. It would swell with oppressive urgency, like machinery about to break itself apart, and would then suddenly die away.

Livingstone, his senses numbed by the interminable sameness, wrote of long marches through '*flat forest*'. In fact, the ground undulates gently, but the huge arc of the sky makes the contours seem as insignificant as the roughness of a cathedral floor.

The Europeans who had come after Livingstone had cast a net of ordered grid lines over this wilderness, registering its existence on the consciousness of an enquiring world. But then they had passed on, daunted by the crackling sterility, and by the electric dryness that sears the nostrils. So the forest remained unsubdued, baking in the quiet heat, as it had done for millennia.

Ipole felt precarious. The wilderness gnawed silently at the fringes of the village. One day the forest would continue its inexorable progress and the village would yield, with a sigh, to the ash-grey dryness. Ipole would sink out of men's recollection, and the tracks, stretched over impossible distances, would fade. The forest would seal over them like skin knitting over an open cut. In the meantime, a perverse doggedness kept people there. They lived, they worked, they loved and they died at the edge of humanity, oppressed by the emptiness beyond, and as small as ants in the eye of the sun.

'This is an uncivilised town,' said Coco, the keeper of the guest house just beyond the skull. He padded off to fetch us a bucket of water, and we stood wondering about his words. Later, I returned into the village. I was to buy food to see us through the next few days and I was to find a guide.

The heat had subsided and the shadows had lengthened. Around the market there were signs of movement. A threadbare dog licked its sores with a glistening tongue. Chickens scrabbled in the dust beneath the rickety market stalls where the women continued to sit behind their mangoes and shrivelled onions. They chatted sporadically. Disconnected fragments of their conversation hung in the air, and their eyes followed me.

There were no customers to justify their long, fly-blown vigils, and I wondered what kept them there – who bought their fruit, who stimulated the weak trickle of money around this isolated community? Perhaps at the end of each day's brooding watchfulness they sold their wares to each other, in an act of miserable self-perpetuation which bucked the laws of economics. A little farther on a group of men and youths was standing at a rough counter erected in the shade of a palm-leaf shelter. They were nursing bottles of beer. This, then, was the complementary part of Ipole's economic cycle: the money gleaned by the women found its way to the men, whose prerogative it was to spend it as they willed.

They eyed me suspiciously. I bought a bottle of beer which prickled with tepid fizziness.

'Mpaka wapi?' one asked.

'We're going as far as Zambia,' I replied in Swahili. There was a pause as the men exchanged glances, the hint of a smile, a raised eyebrow. 'Kwa baiskeli?' he continued, his voice rising with an unpleasant hint of incredulity. Yes, I confirmed, we were going by bicycle.

Over a few days of travelling, this was a conversation that I had come to enjoy. Normally, I treasured the quiet moment, like some small jewel, as I watched people reacting to my explanation. Most were perplexed, impressed even; some were amused. And it somehow legitimised what we were doing: like Livingstone, we were travelling for the sake of travelling, in the great tradition of British explorers. But in Ipole, I felt differently. Perhaps it was because I was scared of the forest. I was not going to play the game today.

'I need a guide,' I said, not smiling. There was a moment's hesitation and then a man in army fatigues, his hat set at a rakish angle, stepped unsteadily forward. He was clutching a bottle, and he smelt strongly of the coarse, rank spirit that is distilled from cassava. He gripped my shoulder with a knobbled hand and gazed through me with blurred eyes.

He moistened his cracked lips and began talking. His Swahili sentence started strongly, but died in the dryness of his throat. He drank deeply from the bottle and started again: 'I can take you. I can take you. I know the forest well…'. But then his gaze slid off my face, and he was squinting abstractedly past the skull, along the track where we were to set off.

Gently I prised his fingers off my shoulder, and asked quietly where I could find the village headman. They pointed down past the dark mud building that was our guest house. I broke away from the small group, and walked over the sandy open space where the light was softening. The cracked skull had flushed primrose as the sun slipped towards the horizon. As I started back down the track there was an ugly shout, and I turned to see my would-be guide standing in the open, his body lax and distorted. One arm was awkwardly straight, sticking out abruptly from his body – the better to protect his precious bottle. He roared a short Swahili sentence at me, slowly creasing with the effort. Recovering, he wheeled around, and the bottle flew out of his grasp in a wide arc. A bright flash of reflected light and the noise of splintering glass, and then silence.

I arrived beneath a flat-topped tree in front of the headman's house. There, in an area of ground worn smooth by generations of bare feet, the headman called for two chairs to be arranged. As I settled myself, the wives arranged chairs for themselves a short distance away, but within earshot. Silent, wide-eyed children were mustered around their mothers. The audience could begin.

Swahili greetings are long and thorough. During the course of the ritualised, drip-feed exchange, particles of information are traded in accordance with a time-worn formula.

'How is your family?'

'Good.'

'How is your home?'

'Peaceful.'

'How are your children?'

'Good.'

'How was the journey?'

'Fine, thank God.'

The possibilities are without limit. Each response adds a tiny piece more to the edifice of mutual confidence.

'From where have you come?'

'From Tabora.'

'And how is Tabora?'

'Tabora is a good place.'

'And to where are you going?'

'Inyonga.'

'Ah. Inyonga. Your journey is a long one.'

That was the cue. I told him that we needed a guide, for no more than two days, to see us along the next stage of the track. Then there was silence. I looked out over the forest, which was bathed in oblique orange light. Pools of shadow had gathered in the hollows, dispelling something of the oppressive uniformity. It was altogether a gentler scene than before.

The village leader deliberated for a long time, drawing with the point of his stick in the dust. When he finally spoke, his sentences came slowly and he used Swahili words that I did not understand. There was apology in the movement of his hands, and reluctance in the lines on his forehead. Twice, his arm swept a wide, slow circle which took in the dusky forest, and once he pointed with an outstretched arm at the track, a dark line of shadow now that the sun was sinking.

There was some problem, but I did not understand. I felt frustration rising inside me, but he still talked on, labouring some words. *Banduki*, in particular, was a word heavy with significance. He said it with a flourish, and then paused, gauging my reaction. I looked across at his wives. They were silent, but they nodded gravely. I nodded too. This word was outside my vocabulary.

I departed soon after that. I would return tomorrow with my dictionary. With startling suddenness, it had become night. Over the noise of the cicadas I could hear that a generator had started up in the village, and now there was the low throb of music, like the heartbeat of a nervous animal. Two flickering neon strips struggled to maintain a pallid gleam over the market stalls and the bar counter. This fragile bubble of light, lapped round by darkness, was the focus of Ipole night life. In the marketplace, the women continued to wait, and the men milled amongst them restlessly.

Lying in bed, I thumbed through our small dictionary. *Banduki* meant gun. I blew out the candle, and Aisling stirred in her sleep.

*   *   *

The ox-cart had no wheels. It ran on skids, which had drawn deep parallel furrows along the sandy track. It was stacked high with hardwoods from the forest, and rocked in time with the heavy steps of the four oxen. Primeval, they plodded past us. They had come from beyond the point where civilisation ended.

We followed the swaying cart into the centre of the village and entered a small *hoteli* to find breakfast. A circle of children settled down to watch us as we ate coarse doughnuts from grease-bleared plates and drank strong sweet tea. On the wall was a yellowing magazine photograph of a white-skinned child with a sunny smile sitting in a European garden. I could tell by the child's clothes that it was a photograph from some decades ago. She would be a middle-aged woman by now, but with her childhood immortalised in Ipole.

I returned to the house of the headman. Already the forest was becoming indistinct in the heat and white storm clouds stood like pillars on the horizon. The headman seemed agitated. He spoke rapidly, irritably almost. I caught some of his phrases; I thumbed through the dictionary for others; and my heart sank. He said that in the forest we would find no water, no food. The track had much sand: when he used the expression for 'very difficult', I was already expecting it. With a slow shake of his head, he drawled out the words 'Wanyama wakali.' Livingstone, too, had been fearful of ferocious animals.

The headman put a sympathetic hand on my arm, and indicated a broad-shouldered man sitting against the tree. This was his friend, said the headman, who would act as our guide and, most importantly of all, he would bring his *banduki*. The man stood up and approached. We argued about money, and then, with a slow smile that gradually revealed a line of brown and broken teeth, he shook my hand. Later, he came to our room, announced that he had changed his mind, and strode off without another word.

At the bar nobody cared. Even the headman, who now sat on a low stool and stared morosely at the forest, was not interested. Twice, I asked about a guide. On the first occasion, no one answered. The small knot of men at the bar was preoccupied. The air of expectancy puzzled me. Two of them argued in quiet, bitter voices, not listening to each other. Another pulled the legs off a butterfly, waiting for time to pass. When I asked again, a man on a low bench kicked a passing dog. Then, without looking around, the headman quietly responded – 'labda baadaye': 'maybe later'.

So I waited with the others, biting back my impatience, until a hollow shout interrupted the sun-glazed reverie. The men looked up, and a bright butterfly wing fell to the dusty ground. There was a drumming of feet, and people surged from among the buildings, either fleeing, or running towards something. The young, the old, the men and women seemed to be impelled by the same empty, directionless energy that strips leaves from autumn trees.

My eyes fastened on a thin line of men snaking around the rocky outcrops of the low hill above the village. Much farther ahead, I saw another figure. From his stumbling, jerky progress I knew that he was being pursued. Some of the men at the bar scrambled to their feet and set off to follow. The air was full of a low, whooping noise and quivered with the excitement of the hunt.

Only the headman did not appear to notice. Instead, he dismissed one of the remaining youths with a few curt words. Then he turned to me and fastened me with sunken eyes. 'I will find another guide…' he said, and then lapsed back into sullen silence. When the youth returned, a man was trailing in his wake. 'This is the village game-scout,' the headman said.

Superficially, the man looked much as he had done yesterday – he wore the same crumpled army fatigues, thick with dried mud, and his hat was still askew. But subtle changes marked the passage of another day in Ipole: a cut on his jawline buzzed with flies, and he was now desolate in his drunkenness, whereas yesterday he had been buoyant.

'He can take you. He knows the forest well. Atakulinda.' I shuddered. 'He will guard you' – it was easy for the headman to say, but my confidence in the scout's abilities drained away as I looked him up and down. He swayed slightly in the noon-time sun. His downcast eyes were half-closed and his head sagged. And he was going to be carrying a gun. No, I would make other arrangements.

I looked round for the headman. He met me with cold steady eyes, alert now.

'Shilingi ngapi?' he asked. How much? How much for a drunken wretch who was more likely to shoot me than a lion? I shook my head.

'Shilingi ngapi?' he repeated, calmly.

The men and remaining youths had gathered around in a loose circle and were exchanging grins. This was an exciting diversion. I pushed past the game-scout, who rocked like a skittle. He smelt of urine. A thin youth confronted me. His head was cocked on one side, his face expressionless. I had a brief impression of matt-dry skin and a hard thin shoulder, and then I had broken away.

*   *   *

'Where are you from?' His English was fluent.

'From Britain.'

We walked on in silence. He had fallen in with me as I beat my retreat from the bar.

'You are not from Germany?'

Strange question. But I was not keen to encourage the conversation. Now I longed for the gloomy seclusion of our room.

'No, from Britain. London, in fact.'

But perhaps this man could help us. I looked around at him, appraising. He looked back at me and smiled warmly.

'I'm trying to find a guide to take us through the forest.'

There was a moment's silence, then: 'I have two friends who will take you.'

'I have to leave tomorrow.' I looked back at him uncertainly.

'No problem. They will come before sunrise.' This all seemed too good to be true.

'Tell me,' I said, 'why did they chase that man?'

'He has the wasting disease and he lay with a woman. Now she will have the disease also.'

The wasting disease. They call it that because that is how people die. I had heard stories of people in the last stages of the disease who were so withered that they could be folded up inside a cardboard box.

'What will they do to him?'

'They will beat him,' he replied.

Perhaps they already had. People were coming back to the village in ones and twos, panting, sweat-stained. Impulsive justice had been executed. Now the village's raw brutality could slip back beneath the surface.

We walked on in silence. I warmed to this man. We arrived at the house of his parents up a small path above the main track. We sat beneath a tree outside the mud house and he sent his young brother to fetch water from the well. Below us wind worried at the trees, and threw the forest into a tumult of ragged waves, whipping leaves and debris away like spume.

'There's a storm coming,' I said.

He remained silent, then he turned to me suddenly, his eyes bright, searching.

'Do you *speak* German?'

'No. Why do you ask?'

His shoulders sagged and his eyes flicked back to the horizon. William was a young man, mid-twenties I would have said. He was a school teacher, but he said he had recently given up his job to concentrate on 'another project'. He was different from the others: he did not treat me with the same hostile fascination as his fellow villagers had done.

'I need the help of a German.' He nodded his head to where a streak of grey rested on the horizon. 'There is gold in the distant mountains. Only a German can break the spell.' He fell silent. I looked round, wanting to ask, but his face was pained.

At last he continued. 'When they left, they hid their gold.' My understanding edged forward. At the end of last century this part of East Africa was a German sphere of influence. Within twenty years it had become a theatre for a white man's war, a savage, low-key affair, fought by a handful of men: the African counterpart to the horrors being enacted in the trenches of Europe. It was a war that was never lost: the future of German East Africa was determined far away, on the battlefields of France. When the final curtain fell on the Western Front, the Germans scuttled their gunship on Lake Tanganyika and melted away, their colonial aspirations in East Africa dashed forever.

'An old man remembers them leaving. They hid their gold in a mountain cave. The old man showed me where.'

'So why don't you get the gold?'

'It is guarded by bad magic.'

William had seen the boxes containing the gold. He described them, stacked deep in their mountain recess, rusted and shrouded in cobwebs. He had stopped short of touching them – the magic could be unleashed by such curiosity – but he had been able to make out that there was a German inscription. This, he believed, was the spell that protected the gold, but he knew no German.

'I need a German to pray to God. With God's help I can break the magic.'

I did not speak German. I was not a Christian. There was nothing to say. I stood up to leave.

As I reached the track, I looked back. William's head was bowed. He was staring at the ground, his mind teeming with the riches that might have been his, the chances he might have had. If only.

*   *   *

Later the wind died away and the darkness became still. The rain broke, the first loud drops coming like the chaotic beginning of a round of applause. Lightning fractured the sky. It snapped the grey forest out of silhouette and into a confusion of twisted boughs. The applause increased until it was a roar. In the lightning's flicker, shadows appeared as yawning voids of darkness, and solids looked like stone.

Still the village waited. Under a tattered awning, a woman was still sitting behind a pile of gleaming fruit. In the next flash, her eyes were dark hollows, a blind gaze as I passed. After an hour the rain ceased, and the trees dripped. I heard a distant tone, like the long night-cry of a mournful animal. I opened the door and watched as the village held its breath. After a few minutes, it came out of the forest, an explosion of sound and light into the market place.

When the bus arrived, the village came alive. People spilled from the huts and flooded across the open spaces towards where the gleaming animal shuddered and coughed. Villagers flocked to where arms writhed from the open windows. In Ipole, they were anxious for trade, for news, for contact with the world beyond the forest. Others had swarmed onto the roof, and were throwing misshapen bundles to the ground. The air was full of shouting and laughter, and yellow light glimmered in the puddles and threw reflected gleams from the forest's long, wet leaves.

In the market, the women were selling their mangoes and an unruly crowd of men had gathered at the bar. Children and dogs had appeared from nowhere, silhouettes hovering uncertainly at the periphery of the pool of light.

At the end of a short time there was shouting and an impatient pulsing of the horn, a surge of people towards the bus, and bodies jumped from the roof. The engine roared, and the bus was away, a small capsule of humanity penetrating the emptiness once more, night and forest crowding back against its windows.

Gradually, the roar subsided to a low throb which rose and fell with the change of gears. Finally there was just a murmur and the smell of diesel lingering in the air. In the market, the women packed away their unsold mangoes and chattered lightly. The dogs and children scavenged beneath the trestles. Two or three men leant against the bar, their voices drifting across to our room. I pulled the door closed. In Ipole, the waiting had started again.

Log Book Extract

DAY 5 – Friday 29th November

PHASE 1

FROM: Ipole

TO: Koga

CAMP: Tent pitched in fisherman's camp.

POSITION: 32°16'11" E
6°13'18" S

TIME CYCLING: 8 hours 30 minutes

DISTANCE TRAVELLED: 75km

AVERAGE SPEED: 14km/hr

ROUTE: Took the long straight track to the right at Ipole into the forest.

TRACK CONDITION: Surprisingly good. Overnight rain had hardened the sand.

BICYCLES – PERFORMANCE: The spring in Col's back brake is playing up – removed during day. Colum is cycling with 5 out of 21 gears as there is some problem with his front chain-ring.

BICYCLES – MAINTENANCE: Checked and cleaned tyres, gears, brakes.

WEATHER: Light rain to start with, soon cleared. Hot and bright all day. Midday temperature 34°C.

HEALTH: Aisling is depressed, and her new boots are hurting her feet.

EQUIPMENT: Still evolving the best way to pack the panniers. We are trying to keep one pannier completely watertight to protect our documents, books etc against the rain.

LANDSCAPE: Continuous flat forest.

EXPENDITURE: Guides Tsh9,000

FLUID CONSUMPTION: 9 litres

FOOD: During day: chapatis and nuts
Evening meal: rice, nuts and mangoes with tinned cheese

COMMENT: Our water consumption has been nothing like enough today. Both were feeling very dizzy by the end of the day. If we don't filter the water, it is easier to put up with chlorine or iodine sterilisation tablets if we use them on alternate days.

Note:
andazi (Swahili) = doughnut
ugalli (Swahili) = maize porridge
shamba (Swahili) = farm, allotment

LIVINGSTONE: It is difficult to pin him down exactly, as he is vague about position: probably some 20km to our north, heading SW. For him, also, it is dry and hot; water and food are scarce.

5
From Ipole to Inyonga
by Aisling

THE BEEP of the digital alarm raced around the darkness. Outside it began to rain again. By 5.30am we were swathed in waterproof ponchos and waiting for our guides in the refreshing cool of the downpour.

There was a movement and two boys emerged from the blackness: John and Pharles had kept their word. Low Swahili phrases murmured over the rushing of the rain. There was nothing now between us and the wild road. Colum turned to me: 'They think we should start immediately.'

We walked our bikes up to the gate. I could feel the presence of its ghastly ornament even in the darkness. To my surprise Pharles reached out absently and knocked at it with his knuckles: it made a dull, hollow noise just as an old piece of bone would. I groped, half-blind, until my fingers, too, touched its cool, smooth wetness. I pushed it gently and it shifted on its pole: it was lighter than I had thought it would be. A stronger push could knock it to the ground. The fresh reality of the rain had altered Ipole, weakened spells, washed away the unfathomable superstition that had shrouded the road ahead.

The dark thinned to grey and the boys swung themselves onto their bicycles and sped off. We followed, and soon the forest enveloped us. Pharles slowed and called to us to cycle close together. I did not ask whether it was bandits or animals that he feared. There was little undergrowth and so we could see far into the forest, spying every so often a movement – monkeys swinging away high up in the trees, animals bounding into the distance. I was nervous but with every extra mile beyond Ipole my mood lightened. The place had intimidated me and I had spent most of the time lying depressed in our dark hut.

Within an hour the rain stopped and the early sun broke through. For a short time, long bars of light cut horizontally between the trees, and the shadows were green and cool. Gradually the heat strengthened and the ground began to steam. The muddy track was transformed into a hard, smooth surface along which we raced with unexpected speed.

As the sun rose higher, distant, outlandish bird cries pierced the forest silence with an urgency that made the tweeting of English birds seem mere prattle. The cry of one surged up and down the cadences, growing louder and more pungent until it seemed to scream into the loneliness: 'Get the hell out of heeeeeere.'

They were probably the same species of bird whose calls had punctuated Livingstone's journey and which had fascinated him: near here he had written: '... *a flock of small swallows now appears: they seem tailless and with white bellies*'. And later: '*Under a lofty tree a kite, the common brown one, had two pure white eggs in its nest, larger than a fowl's and very spherical.*'

Farther on he noted '... *a purple ginger, with two yellow patches inside, is very lovely to behold, and it is alternated with one of a bright canary yellow*'.

Often his observations betrayed the obsession of the scientist: '*We found many lepidosirens in a muddy pool, which a group of vultures were catching and eating. The men speared one of them, which had scales on; its tail had been bitten off by a cannibal brother: in length it was about two feet: there were curious roe-like portions near its backbone, yellow in colour; the flesh was good.*'

The fulfilment Livingstone drew from these treasures of nature was not merely scientific. His fascination was also a renewal of his religious faith. He came from an age which had embraced the Argument from Design – which asserted that the complexity of the world is evidence of the existence of God. In every little twist of nature Livingstone found God's signature and, as he weakened with illness later on, his journals were to fill with extraordinary description. Tiny details of the lives of caterpillars, spiders, birds and fish laced the dark comments that revealed he was almost too weak to hold his pen. When he finally realised he was dying, beholding God's craftsmanship brought him a profound sense of nearness to his Maker.

Livingstone had harboured this sensitivity to nature from boyhood and it somehow survived his rude upbringing, like a tenacious desert flower. As a child, however, his fascination with the natural world had not lain so easily with his religious beliefs. Livingstone's father Neil instructed him that God's only textbook was the Bible. To practise science was to meddle with the Creation.

Neil Livingstone was uncompromisingly religious, and David spent his first nineteen years in tearful certainty that his future lay in eternal damnation. According to his father's Calvinist doctrine, if one was predestined for heaven one could already feel the breath of the Holy Spirit. Livingstone could sense no such thing and so he believed that Hell was his final destination. Those childhood years of private torment and desolation show that even as a child he had a vivid and often morbid inner life – and they marked his personality for ever.

One day, when Livingstone was nearly twenty, a bright new message burst in upon his troubled spirit in the form of sermons from new, more liberal preachers. These men, part of the early nineteenth-century Scottish religious revival, had rewritten the rules to say that atonement was available to anyone who asked the Holy Spirit into their lives.

Dr Thomas Dick was one of the revivalists and assured Livingstone that science was a way of confirming God's existence. For the first time the young man could study the natural world with inner peace.

With the religious and the scientific reconciled, Livingstone blossomed and acquired a direction. He joined the Protestant revival, subscribing to its creed that people needed practical help in this world as well as a ticket to the next. It was then that he decided to become a doctor and practise as a medical missionary, healing people and winning them to Christianity at the same time. This faith in God was one of formidable strength and an element of his character for us to cling to when his behaviour resisted explanation.

*   *   *

The heat stole up on us. The boys were always ahead, their backs bent over with the effort of shifting gearless bicycles with bare feet that strained against the stumps that served as pedals. Their knees stuck out to the sides. One of them laboured with a twenty-litre tank of water strapped to his back carrier, while the other was weighed down with a big grey sack containing, I presumed, what they needed for a few days away. Their tyres were smooth and every so often we would have to stop to pump them or to flip a loose old chain back into place. Neither had brakes, but then nor did Colum. He had removed them because his back panniers pinned the elaborate braking mechanisms into a permanently closed position. But, as we both were realising, African tracks provide sufficient friction to make brakes superfluous.

In the early afternoon the boys drew up at a small clearing. It was empty and silent, but amongst the trees that fringed it we found a wooden structure whose straw roof provided a square of shade. Near it was a large straw wigwam with rough planks for a door. There was no one about, unless they were watching us from the forest. Even though there was no water source marked on the map, this hunters' camp was dignified with a name. Here, at Isuwangala Kamanga, we had planned to spend the night, nothing between us and the wild but a few wisps of straw.

Colum was frowning. 'Not much to the place, is there?' He looked at his watch. I sighed. I could see that there was going to be no long afternoon recovering in the shade. 'We really ought to get on – we could save a day that could be useful later on.' I began to protest but he was gone – in mind if not yet in body.

'Can we at least stop for lunch?'

'Well, OK then, but let's make it quick.'

John and Pharles opened their sack and drew out a large battered cooking pan, a long wooden spoon, a hefty bag of maize flour, a smaller bag of dried fish and a tank of cooking oil. They found the ashes of the last hunter's fire, rekindled them and soon had a pot of bubbling porridge and a pan of sizzling fish. I delved into a pannier and pulled out lunch for Colum and me: a small bag of peanuts and two floppy chapatis that our hosts in Tutuo had provided.

While the boys cooked, Colum prodded the bicycle tyres, found them wanting and unhitched the pump. For a moment he gazed at the unscrewed valve in uncertainty and then he began to pump.

'Ais, hold this.' I kept the bike steady while he sweated but the tyre did not fill.

'The valve won't let the air in.' Irritation edged his voice. I looked at the valve – a green liquid had seeped out of it and was turning to jelly.

'That stuff's meant to clog up punctures – but it's stopping me getting the air in.' His voice was fierce. Soon the ground was spread with spanners, pliers and the exotic instruments required to fix a modern bicycle, while Colum was engrossed in the maintenance manual, oblivious of the scorching sun.

It took him half an hour to fix a new valve to the tyre and coax air into it. As I watched him I realised that he was as scared of the bikes as I was, but he was at war with them, quelling uprisings with novel weapons he did not yet understand. Which side would win was not yet obvious, I concluded, feeling rather depressed.

After lunch we plunged back into the blazing heat. Livingstone, too, was contending with the hottest time of year and some of his men had already fallen sick, exhausted by their heavy loads. Soon he would write:

> *The sun makes the soil so hot that the radiation is as if it came from a furnace. It burns the feet of the people, and knocks them up. Subcutaneous inflammation is frequent in the legs, and makes some of my most hardy men useless. We have been compelled to slowness very much against my will.*

By 4pm the track became sandy, the forest dwindled to bush and we began the descent to the river at Koga where we would part from the boys. We had crossed the first expanse of lonely forest and, to our relief, Ipole was now a two-day walk behind us.

Koga is a fishing village, a messy sprawl of rough straw shelters. A dozen men snoozed, smoked or worked at their nets. The ground was untidy, scattered with wisps of straw and the paraphernalia of fishing. The fishermen welcomed us, offering us wooden chairs and I sank down in exhaustion hoping for a few hours of inactivity. But within half an hour Colum sprang up. He began to dismember his bicycle to clean out the sand and, since I showed no initiative, to instruct me on how to do the same with mine. Irritably, I began to work, but the intricate mechanisms defeated me.

I felt defeated by most of my allotted tasks. I abandoned the bicycle to Colum and pitched the tent instead. Soon it sat like an alien craft amongst the fishermen's huts. I crawled inside and, in the privacy of that small blue world, began to cry. From the very first day the journey had overwhelmed me, and now I just wanted to give up. A pattern was starting to form. I could endure each day's trek, but my failings really began when the cycling stopped – I stopped too, frozen into tired helplessness. It was time to meet the village chief, explain ourselves, negotiate for water and for a site for our tent. It was time to prepare for the next day's journey – and all had to be done before dark. Yet just then something switched off inside me and I left all the tasks to Colum. He had become like a machine, organising, planning, calculating, and I had become just another expedition factor that he had to overcome. My troubles evoked no sympathy with him, no sense that perhaps I was being pushed beyond my limits. Instead I seemed to be the enemy – my protests were regarded as mutiny.

Colum exuded a stale smell. Huddled in the tent, I found my own odour to be equally powerful. Our clothes were coated in red dust and assorted stains and I yearned to scrape away the dirt, to feel smooth and light and cool again. But to achieve such a simple state was defeatingly complicated. To wash I needed water – for that I needed the Swahili for 'river' and the courage to ask a fisherman where it was. I would have to walk to the river to fetch it. But the late afternoon was fading and mosquitoes were emerging – I would need to change into trousers which lay at the bottom of a pannier stacked outside. But the trousers were ripped – I bore the bites of earlier insects which had found their way through the tear to my skin. I needed the sewing kit first.

No job could be done until a hundred others were seen to. To wash my clothes I needed a large bowl which I didn't possess. I would have only cold water, which in my inexpert hands would produce a bleary version of cleanliness. I knew my energy would expire after just one garment. So, I thought, by this time tomorrow I would be as helplessly dirty as before. I longed for a cup of coffee to kick some energy into me. But the stove was explosive and uncontrollable; the coffee powder was no doubt hiding with the needles and soap; and the water – well, it was still in the river.

Instead of washing I was supposed to be filling in the log: distances, times, health, terrain and expenditure. I was also meant to be maintaining a supply of purified drinking water. That task was far more important than washing or brewing coffee but I had let it run out and we needed twelve litres before we could leave the next day. I decided to rebel: tomorrow we could drink mucky water sterilised merely with a blast of iodine.

Even on rest days there was time only for urgent tasks. Before the journey began I had imagined long African afternoons dissolving into giant, red sunsets, inspired prose written at leisure in elegant, marble-backed journals.

'I can't stand it,' I scratched furiously in my tatty Tanzanian exercise book. 'This toil, toil, toil, just to stay in one place.' I was tasting authenticity, and it was bitter.

Colum, on the other hand, was stretched to his utmost, living on adrenalin. He unzipped the tent and looked inside.

'Is there any drinking water?' he asked. The voice was deliberately mild.

'No,' I said.

'Will you be getting some?'

'No.'

'Right… and the log?'

'I haven't done it.'

'Well as soon as you have could you let me know because I need it for planning tomorrow's journey.'

He rezipped the tent and I burst into tears again. When I had recovered it was dusk. Outside, Colum was cooking a rice and peanut supper in water he must have fetched himself. I unzipped the other side to peer out unseen at the fishermen. They had lit a fire under a large grid balanced on a structure of sticks. On it lay the day's catch. Two of the men were settling down on sackcloth by the fire to keep watch as it gently smoked the fish through the night.

*   *   *

The wife of David Livingstone, Mary, suffered deeply as she followed her husband on his demanding journeys. Her youth had been harsh – she was the daughter of the pioneering missionary Robert Moffat and had grown up in the lonely outpost of Kuruman in southern Africa. In her early twenties she was whisked by Livingstone to a new – and tougher – life farther north. Their home was remoter even than Kuruman and Livingstone dreamed of exploring ever farther.

Once, when Mary was five months pregnant, Livingstone loaded her and their children into an ox-wagon and they crawled north across the Kalahari Desert. The children, aged four, three and one, endured a diet without vegetables for four months; for two parched days they had no water to drink. They suffered from fever, brushed close to death. They were too weak to stand by the end of the four-month journey. When Mary bore a new baby daughter shortly after their arrival home it lived for a month and then died screaming.

Later Mary crossed the Kalahari with her husband for a second time. Again they endured the scorching desert. Again Mary was pregnant. Before they left, Livingstone had trouble explaining to Mary's parents how a devout Christian could behave so inhumanly towards his wife and children, as they urged him not to risk his family's lives again. His defence was illuminating: '*It is a venture to take wife and children into a country where fever, African fever, prevails. But who that believes in Jesus would refuse to make a venture for such a Captain?*'

In that utterance lay the defining strands of his character: the courage, the endurance, the obstinacy, the carelessness with other lives. The Christian conviction that had gripped him in childhood now convinced him he was God's instrument, intended for a career doing great works for his Maker. Livingstone's response to hardship and danger was correspondingly straightforward: '*If God has accepted my service then my life is charmed till my work is done.*'

At the age of fifty-seven, with so much successful exploration behind him, it would have been tempting for him to believe that his life had indeed been charmed so far. There was therefore every reason to be optimistic that his failing health would last until his mission was done. From day to day his task was to rise above the trivia and petty obstacles of life. For Livingstone, trivia included human relationships and human suffering – his own and anyone else's.

Later, I told Colum how overwhelmed I felt, and how he didn't seem to care. He continued to brush at my bicycle, without appearing to have heard me.

'Colum…?' He shifted slightly to better reach the chain he was cleaning. The sun had set and the mosquitoes were whining in the failing light. Finally, he put down the oily rag.

'OK. I shall try and be more sympathetic. But you've got to try harder too… you've just got to be more courageous.' I didn't reply.

*   *   *

'Fine fish…' Colum said doubtfully in Swahili. The young man nodded and grinned. The gently cooking fish were ugly, primeval creatures, a metre of muddy greyness. Tentacles protruded from their heads. Their bodies were eel-like. I shuddered as I watched them withering above the fire. They had had 400 million years in which to evolve but they had wasted it scavenging amongst sediments, and now a human – a pretender merely hundreds of thousands of years old – was roasting them for supper. The man, sleek and youthful, led us away from the fire to a small, wooden bench outside the only mud building in the camp. There his friend sat, a thin man with bloodshot eyes. Under the eaves of the wall above them, which had cracked profusely in the heat, was pinned a great shell which looked like the armour of some primitive, bottom-dwelling beast. The men said it was the head of a giant catfish: its body must have been at least the length of a man, maybe two. We nodded, impressed.

Under his baseball cap the youth smiled again, gratified at the impact the shell had made. He raised an old Fanta bottle towards us, now filled with a murky liquid. He gestured to Colum to sit down with them.

'Nina mtaka mdogo sana,' Colum said as he squashed himself amongst them. A cackle burst from the men.

'Mtaka mdogo,' repeated the bloodshot man, bending over in laughter so that his dirty shirt and decaying trousers crumpled around his scrawny body. He balanced a fragile rolled cigarette between his fingers.

Colum stood up again and turned his bottom towards them: 'Kwele,' he said, pointing at his khaki-covered buttocks, '... mtaka mdogo.'

Another explosion of laughter. Colum turned to me: 'I was just pointing out that I've got very small buttocks so I won't take up much space.'

The young, smooth-skinned one offered me his drink. It was *wanzuki* – fermented honey, silky on the tongue. I practised my fumbling Swahili: 'Where do you come from?'

'Some of us live in Ipole, some in Inyonga. We live here maybe for nine months of the year. When the water drops we go to other rivers.'

'But you have a house in a town?'

'Yes.'

I tried to think of something else to say. 'Are there many wild animals here?'

The smoker leant forward, cigarette held precariously between his fingers. His eyes narrowed: 'Yes, there are many animals.' He paused. 'Two nights ago there were seven lions around this camp.'

'No,' I said in disbelief. Smoker was enjoying my wide-eyed reaction. 'Yes, and there are many hippos at the river. They are there now,' he added eagerly. Of all East Africa's fauna, the protective mother hippo is the biggest killer.

'Here,' one of the men said to Colum, 'try this', and he passed him a plastic beaker half-full of a colourless liquid. Briefly, Colum examined it and I saw him brace himself. Then he put the beaker to his lips and emptied it with one gulp.

'Kali sana': 'Very fierce'. His voice was unsteady and his eyes were watering. There was a roar of laughter at his colloquial Swahili. Colum had been accepted.

Soon they were swapping the banter that unites men across the globe. My loneliness surged: I was not just a European struggling in Africa but a woman stranded in a world of men. But at least I did not feel threatened in Koga, so I gradually relaxed, lulled by the mellifluous Swahili. The day drifted towards evening, the light became heavier and softer. It yellowed the straw of the huts and turned the *wanzuki* golden. I breathed the sharp aroma of the men's hashish and my mind softened with the laughter and the coarse honey drink.

Then someone cried 'Gari!'. In the distance a dust cloud was forming in the orange evening light, and before long, the shambling weekly bus had shuddered to a halt. It was a precarious, multi-coloured contraption, with people hanging from doors and windows.

The road from Koga to Inyonga was the waterless stretch we had identified in London. In Tutuo, our Arab host had confirmed that we would never be able to pass by bicycle. The sand, he said, was knee deep – even the weekly bus laboured with extraordinary difficulty. Here, then, we were to make our only concession of the whole expedition.

All was rushing and noise as we passed our bicycles up to be tied amongst the sacks of maize, the buckets and the mattresses that festooned the roof. I handed a bag to one of the fishermen: 'Rubbish,' I said in Swahili. His eyes gleamed.

'Thank you,' he replied, cradling the bag.

'No, it's rubbish,' I insisted.

'Thank you,' he bowed and smiled, revealing three brown teeth. I gave up and scrambled inside, and with a long, ambling farewell melody on its horn, the bus creaked away from Koga and into the forest.

Outside it quickly grew dark, and hefty unseen tree branches constantly brushed the bus. It was easier not to consider what was happening to Colum, who had decided to stay on the roof with the bicycles. The bus dropped into craters and heaved itself out of them, throwing its hardened passengers from side to side. Eventually it descended into one hole too many and stopped there. We all climbed into the insect-infested night and pushed. Three times this happened and then, on the fourth time, the engine died.

A lithe lad in rolled-up trousers produced some heavy tools from nowhere and within an hour the engine roared into life again. We heaved onwards. As I gripped the seat to counteract the jolts I wondered what my fellow passengers were thinking. Perhaps they were delighted that technology had produced a way of getting from Tabora to Inyonga in a day once a week. Or did they feel paralysed – did they have any inkling that they had been dealt the shoddy part of the world's bargain? I stared out of the window and thought of Livingstone, inspiration for a century of meddling in East Africa. What difference had it made?

Night simmered in Inyonga. The naked flames of oil lamps cast balloons of gold into the darkness and gave us erratic glimpses of the little crowds that bubbled from the bus, swarmed up its sides or dispersed noisily home. Someone led us to the house of an old man with a white beard that drooped to his feet, an Arab so ancient that he might have been from that ancestral generation which ventured this far west in Livingstone's time – and never returned. Though it was late the frail man welcomed us and soon we were drifting into a milky, cardamom-fringed slumber.

*   *   *

'It's not possible to cycle on that road. And it's not possible to walk either. It's too far.'

'And there's lots of sand?'

'Yes,' the plump man leant against his Land Rover, pleased that we had grasped the point. His shirt hung open and sweat moistened his generous stomach. Below him the mechanic's bony legs jutted from under the vehicle. I turned to Colum: 'Does he mean it's absolutely impossible to cycle it or just that it's very difficult?'

Colum spoke in Swahili to the man, whose reply was unambiguous.

'Nobody cycles on that road.' He banged the vehicle's bonnet with his hand, and the mechanic stirred uncomfortably. 'I tell you there's too much sand.' They were the words we had come to dread: 'Changa mengi. Changa mengi mengi.'

The driver bent down to help the mechanic who had pulled out what looked like the vehicle's entire alimentary canal.

'Do you take the Land Rover along that road?' Colum asked.

'Yes. I go to Mpanda one day and I come back the next day.'

'So you're going tomorrow?' Colum was disbelieving.

'Yes.'

It was hard to imagine that the vehicle would be mobile within less than a week. The driver twisted a dirty rag in his hands, recovering from his exertion, and watched us.

'What time do you leave?' asked Colum.

'About three.' In Swahili, that means three hours after sunrise. As we said no more he wandered off down the street, leaving the mechanic staring morosely at the Land Rover's entrails.

Maps spread, we looked at the track that headed south west to Mpanda. It was a little south of the route we calculated Livingstone to have taken but it was the nearest we would get to it. Half way along it, fifty kilometres after Inyonga, there was a steep escarpment where a camp was marked, and a spring of water. If something went wrong on that track we would be stranded, with no prospect of a vehicle for two days and with less than one day's water.

We trudged down Inyonga's main street. At a nondescript mud building with a rag hanging in the doorway we found the town's only *hoteli*.

Inside, the heat seeped around three tables covered in patchy green linoleum and scattered with spilt sugar over which the flies swooped. In a wooden cupboard with glass windows sat a plate of forgotten *andazis*. We were the only customers. 'We are so poor here,' the proprieter told us with no prompting. 'The problem with Tanzania is that we have the resources but we have no money.'

We ordered the customary black tea with its compulsory spoonfuls of sugar, and drank it out of plastic beakers. I watched Colum. The relaxed man I had known for so many years was disappearing by the day. Tanzania had hardened him almost into aggression, and it frightened me. Now he was determined we should walk or cycle along that road.

I gathered some energy to fulfil my part of the bargain I had made in Koga.

'We have got to travel on that road and we've got to go under our own steam. What else did the Land Rover driver say?'

Colum was drawing patterns in the spilt sugar: 'He said his is the only connection for people who want to travel between Inyonga and Mpanda.'

I knew his moods well, but nowadays there was something else about him, as if he himself was exploring a new side to his character. He gazed out through the door, his eyes set: 'I'm not convinced that track is not walkable or cycleable. We just need to find one person who's done it...'

We returned to the house of our Arab hosts, pausing in their front room shop to explain the problem. Colum was quiet, so I stumbled on in Swahili until a small man emerged from the recesses of the room and asked to see our map. Wearily, Colum traced the thin pink line that, in theory, connected us with Mpanda.

'Ah,' said the little man slowly, 'the road to Mpanda. It's a difficult road but...' – suddenly he had our attention – '... I have cycled it.'

Clean Clothes, Shining Bicycles

Thick sand on the track

(*opposite*) Livingstone's men were without food. He wrote 'The women collect mushrooms.'

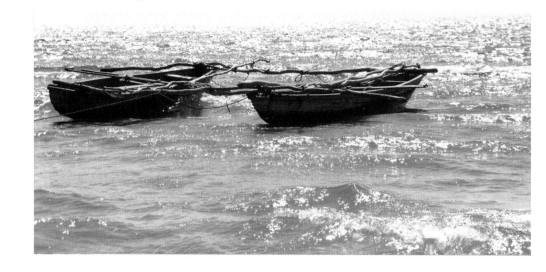

Karema - The White Fathers' palace

(*Opposite, top*) A dhow
(*Opposite, bottom*) A fishing catamaran

Chickens often had comfortable accommodation.

(*Opposite, top*) Our bicycles arrive at Wampembe
(*Opposite, bottom*) Aisling crosses the Luena

His Royal Highness
Chief Chitambo IV,
whose ancestor met
Livingstone.

The Livingstone
Memorial marks the
spot where his heart
is buried

Log Book Extract

DAY 8 – Monday 2nd December

PHASE 1

FROM: Inyonga

TO: Kanono Camp

POSITION: 31°42'33" E
   6°29'31" S

TIME CYCLING: 9 hours 30 minutes

DISTANCE TRAVELLED: 48km

AVERAGE SPEED: 5km/hr

ROUTE: Took track towards Ulende out of Inyonga

TRACK CONDITION: Very sandy. We estimate that we pushed the
   bicycles for 23 of the 48km.

BICYCLES – PERFORMANCE: Aisling's back brakes playing up.

BICYCLES – MAINTENANCE: Removed Aisling's back brakes.
   Routine check of gears, spokes, chains, brakes, tyres. Thorn
   discovered in Aisling's tyre this evening. Slow puncture – which may
   seal itself.

WEATHER: At midday our thermometer showed 43°C in the shade.
   No cloud, no breeze.

HEALTH: Backs of hands badly burnt. Aisling has blisters on feet from
   pushing bike much of day. Anti-histamine ointment applied to tsetse
   bites, which cover all exposed skin like a rash of red dots.

EQUIPMENT: Nothing to report.

LANDSCAPE: Early on, some tobacco cultivation and drying, then
   dense, flat forest, though more jungly than before. Many palms.

EXPENDITURE: None

FLUID CONSUMPTION: 18 litres

FOOD: During day: peanuts, andazis, eggs, salt.
   Evening meal: rice, stock cube, and onions, mango and peanut
   crumble.

COMMENT: Lost a valuable hour this morning by oversleeping – we did not leave until 6.30am – then a very hard, hot day. The forest is severely infested with tsetse. Headnets and heavy clothing worn all day. Tsetse appear to find light clothing less attractive than dark clothing, but they are completely indifferent to insect-repellent. Saw no one all day except two honey collectors. When camping, we have taken to tying a string between the tent frame and the bikes before going to sleep – then at least we will know if anyone is nicking them. Probably unlikely round here.

LIVINGSTONE: To our north. Our paths are now parallel, due west, 20km apart. Livingstone is ill.

6

From Inyonga to Mpanda
by Aisling

Fortitude is far rarer than physical fitness. Fortitude: that courage in adversity, that gritting of the teeth when there is no food and the tent has blown away.
Nicholas Crane, *Expedition Planners' Handbook and Directory*

IT WAS the only enjoyable hour of the day: very early morning, so early that it was still too dark to travel. But there was a faint lightness in the sky. I stopped unpegging our tent from its site on the foothills of the escarpment and watched. The sky looked vast when there was nothing below it but miles of flat, uninhabited African landscape. Silent cracks of lightning raced across it. There was no thunder and no rain, just monochromatic mass entertainment for an indifferent forest audience.

The moon began to fade and the rising sun coloured the eastern clouds crimson. I gazed down onto the flat land we had crossed the previous day. The dusty greenness of the trees was emerging with the dawn. There were low mountains in the far distance and yesterday's track, or the last kilometre of it, was visible below.

The previous day had been ten hours of strain, most of it spent off the bikes forcing a furrow through the heavy white sand. By nine in the morning the heat was like a sponge drawing the sweat from us. There was nowhere to hide from the sun – not a cloud slipped over it – and there was no tree tall enough to offer our path a fringe of shade. We greedily gulped our water ration every half hour, and in between it offered itself back, drop by drop, from our pores.

My arms ached, my feet and hands were sore. I would try to cycle, weave to a halt, dismount, plod and then try again. Worse even than the heat and the sand were the tsetse flies, driven wild by the delicacy of soft pink flesh after months of animal hide. They landed in ones and twos at first – each as big as a horsefly, each sinking a stout needle into the skin in search of blood. Soon they were swooping in their hundreds in an orgy that lasted all day. Infuriated, I learned to control the bicycle with one hand and use the other to keep swatting. The flies can bore through a layer of cloth, so we sweated under extra trousers and shirts while headnets kept them off our faces. Once, when a fly crawled inside my headnet, I groped for it and fell off the bicycle, kicking at the metal frame and screaming in tearful anger.

We managed to kill a good many. I perfected the knack of trapping one in a corner of the headnet and squeezing it into a bloody little mess onto which, with dull satisfaction, I projected a sermon: 'Let that be a lesson to all of you'. Colum would catch them, pull off their mouth parts and release them again in the hope that they would breed along Lamarckian principles into a less aggravating species. But our massacres were trivial, and we soon learned to drink through the nets and to untie them just for a second in order to poke food into our mouths.

Tsetse flies can carry sleeping sickness, a disease that humans catch infrequently but from which their animals regularly die. Livingstone recognised that tsetse were one of the barriers to the colonisation of East Africa, and so on previous journeys he had brought with him buffaloes, mules, cows, camels and donkeys to test their immunity. The donkeys seemed to have fared the best, and he had convinced himself that they were resistant, so he brought two with him from Tabora. Their health was important not just for supporting his colonisation plans, but also because they could carry him when he was too tired to walk.

The animals did well at first, remaining healthy through the forest and until the southern tip of Lake Tanganyika. Then, to Livingstone's distress, the larger one fell ill. '*It was distinctly the effects of tsetse,*' he wrote, '*for the eyes and all the mouth and nostrils swelled.*' It recovered briefly but relapsed again, and within ten days it was dead.

With a stoicism that exasperated us, Livingstone barely mentioned the frustrations he and his men must have endured in the tsetse belts. He simply referred to the need for forced marches '*on account of tsetse fly*'. It was typical of his attitude towards adversity. Hunger tormented him and his men. They had beads and calico with which to barter for food, but often the land was empty and there was no one with whom to exchange them. Already his group was passing through country ravaged by war – Arabs plundering Africans, tribes raiding their neighbours for slaves. The legacy was a string of abandoned villages and barren fields. Even when the fifty-seven travellers found an inhabited village they often discovered that the people cultivated little '*for fear of enemies*'.

Yet Livingstone's response was phlegmatic. Arriving one day in a ghost village, they found an abundance of sweet potatoes. The famished people fell on them, scrabbling in the earth for the misshapen bundles of starch.

All Livingstone wrote was: '*A great help, for all are hungry*'. Neither did Livingstone complain about his fickle health. For six days of his trudge through the heat and tsetse of the forest he ate nothing and did not mention the fact in his diary until the sixth day, when he was briefly clinical, recording that he was '*ill with bowels*'.

He had always persevered through the most debilitating of illnesses. Two years before, he had developed foot ulcers that took eight months to heal. His description of them was more emotive than usual. The ulcers '*eat through everything – muscle, tendon and bone, and often lame permanently if they do not kill... If the foot were put to the ground, a discharge of bloody ichor flowed, and the same discharge happened every night with considerable pain, that prevented sleep*'.

Livingstone's phenomenal powers of endurance developed in his childhood alongside his religious conviction. From six in the morning until eight at night, six days a week, the children of the cotton mills ducked and darted around the machinery to retrieve thread. In his desperation to learn, Livingstone propped his books on the noisy machinery. When his peers escaped, exhausted, at the end of the day, he ignored his body's protestations and went to school for another two hours. Then he would read in bed until late at night. The conditions wore down nearly everyone but Livingstone, who had a rare set of qualities that allowed his strength to grow, rather than be destroyed, in the harsh surroundings. On the first of his three journeys in Africa, when he explored as far as the west coast and then crossed to the east, he survived three weeks in a canoe on a furious river while suffering from fever, vomiting and diarrhoea. Later he grew so weak that he often slid from his ox to the ground. But he went on.

His hardiness surprised me because I could not at first reconcile it with what I already knew of Livingstone – his deeply personal relationship with God and his sensitivity to natural beauty. It seemed to me that a man with such a tough shell must also have had a mind like sandpaper, not one that could take pleasure in the shade of a flower petal or which could rejoice in theological meditation.

There are different species of endurance. Some people are born with diminished sensitivity, while others are dulled by a harsh life which they survive through passive resignation. There is no doubt that Livingstone was from hardy stock, that his childhood toughened him tremendously. But that was not the key to his powers of endurance. Livingstone was an ascetic. In a sense, he sought pain. His was a conscious and deliberate endurance, a summoning of the mental faculties to find and defeat the merely physical. He had an indestructible will, and it was a point of pride for him that his body was utterly under his control.

I was trying to exhibit fortitude, a word I had belatedly remembered was my expedition motto. Boundless fortitude was impossible for me. I needed goals to be finite, so I made a rule with myself. I would display fortitude on three successive occasions – perhaps two falls from the bike followed by one tsetse fly in the headnet. On the fourth occasion I could have a reward: a scream, five minutes in the next bit of shade or a glucose tablet.

Five hours passed.

'What shall we do when the Land Rover comes?' Colum's mildness disguised the import of the question. We had come to an agreement with the Land Rover driver the day before. He would carry water for us and drop it off as he went past, but if he found us in trouble he would load us into his vehicle and carry us to safety. The Land Rover was due to pass soon so we had a sore decision to make.

'It's up to you, really. Whatever you decide, I'll go along with it,' said Colum, and we continued in silence for a while. We both knew that we had only planned to take transport on the stretch from Koga to Inyonga. Then he went on: 'But we've already shown this morning that we can do this. If we really want to, we can win through.'

I did not agree. For the last few hours I had sustained myself with the thought of the Land Rover's arrival, and of how I would fall sobbing in front of its wheels so that it could not continue without us. The drama would show Colum how much I was suffering.

'Really, it would be a sort of a failure to accept a ride anywhere else…' Was his tone slightly imploring? I glanced across at him. He had stopped pushing, and was leaning over his handle bars, his headnet pulled up. His face was tanned deep brown, unshaven and smeared with sweat and dust. Our eyes met.

'I mean, I know it's hard work…' Did that count as sympathy? Despairingly, I swatted at a tsetse, and considered the parameters of the deal we had struck in Koga.

As I wrestled with the decision, plumes of dust formed in the distance behind us. Soon the jeep materialised, labouring along the sandy track. The vehicle was overflowing with life and luggage, packed according to the creative African style and, as I gazed at the men who clung to its sides and the mountain of goods stacked on the roof, I realised, almost with relief, that the decision had been made for me. There was no room – no space for two more people, their bikes and their panniers. Land Rover man swung ten litres of water to the ground and grinned. Twenty curious faces watched us from the windows as we waved him on. Then they were gone, and just the dust cloud remained, hanging in the hot, still air.

We struggled on. For more than twenty kilometres we had been pushing the bicycles. Progress was so slow that the speedometer on Colum's handlebars registered a zero. Then there was a flicker of movement in the forest. Instantly, my sweaty sulkiness was forgotten, and my heart was beating hard with panic. Colum reached for the machete.

Cautiously, we drew level with the point on the trackside where the movement had caught our eye. Now we made out two men. One lay asleep under a straw shelter at the edge of the trees, almost indistinguishable from the earth. The other was on his feet, stretching. When he saw us he blinked twice and kicked his sleeping companion who gave a sharp grunt and scrambled clumsily to his feet. Then both men froze, staring at Colum, and I had to concede that he did have a sinister air about him. His dark green headnet completely hid his face, and he was swathed from head to toe in heavy clothing. The machete was unsheathed at his side.

'Habari za kulala?' – 'How was your sleep?', he asked.

One of the men slowly motioned us to their small patch of shade. They were honey collectors, he said, living here amongst the wild animals. In the cool of the mornings they slipped up trees to tend their hives amongst the branches. During the day, they slept – the best way to behave in such heat. If you stay perfectly still you can also hide from the tsetse fly which is attracted by movement. Back in Tabora a tsetse expert had told Colum: 'Either peddle very fast or stay still – above all, don't behave like a cow.' A cow, we now realised, behaves approximately like a human pushing a heavy bike through sand.

We shared our biscuits and peanuts with the men, and one of them dipped into a large barrel with a flat stick and scooped out thick, brown honey which we licked from our hands. At last we dragged ourselves back into the sun and the flies.

I began to realise that there was a way of dealing with the pain. The heat was constant; the tsetse flies attacked at a steady rate; every physical onslaught had a rhythmic predictability like the beat of the rain. With a trick of the mind one could forget time and just steadily put one foot in front of the other. I knew that in a day – or an hour, or a minute – Colum would tell me that I had taken the last step.

It was 5pm and we had been trudging for nine hours. The world seemed very bright, and the exposed metal of my bike frame shone like flame, burning my hands. My throat had stiffened like parchment. All at once, my resolve folded, and I sank to the ground. Scalding tears began to course down my cheeks. I fumbled through the headnet to save them and guide them to my mouth. I watched Colum's receding back as he pushed onwards, oblivious of me, again. Before long, he was a shimmering figure only a few inches high.

'*Why?*' My voice cracked like dry bark, and I tasted blood on my lips.

'Why are we *here*?' Silence. Nothing but stark branches against the incandescent blue of the sky. My head sagged and I felt comfortably sleepy.

It had been all right for Livingstone. He had a tried and trusted strategy for dealing with the hardship. He had his fortitude and his God: something inside and something outside, or perhaps they were both inside. But what was there for us? Colum had become like a stranger – I did not know what drove him on. And for me, there was nothing. There was no reason for me to put myself through this, driven like a machine with no time to reflect.

I picked at the hem of my trousers. It was solid with tiny white crystals of sand, each sparkling like water. With surprise, I noticed that my hands were dry. I had stopped sweating long ago. I drowsed. I did not feel hot anymore.

Then Colum came back. I felt his solicitous hands putting water on my face, and in my mouth. At last, I opened my eyes. He had lifted his headnet, and his face was pale. 'Look,' he said, and he opened his hand. In his palm was something that was caked with dirt, but which glowed livid orange. I looked at him questioningly. For the first time for a few days, he smiled. Then he winced. Tiny beads of blood had formed on his lips as well.

'It's a mango stone. I found it on the ground. There must be people about.'

He lifted me to my feet, and we continued. Colum stayed beside me now, casting anxious glances at me from time to time. At last, he pointed ahead. 'There.' I raised my eyes. There was a wrinkle in the flatness in front of us, and on its lowest slopes was a white-painted building with a thatched roof. After the endless chaos of forest, it seemed like a mirage.

Within ten minutes we were installed in Kanono camp, a row of empty and decaying houses built years ago when the government had enough money to consider issues such as track maintenance. At Kanono lived three men and some hens beside a clear, cold stream which cascaded down the hillside. The men cooked their chicken and porridge on wood fires and slept in the doorless, glassless, furnitureless buildings. We pitched our tent beside the broken houses and Colum cooked peanut, onion and mango stew with rice. For pudding, we ate mangos in sugar with peanut topping.

*   *   *

The next day we tramped for another ten hours, up the Kanono escarpment and across a plateau. We pushed our bicycles for much of the time along a river of sand with forested banks. The land was as abandoned as it had been in Livingstone's day when he wrote: '*No people, or marks of them.*'

The plateau was uncomfortably quiet except for the eerie creaking of palm trees, their great leaves shifting like gates on rusting hinges. Each creak startled me, and provoked a lone bird in the forest to break into a ghostly call.

'Ais,' Colum barked with an urgency that made me jump. 'Look.'

'What? What is it?'

'Look at the ground, carefully.'

We stopped and scrutinised the track. It was indented with the prints of animals – big prints, small prints, unmistakeable lion prints, prints so large they could only have been an elephant's. They were all heading in the same direction, as if they were fleeing from some calamity. I shuddered.

'We must keep making a noise,' I whispered. Several times we stopped and silently scanned the track ahead and behind. Nothing moved but the tsetse flies.

In the late afternoon, we saw a twist of smoke curling up from amongst a copse of mango trees. It marked the outskirts of a village – the first for 100 kilometres – and the end of Livingstone's '*flat forest*'.

Urawira was a run-down place, with shanty buildings of mud and corrugated iron. A single shop sold soap and biscuits, and there was a *hoteli* where we drank strong black tea. That night, we shared a rickety outhouse with a startled hen. By morning, it had presented us with an egg.

*　　*　　*

As the moon was setting next morning we slid out of Urawira, and the sun rose on a land that had relaxed. Rivers brimmed with water and there was greenness and plenty. Strung along the road was a suburbia of mud-walled compounds, the red earth around each one neatly swept and bordered with flowering bushes. Hens foraged and people dug in preparation for the rains. Green shoots of cassava poked from freshly shaped furrows.

Now our road joined a broader one and filled with people cycling to Mpanda. They mustered only a teetering pedal power but their cargo would have challenged the capacity of a small car. One man laboured uphill beside us with an old woman on his handlebars and a younger woman, who carried a baby, on the back carrier. A haystack, out of which protruded a head and two wheels, overtook us. Live hens squawked from a box the size of a washing machine as their owner freewheeled down the hill we were climbing. Perhaps they were urging him on.

When Livingstone stopped near here he was still recovering from dysentery. '*Rest here, as the complaint does not yield to medicine or time; but I begin to eat now, which is a favourable symptom.*' Soon we would rest too and I would write copiously about thirst, hunger, fatigue and self-discipline.

Fortitude: I did not yet possess it but I knew, intimately, what it was.

7

In Mpanda
by Colum

The chiefs, the chiefs to whom do they pray?
To the shades! To the shades! ...
The Europeans, the Europeans to whom do they pray?
To money! To money! ...
The baptised, the baptised to whom do they pray?
To Jesus! To Jesus!
From a song sung by East African Christians (1930s)

THE MISSIONARIES had spotted us as we arrived in Mpanda and had invited us to dinner, but now we hesitated at the threshold, diffident in our filthy clothes.

'Come in, come in,' Celia called. Simon emerged from a tumble of children and table-laying, and they intoned together: 'Shut the door,' with a sharpness that surprised me, and sent us both darting for the handle.

'The mosquitoes are bad at this time of night,' explained Celia as she came towards us, wiping her hands on a cloth.

'Welcome,' she said, her face shining with eagerness: 'It's so nice to have other *wazungu* to talk to.'

She led us across the large, bare room, picking her way over a detritus of dog-chewed toys. Through a wide archway, up a step, we squeezed ourselves onto benches around a table.

A child kneeled up on a chair beside me and demanded my admiration of a picture of a snake. 'Very, very bad,' he said in an awed voice, his blue eyes wide with wonder. He had straight white-blond hair that curled at the ends. He looked like an angel. The oldest child – a girl – stalked silently past us with the full-blown self-consciousness of adolescence. The youngest was a toddler.

Celia returned to her preparations in the kitchen. She issued instructions and the family responded mechanically, a stream of fluid movement around us. Finally she joined us and Simon took his place at the head of the table. With an unspoken consensus, the family bowed its heads. Simon uttered a brief prayer, his face as closed and inscrutable as Celia's was open, and then the hubbub returned, as if someone had thrown a switch.

'Mosquitoes are rife here,' said Simon with a sigh. He had a young face but it showed little trace of light-heartedness. 'I suppose one day I'll get round to the nets.' He nodded towards the windows, where the mesh was punctured and ripped.

'We just haven't found time,' Celia explained.

'We came here to be missionaries but it's so easy to spend the whole time on maintenance.' He paused and then, with unexpected intensity: 'I'm *not* going to let that happen.'

Celia passed us a plate and, with an appreciative smile, Aisling helped herself to a piece of white cheese.

'Yes, cheese is really quite a luxury. It came from Mwanza, up north by the lake. We were up there recently, visiting old friends – it's where we trained, you see.'

'And how long did that take?' I asked between mouthfuls.

'A year of classes and seminars.' She shifted dishes round the table. I raised my eyebrows.

'Oh, but there's a lot to learn. We have to know about language, culture, how villages work, how to approach people – all the things that are specific to Tanzania. Gone are the days when missionaries just arrived and had to find out these things for themselves. It's all very thorough today.'

'So how long have you been here for?'

'Just under a year. Mpanda's our first posting.' She paused and looked at me, her brow creased into anxiety. 'We still feel very green. There's so much to learn.' She had a face across which a shadow of every emotion drifted like weather across the sky. Now her eyes were wide with almost confessional honesty: '... sometimes it's so difficult to know how to behave.'

Simon was chewing with patient deliberation and gazing abstractedly at his wife. He showed no hint of unease at her candidness about their fallibility in doing God's work.

'So what, exactly, does a missionary do?' I asked him.

His adam's apple moved up and down as he swallowed, and then he engaged me with a deep, steady gaze.

'Well, I travel all over the place, often deep into the forest. Sometimes I'm away for a couple of weeks at a time. We try to concentrate on people who have had no contact with the outside world.'

'They're the ones who stand to gain the most,' Celia added.

'How do you get to them?' I asked.

'By bicycle. They're the only things that can get down the paths in the forest.' He wiped his mouth with the back of his hand.

'The rainy season is the hardest – wading through swollen rivers, and pushing through the mud to reach a few families living in the bush. That's difficult.' I searched his face for traces of self-congratulation, but all I saw were the circles under his eyes. One sensed he would do anything to touch the lives of the pagans in the forest. He seemed a driven man, compelled by faith and also, perhaps, by the same pioneering stoicism that had pushed Livingstone '*beyond every other man's line of things*'.

'But using a spotter plane should make things easier,' Celia added in a comforting tone. Simon's face brightened.

'Yes, it should help.' He nodded towards a large map hanging on one wall, sprinkled with red pins. 'We've started identifying target tribes from the air before going in on the ground. It should be far more effective that way.'

'But what do you actually do? I mean, when you arrive in a village what do you say?'

'Our method is to go in and to ask questions,' Simon replied, 'to leave people perplexed – then they want to find out the truth... let me show you.' And he left the table, returning with a worn volume from the bookcase. He began to read out loud: 'What happens when you die? Where do you go when you die? Does how you have behaved in this life affect what happens when you die?' He closed the book with a snap and looked up.

'These are the sort of questions we raise, you see, and if they really start to think about them, if they are really concerned about dying, they soon want to know the answers.'

'What happens to their traditional beliefs?' Aisling's question surprised me. I looked at her. She was sitting back in her chair, gazing at the fork she held in her hand and tilting it so it caught the light. Simon took time to sit down again. Then he put his hands together and frowned.

'The trouble is that their ideas are so contradictory.'

'You see, Christianity is the only religion that is self-consistent.' We both turned to Celia.

'The truth that we offer is so much better. When they start thinking about these questions, their own beliefs can't provide all the answers.'

Perhaps it was the intensity of their spiritual life, or perhaps it was their isolation from the outside world, but it seemed to me that Simon and Celia shared an extended consciousness. Their thoughts were always in tandem, always circling together around familiar issues which stood out like landmarks on their spiritual map. Together, they were in a perpetual round of rehearsing arguments and questioning anomalies.

'In the West,' Simon continued, 'most people's ideas about what happens after they die don't make sense either. Questioning can often lead them into difficulties...' He paused, and looked directly at me: 'but perhaps we'll get on to that later.'

Celia cut across the uncomfortable silence: 'At least in this culture there is a general belief in God – we are starting one step forward from where we are in Europe...'

'... it's certainly easier to win Africans over...'

'... but making people stick is harder...'

'... whereas in Europe,' said Simon, 'winning people in the first place is difficult. But when Europeans are converted, they tend to stick to it much better. When they know the Spirit, that is.'

They paused in their train of thought. It was so familiar to them, and yet it resonated with the influences of another era. Simon and Celia had been sent by the African Inland Mission – one of a group of religious societies known as the 'Faith Missions' founded shortly after Livingstone's death. One of the new brand of missionaries was CT Studd. In 1915 he summed up the zeal which had, from the outset, typified the movement: 'Christ's call is to capture men from the Devil's clutches. But this can only be accomplished by a red-hot, unconventional, unfettered Holy Ghost religion...'

The Faith Missions were romantically inspired and had no time for the comforts of home: Studd spurned 'the artistic musical performances, the fancy collars, the silver croziers, the embroidered altar cloths' in favour of a religion of the heart and direct confrontation with Satan. In the African Inland Mission, the emphasis has always been on individual spirituality and evangelisation.

I looked around the sparsely furnished living area, through the door into the primitive kitchen, where buckets of water still served in place of plumbing despite the passage of a year. I looked again at the windows, where Simon had not had time to fix the mesh. Mosquitoes darted in through the gaps around the ill-fitting shutters, and wove through the light and into the shadows beyond where we sat. This was the spartan homestead of crusaders in Africa, Christians with a formidable missionary pedigree, and a dream of the past.

Celia turned to Aisling, an open smile on her face.

'But how about you?' she asked. 'What on earth brings you on a journey like this?'

'We're trying to recreate the very last journey of David Livingstone...'

'He started in Tabora and he passed through here...' I began, but suddenly everybody was talking at once. The white-haired boy was bouncing on his chair chanting 'the explorer, the explorer', Celia was finishing a sentence with the words '... a truly great missionary', and Simon was glancing from my face to Aisling's, looking for some reflection of the religious fervour that now glinted in his eyes. He was talking rapidly, intensely. It was Livingstone who had inspired the founder of the African Inland Mission to stretch a chain of missions, like beacons, across Africa. It was Livingstone who had provided the impetus for the great surge of missionary endeavour during the nineteenth century. It was Livingstone, ultimately, who had brought Simon and Celia to Mpanda.

*   *   *

In East Africa, the nineteenth-century missionaries made their entrance into a turbulent world. Far away in the south-east a powerful warlord had risen up and was devouring neighbouring tribes and laying waste the land. At the head of a disciplined army of warriors, Shaka Zulu practised a new kind of warfare, the brutality of which had never been seen before. He built an empire, sweeping all before him. The Zulus called it the Mfecane, which means 'the grinding'.

Shattered bands of the conquered fled northwards, their advance pushing other tribes as far as southern Tanzania. The flood of refugees imposed an unsustainable burden on the meagre resources of the scattered communities east and south of Lake Tanganyika. Cattle disease and famine caused thousands to die in the long, hot dry seasons.

At about this time Arab traders were penetrating the interior from their foothold in Zanzibar. They came for ivory and for humans to fuel the burgeoning trade in slaves. Those too feeble or too old to manage the journey to the slaving stations were shot, or were left to die by the side of the track. Others simply pined away. With their tribes and families in bondage or slaughtered, they were without hope. The point of departure from mainland Africa for slaves being shipped overseas became known as Bagamoyo. In Swahili, Bagamoyo means 'lay down your heart'.

However, in spite of their inhumanity, the Arabs never had any aspirations to build an empire or proselytise the heathen, or even to develop the region for future commercial activity. Their interest was limited purely to short-term gain. Ultimately, it was another, far less rapacious interference which would have a greater impact in East Africa.

In the 1860s, in a small village on the shores of Lake Tanganyika, it is said that a diviner went into a prophetic trance and spoke of a spear that would come from the far distance, and against which the fortresses of the chiefs would have no power. Within a decade, the first white missionaries had arrived.

The Victorian missionaries were men of considerable hardiness, and were fortified with the unshakeable self-belief of a people whose nation was at the peak of its imperial power. In the face of their zeal, it is surprising that the nineteenth-century missionary endeavour did not meet with more success. Robert Moffat, Livingstone's father-in-law, had been one of the earliest missionaries in central Africa, but all he had to show for fifteen years of unremitting work was a congregation numbered in tens rather than hundreds.

However, the missionaries were not destined to stay on the sidelines for ever: the 'magic' which they offered was too powerful to be ignored. From the outset, resourceful tribal chieftains saw the strategic advantages that the missionaries' fire-arms could offer in inter-tribal wars. Other chiefs were impressed by the Europeans' wider technological skills, and demanded teachers to train their people as blacksmiths and carpenters.

From here, it was a small step to identifying Christianity with prosperity and advancement. With cunning that verged on the disingenuous, some missionaries moved to exploit the power of their wealth and technology. In southern Tanzania, one recorded how he '... showed them a Bible and told them it was *it* that made our nation rich and powerful'.

*   *   *

After dinner we moved into the spartan sitting-room where our voices echoed, muffled only by a few cane chairs and a single bookcase. A large, incongruous television occupied an alcove. Simon followed my gaze: 'We use it as a preaching tool.'

Aisling and I nodded, as if it was the most obvious explanation in the world.

'Have you heard of the *Jesus Video*?' Celia's question was sudden and her gaze disconcertingly intense.

'No,' I replied uncertainly.

'It's all about the life of Christ – dramatised. It's very good.' She made a movement towards a small untidy pile of videos on the floor.

'And you use it for teaching about Christianity?' Aisling asked quickly.

'Yes,' replied Simon. 'And the great thing is that they can easily identify with it.' He stretched back in his chair while Celia leant forward enthusiastically: 'You see, the life of an African farmer is very similar to the way of life described in the Bible. Their food, their clothes, their houses – it's the peasant way of life. It's much closer to the Bible than our lives are in the West.'

She paused.

'And it's very realistically done. It's really been very well put together.

Do you know, when people come in here to watch it they actually believe that what they are seeing is happening? They actually believe it.'

She drew the last sentence out, savouring each word. Her eager gaze searched our faces. I made a movement with my eyebrows that I hoped would pass as a nod.

'Of course, they are new to television, and theirs is a culture in which there is no acting,' Simon added. He smiled indulgently: 'When it comes to the Crucifixion, they are on their feet and really angry. We have to ask them to leave their sticks outside before we turn the video on.'

I dropped my eyes to where I would not meet either Celia's or Simon's – to the puppy which was lying on its back by our feet. Aisling reached down, and slowly rubbed the soft pink skin of its belly.

'They go away so fired up, and so excited about the Gospel...'

I was just out of reach of the puppy. I moved along the sofa slightly, and extended a foot. Contentedly, the dog took my bootlace in its mouth and started chewing.

*   *   *

By Tanzanian standards, Mpanda is a town of medium size, with a railway station, several bustling markets and a grid of dusty streets. The town's other Europeans lived and worked at the Moravian Mission. Their house stood behind high walls lined with wire at the junction of two wide and pot-holed streets. There was a satellite dish on the roof.

I knocked at the door. Through a small window, I looked into a silent hallway where a fan moved lazily overhead. No answer. I knocked again.

As we turned to leave, we heard the weak clicking of a bolt, and the door opened a little; there was a glimpse of a beautiful woman. She opened the door wider. She was pale and exquisite, with skin like a waxy magnolia flower. She had an air of serene fragility, a slender carving in polished bone.

No, it was just her here today. The other missionaries were out working. Her voice was no more than a murmur. She was so sorry not to be able to invite us in, but she had had a touch of malaria. She spoke of it lightly, but she held the back of a chair for support, and taut sinews stood out on her wrist. Where were we going?

It felt like a guilty secret, and an old uneasiness stirred. Why were we deliberately seeking out hardship and possible danger when this woman had been reduced to a shadow? Vagueness was the only way out.

'We're touring,' I said. 'We may try to get to Karema, and then see if we can head south down the shore of the lake.' It sounded very plausible, and much more palatable than some mad idea about following the meanderings of an explorer. Her eyes grew wide in the gloom. 'You'll never make it,' she said softly, 'There are no paths.'

As we walked back towards our guesthouse, I seethed with agitation. The woman had put into words a fear which had been growing unacknowledged in my mind. Even on our large-scale maps, few paths were shown on the lakeside. Farther south in particular, I had to concede that there could be a problem. In these areas the contours were tightly bunched close to the shoreline, and the tree symbol pressed right down to the water's edge. Paths that were shown were no more than disembodied shreds, like random stitches at the edge of a piece of material.

And yet the lakeside was studded with villages. That they drew their livelihood from the water was not in question – no road serviced the eastern shoreline of Tanganyika for more than 200 kilometres. To the east of our route down the shore there was nothing but a vast, empty hinterland between the lake and the main road south from Mpanda.

Spreading the maps out on the floor in our room, we tried to convince ourselves that what we were attempting was possible.

'There *must* be paths linking the villages…'

'Either that or they don't travel…'

'Yes, but they need to trade…'

'Well perhaps they all go by boat…'

We lapsed into silence, speculating about the marine and terrestrial trading patterns of rural Tanzania. Then, with grating cheerfulness, Aisling said: 'Let's go as far as Karema.' That was where the road from Mpanda hit the shore. 'They'll tell us pretty soon if what we're trying to do is possible.'

*   *   *

On our second evening in Mpanda, Simon and Celia again asked us to eat with them. During dinner I asked Simon whether his work had taken him down the side of the lake.

'No, the paths aren't great. I couldn't get my bicycle through – in fact, I had to walk when we were preaching down there.'

'Isn't that the time you got cut off?' asked Celia.

'Yes – we ended up fording a river chest-deep. It was just after the start of the rains last year.'

'Which month was that?' I asked quietly.

'Oh, it must have been late October… it was very bad last year.'

Today was 6th December. The rains were already overdue. The possibility of being trapped by the rainy season in a lakeside village was not one that I had seriously entertained before. Simon was unaware of the chilling effect his comments were having on my spirits, and continued talking: 'But it was worth it. They really needed our help down here. Satan was amongst them.'

I looked up, the prospect of prolonged isolation on the lakeside momentarily forgotten. His voice had remained level.

'Do you encounter Satan very often?' I asked, hoping that I matched his matter-of-factness.

'Oh yes,' Celia answered. 'We drive out a lot of demons – mostly by sessions of prayer. Simon sometimes lays on hands.' She was beaming now. 'We can do things here that you could never, ever dream of doing in Britain.'

'And does Satan… Is there a problem with Satan in Britain?'

'Yes, but they call it psychiatric disease back there. It all gets categorised medically because we find it so difficult to accept the existence of spirits in the West.' Simon's expression had grown intense.

'And so you work in Africa because –' but he broke in:

'… because they understand and accept spirituality here.'

'Yes,' said Celia, thoughtfully, 'we can really return to our Biblical roots here.'

For a while there was silence, interrupted only by mealtime noises. And then Celia looked up. 'But it's very tricky. We work very hard not to break up their traditions, or undermine their culture… Much of the so-called religion in Europe is nothing more than cultural trappings.' She was frowning earnestly. 'Here, we have to think very hard about everything we do – we have to decide whether it is strictly Biblical, or whether it is just Western baggage. That's one of the issues we were taught about when we were training in Mwanza.' She stopped and sighed. 'But sometimes it can get so…', her voice petered out, fretful. With their never-ending diet of self-examination it was hardly surprising if they stumbled on difficulties from time to time. The difference between Celia and Simon was that she was prepared to confide their perplexities to us while he preferred to keep them locked within himself. She looked at me beseechingly.

'Complicated?' I offered.

'Yes… complicated. Let me tell you what happened the other day. Two of our congregation were to get married. The bride came here and asked me if I would bake a wedding cake for her. She said she wanted one "like the cakes you have in Britain".'

'So what did you do?'

'I refused.' She was frowning indignantly, and her mouth was set in a determined line.

'They've got perfectly good marriage rituals of their own without borrowing ours.' Her chair scraped on the floor as she got up. With fast, efficient movements, she started gathering the dishes. 'And she wanted to wear a white wedding dress.' The plates clattered jarringly as she stacked them. Simon wiped his fingers on his handkerchief, and then made an unexpected gesture with his hands, as if appealing for understanding.

'We're *not* here to turn them into Europeans. We're here to tell them about the Word of God.'

It was evidently one of their familiar debating grounds. But then Celia paused and added: 'But, really I was very hard on her and now, well, now I wonder whether it was right. Who are we to tell them they can't have things that they want? They have a right to self-determination after all.'

There was a knock at the door. Simon left the table. Soon he returned.

'Who was it?'

'It was old Phillip. He wanted to charge his battery again from our mains.'

'Oh no… well you can't let him, I mean really, we mustn't. We'll have everyone here soon asking us for electricity. It would just be impossible.' Anxiety had raised Celia's voice. 'They've just got to learn that we're not here to give them easy ways out of problems. They've got to learn self-sufficiency, really, they have.'

Simon sighed: 'I know, I know, I know'. He sat down. Apparently he had already dispensed some version of this philosophy to Phillip before dismissing him.

* * *

Celia's and Simon's misgivings about cultural interference did not torment the first missionaries to East Africa. Their work was clearly defined – they were to evangelise and to civilise. They perceived traditional culture as a recurring impediment to their work, and something to be dismantled. From the beginning, they set about attempting to expose as false the traditional belief systems in which ancestors are venerated. Convincing themselves, no doubt, that the end justified the means, some missionaries went a step further and told their new flocks that their old tribal gods were Satan in disguise.

Far more innocuous but almost equally repugnant to the missionaries were traditional rituals and customs. The missionaries were uncompromising: those who sought baptism had to abandon tribal ritual. Traditional puberty rites and marriage ceremonies were condemned as sinful.

It was through the children that the missionaries effected the change. Throughout the second half of the nineteenth century, the Church held a monopoly on education, and to read became synonymous with being a Christian. At first there was just a trickle, but before long, East Africa was scattered with a generation of mission-educated natives.

At one educational institution whose foundation was inspired by Livingstone, pupils were taught to recite the names of the capes of the east coast of Scotland. While the unfamiliar sounds may have puzzled them, at least this knowledge did not undermine their attitudes towards their own society. Far more dangerous than a grasp of Scotland's geography was the cynicism which students imbibed about their traditional way of life. They were taught that Christianity was modern, and that the religions of their fathers and grandfathers were nothing more than hocus-pocus.

To the educated generation the spectacle of the chief performing elaborate rituals to 'make rain' began to seem risible. Educated youth began to represent a threat to the standing of the village elders, traditionally the upholders of tribal values and customs. A generation of old men who might have expected to live out their autumn years at the hearts of their communities now felt marginalised and uneasy.

It is recorded that a diviner in Ufipa anticipated the implications of the changes: 'The people will eventually forsake their beliefs and become converts to new religions, and a degeneration of the people will be seen.' What she had recognised was the central role that spirituality played in tribal society. She had foreseen that the abandonment of traditional religion and ritual meant the unravelling of East African society.

In the short term, aspiring converts found themselves in a spiritual and cultural wilderness. Forbidden by the missionaries to wear the amulets and charms which traditionally protected them from malevolent spirits, they were forced to wait for baptism into the Christian Church. This could take up to fifteen years, and their frustration was deep and self-righteous. An aspiring African clergyman, waiting year after year for ordination, saw Christianity as part of a sinister imperialism which he described as 'altogether too cheaty, too thefty, too mockery'.

While the Africans fretted, the ambiguity of missionaries' attitudes became more apparent: they were offering education and Christianity on the one hand, but were not prepared to countenance African advancement on the other. Just after the turn of the century, Bishop Weston of Zanzibar wrote: 'I view with great alarm the movement for "educating Africans as quickly as possible". It is a false movement, it is untrue to history, and is poisonous in its effects.' His words summed up an attitude felt by many missionaries who tacitly acknowledged that African advancement would undermine their role.

As late as 1908, Winston Churchill expressed a view which combined the white man's insecurity with romantic notions from the previous century of a rural idyll peopled with Noble Savages: 'The African is secure in his abyss of contented degradation, rich in that he lacks everything and wants nothing. To live with the long nightmare of worry and privation, of dirt and gloom and squalor, lit only by gleams of torturing knowledge and tantalising hope, is to feel the ground tremble under foot.'

*   *   *

At the ragged edge of the town, where the mud shanties petered out into a patchwork of *shambas*, Simon showed us where he was directing an embryonic Christian community to build a church. There was a hot, still silence around the building site – every man, every woman and every child was working in the fields in a final spasm of activity before the rains broke.

The church was, as yet, no more than a roofless, mud-brick shell with frameless gaps where the doors would be. Around it lay piles of earth and bricks. We peered down a square pit several metres deep which was to be the latrine. By now, at the end of the dry season, the soil had been baked rigid by the sun. Hoes had left faint scratchings on the walls of the excavation. Each blow would have yielded nothing more than a few fragments of hardened earth, which would have been painstakingly clawed together and passed to the surface in a headpan.

'This is the women's work,' Simon explained. I shook my head in disbelief. There was a dull thud as his son dropped a rock into the pit.

'Don't do that, Benjy... Well, what would the womenfolk be doing otherwise?' He stood up from where he had been squatting on his haunches and dusted his hands on his trousers. 'I mean, if they weren't doing their domestic chores and then coming to labour on the church, how would they fill their time?' His voice was level and did not invite an answer. 'If they had modern technology to save themselves time, would they be any better off?'

There was another thud. 'Benjy, I *told* you not to do that!' The child looked round, his hair brilliantly fair and his eyes deep and wide. Simon settled himself against the side of the vehicle and absently stripped the outer layers from a grass stem. 'I remember when we last visited the UK we wanted to see a relation of mine. He had to consult some electronic gadget he'd got to be able to tell us that he was free on Tuesday afternoon, in ten days' time, for half an hour.' He paused and inspected the flayed grass stem. 'I don't think technology had enriched his life. And yet that's what we call "development".' He discarded the grass stem. 'Better to leave the Africans alone, I say.'

A small rabble of children had gathered. Staring and barefoot, they followed us as we moved around Simon's new church. They always kept a wary distance and made no sound. I could not gauge their silence –

whether it was speechless curiosity, timid hopefulness, or sullen hostility. When Simon called to Benjy, I heard a murmured echo of the name, so soft and musical that it could have been a fragment of birdsong. The European child spun round and, for a moment, he locked eyes with the tallest of the African children.

Broad grins broke across the African faces. Here was the chink in his armour then: the self-possession of the white boy had been dispelled in a most satisfactory manner. Before long the knot of kids was following him, calling him in gently caressing tones that were intended to infuriate. Finally, Benjy was goaded into lashing out. He took a wide swing with his foot which sent his tormentors into raptures of delight. They cavorted around him like butterflies, experimenting with the alien sound of his name, their light laughter ringing in the sunlight.

Benjy stood, white and still, the focus of the circle of the dancing children. He frowned and then gave a sharp retort in Swahili. Instantly, their glee evaporated. They faltered to a halt, just a rabble of tatty African children, uncertainly regarding the white boy in their midst.

*   *   *

Something strange happened on our last evening. As Celia was clearing the table, she froze, her head cocked on one side: 'It's started again,' she said, just loud enough for Simon to hear. I strained my ears and could just make out the beating of a drum, so low that it seemed no more than a rhythmic trembling of the air. The effect on our hosts was instant. Celia's eyes turned hard as she looked round the sitting room: 'Come on, children, let's play a game.'

Simon was moving calmly but swiftly from window to window, checking that the shutters were secure. He spoke to us over his shoulder in a voice that was level: 'I'll have to drop you home now, I'm afraid.'

A hurried goodbye to Celia, and the slamming of car doors. Then we were labouring back along the pitted track towards the town centre, the beams of the headlights dancing across the scrubland. Once, fleetingly, the lights picked out the yellow eyes of some night animal in the thick grass.

It was only a few minutes to the guesthouse and soon we were alone, the dust settling around us and Simon's tail lights bouncing away down the rough road. No sound now, just the dull noise of the cicadas in the warm, close night. Aisling shivered.

The following morning we were to leave early. The stars were shining brightly when I opened the door to find a small package on our doorstep. I tore off the paper and uncovered a battered book which I examined by the light of a candle in our room. It was a New Testament Bible, English and Swahili texts facing each other on alternate pages. There was also a letter.

Colum and Aisling –

I hope you find the enclosed useful – it was the New Testament I used when I first arrived out here. So sorry the evening was cut a bit short. I thought a few words might explain what was going on, as I'm sure you thought our behaviour a bit odd!

Recently we had a run-in with the local witchdoctor. He sent a woman round to see us with her son, who had earache. The woman told us that the witchdoctor reckoned her child would recover if his ear was packed with the excrement of a black dog! Because he lives just down the road, he knew full well that we have the only black dog in town. So the witchdoctor had sent her to see if we could help out.

Well, of course, we could never be party to such a thing. We did try to help – we offered to see what we could do with our medicines, but she was not interested in that, and went away pretty unhappy. After that, I had to chase some kids out of the garden when they tried to help themselves to some dog poo, and we thought that was that.

Later that night the drumming started. It was so distant at first that we thought nothing of it. But gradually it came closer and closer, and we saw that a procession was heading this way. There were flaming torches, and soon we could hear chanting. It was all a bit unsettling. The noise grew very loud, and the procession came right up to the edge of the garden.

We gathered in the sitting room and prayed and they went away, much to our relief. So the witchdoctor finally got his dog excrement – at least we assume that's what they were after – and put on a good show at the same time. Anyway, ever since we've been a little uneasy whenever we've heard drumming – specially at night. In fact, tonight was a false alarm. Hope that our behaviour makes more sense now!

So good to have met you. Do drop a line to us to tell us that you have arrived safely.

God protect you.

Simon.

With a hiss the candle went out and darkness pressed into the room. I thought of the little missionary family, stoical in the bright light of their bare sitting room, listening to the blood-pulse of the drum through the heavy darkness. And I thought of the missionary anguish that Celia had described – trying to draw the fine line between the spiritual and the cultural. It was a delicate distinction that seemed pale and without meaning in the face of the primeval, visceral drumming, the embodiment of immutable, timeless African belief.

Since Livingstone's day, each generation of Europeans had come with its panacea for Africa. Some ideas streaked the sky like shooting stars, and others gleamed momentarily and then faded, as ephemeral as glow-flies in the forest. All left an imprint in the darkness like the coloured memory of lightning behind the eye. But they were fickle impressions, rife with ambiguity. The bride who sought the paraphernalia for a Western wedding would have been puzzled, hurt even, by the apparent coldness of the missionaries. It would have seemed altogether too cheaty, too thefty.

Now the darkness in the room was tinged with the milkiness of dawn. I folded the letter, and enclosed it in the Bible. Outside, the world was awash with pellucid dream-light, and Aisling was watching the east as she waited for the sun to rise.

Log Book Extracts

DAY 13 – Saturday 7th December

PHASE 2

FROM: Mpanda

TO: Sibwesa

CAMP: Tent outside headman's house.

POSITION: 30°45'3" E
              6°29'39" S

TIME CYCLING: 7 hours 45minutes

DISTANCE TRAVELLED: 54km

AVERAGE SPEED: 7km/hr

ROUTE: Heading north on main, unsurfaced road out of Mpanda, turn left after 10km onto track to Karema.

TRACK CONDITION: Good.

BICYCLES – PERFORMANCE: Good.

BICYCLES – MAINTENANCE: Checked tyres, brakes.

WEATHER: Cloudy at the hottest time of day. A sprinkling of rain. Midday shade temperature 25°C.

HEALTH: Colum's knee playing up. Aisling has problem with strength of grip on handlebars.

EQUIPMENT: We are using up camera film too fast.

LANDSCAPE: Flat, and then low foothills. Then remote and lovely forest.

EXPENDITURE: None

FLUID CONSUMPTION: 8 litres

FOOD: During day: bread, peanuts, biscuits, mango.
        Evening meal: onions, garlic from Mpanda, curry powder, rice. New tin of cocoa bought in Mpanda.

COMMENT: We are storing used film in a water-tight tin with a desiccant sachet.

LIVINGSTONE: Livingstone is ill; trouble with porters, and guides who attempt to mislead him.

*   *   *

DAY 14 – Sunday 8th December

PHASE 2

FROM: Sibwesa

TO: A small farming settlement.

CAMP: In a low valley, beside a farmer's hut.

POSITION: 30°39'39" E
             6°36'24" S

TIME CYCLING: 9 hours

DISTANCE TRAVELLED: 19km

AVERAGE SPEED: 2km/hr (effective – but see below)

ROUTE: Continue on track linking Mpanda to Lake Tanganyika.

TRACK CONDITION: Hardened sand for 19km. Then encountered heavy, thick mud which forced us to retrace our steps.

BICYCLES – PERFORMANCE: Completely caked with mud to the extent that the wheels no longer go round.

BICYCLES – MAINTENANCE: Attempted to clean, but the complete strip down carried out in Mpanda will now have to be repeated.

WEATHER: Heavy rain overnight continued sporadically throughout the morning. It feels cold. Midday temperature 18°C.

HEALTH: Tsetse fly persist and have caused swelling in Aisling's wrists. Aisling v. tired. Colum has some pain in his right knee, pins and needles in both hands. Both irritated and depressed.

EQUIPMENT: Mud seems to have penetrated everywhere.

LANDSCAPE: Thinner forest with thick green grass between trees. More hilly as we approach lake.

EXPENDITURE: None

FLUID CONSUMPTION: 4 litres

FOOD: During day: peanuts, biscuits, mango.
Evening meal: Ate *ugalli* and peanuts with locals. Provisions will run low tomorrow.

COMMENT: Terrible day where we were forced to turn back because of mud. The waterproof ponchos are pretty tricky to cycle in, as they have a habit of getting caught in the spokes. There seem to be few people around here, although we were passed by two vehicles on their way to lakeside market.

LIVINGSTONE: 20km north of us, heading west.

8

From Mpanda to Sibwesa

by Aisling

Ku-zunguka (v.i. and t.) to go round and round, rotate
M-zungu (n.) European, white person
Swahili–English Dictionary

OUTSIDE the Moravian Mission just before dawn I breathed the chilly air. It was tinged with the acrid smell of Mpanda's rubbish dumps which smoulder night and day. In the battered porch of the Moravian Church a single bar of fluorescent lighting emitted a dull white glow, a privilege also enjoyed by MOHAMMED'S SPEA PARTS SHOP farther down the street.

A cockerel called. All over town the rest replied. A mosquito hummed by my ear. The sky grew lighter and, across the road, the angles of the market's rickety wooden tables slowly protruded into the day. There was a rattle in the dimness and shadows filled with the bulky forms of women carrying empty buckets. Now the early morning sounds were gathering strength – the clinking of metal on brick at some distant well; the revving of an old Toyota truck. In the east the sky brightened and flushed gold, and the street became alive with colour – the rich hues of women's clothing, of gawdy shop signs and of the red, red dust. The town had woken up. It was time to go.

Mpanda is on the sketchy main road that runs north-south, parallel to Lake Tanganyika. Between the road and the lake is a broad ribbon of blankness, as untamed as the empty forest that we had crossed from Tabora. It is a transition zone. To the east is the dry interior through which we had ridden, where farmers scratch in the dust, and where honey-collectors sleep through the day. To the west are the maritime folk who depend on the lake, which fills a deep cleft between the mountains.

We turned west, following a track drawn like a tight thread across the transition between the two worlds. We were in an empty space peopled only by travellers, their minds fixed on what lay beyond the distant mountain rim. Once we passed a family: the man cycled, his wife and child balanced on a large pink cushion on the back-carrier. He hardly

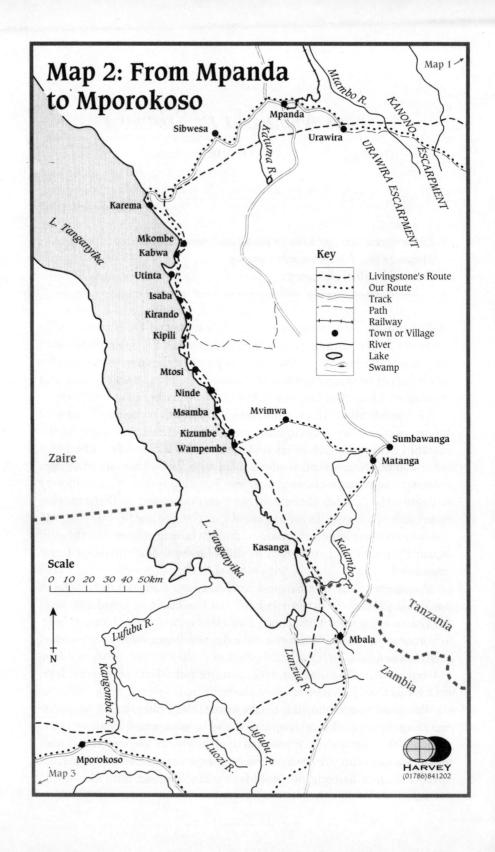

Map 2: From Mpanda to Mporokoso

Map 1 →

Mtambo R.

KANONO ESCARPMENT

Mpanda
Sibwesa
Urawira

URAWIRA ESCARPMENT

Katuma R.

Karema

Mkombe
Kabwa

L. Tanganyika

Utinta

Isaba

Kirando

Kipili

Key

Livingstone's Route
Our Route
Track
Path
Railway
Town or Village
River
Lake
Swamp

Mtosi

Ninde

Msamba   Mvimwa

Kizumbe
Wampembe

Sumbawanga
Matanga

Zaire

L. Tanganyika

Scale

0 10 20 30 40 50km

Kasanga

Kalambo R.

Tanzania

N

Lufubu R.

Mbala

Kangomba R.

Lunzua R.

Zambia

Mporokoso

Luozi R.   Lufubu R.

Map 3 →

HARVEY
(01786)841202

acknowledged us – absorbed, as we were, in making the dash across the no-man's land.

We cycled through gentle hills, pausing from time to time to eat soft white bread we had brought from Mpanda. Then we descended to a wide, sunlit plain. It was a still, breathless place – withered grass under a bald sky. In the distance, the scrub was mottled with patches of low forest and by afternoon we came again to low foothills. Reaching a shoulder we paused and looked back at the plain. The bright pools of light remained, but now the grass and patchy forest were whipped into a tumultuous sea and an armada of grey clouds billowed above, releasing volleys of rain and broadsides of silent lightning.

Deeper into the hills, the forest closed around us once more. '*Through forest, along the side of a sedgy valley. Cross its head water, which has much rust of iron in it, then W. and by S. The forest has very much tsetse. Zebras calling loudly, and Senegal long-claw in our camp at dawn, with its cry O-o-o-o-o-o-o-o-o-o.*'

Along a valley we came to a small village, a scanty staging post clinging to the track. We camped by the chief's hut on a faint slope.

'There will be rain tonight…'

I paused as I was pitching the tent. The villager was sniffing the air like a dog. I weighted the flysheet with stones. Colum was muttering to himself, the messy cooker-lighting ritual proving more difficult than usual in the mounting breeze. Our friend drifted away, and a light rain swept up the valley so that, before the meal was ready, we retired into the tent clutching a plateful of gritty rice and cold peanuts.

'*The m'jure, or water-hog, was all eaten by hyenas during the night; but the buffalo is safe.*'

After dark the storm crashed around us and the rain poured into the land, etching the ground with new streams and river-beds. The tent flapped and heaved and its walls vanished with every shock of lightning so that we felt naked in the storm. By morning the rain had stopped: the sky was grey, the wind chilly. We were dry but our panniers and tent were sodden. The night's rain had improved the sandy track, however. The damp surface was now firmer than before and for the first hour we made swift progress, our spirits buoyant.

Then we turned a corner and stopped, abruptly. For as far as the next bend several hundred metres away, the track had been transformed into a sea of deep red mud, hemmed in tightly by the forest. There was no question of cycling through it so we dismounted and I found myself shin-deep in a porridge-like substance that was almost alive – after a few metres it had already licked my bicycle with adhesive tongues that reached every moving part. For the next half hour we eased forward inch by inch until the wheels could no longer turn and the bikes were too heavy to lift. We half-dragged them on.

Finally I lost my balance and staggered backwards, vainly trying to wrench my feet free of the sucking mud. As I sprawled on my back and felt the cold dampness seeping into my shirt, Colum turned and regarded me. He was a few precious metres farther on and I called to him, but his face remained expressionless. Mud had covered his bicycle frame and had coated his poncho and trousers. He raised a weary hand to his face and inadvertently daubed a smear of red across his forehead and cheek.

'Livingstone would have managed…'. His voice was flat and lifeless. He looked away. Inside me, something that had been lying dormant reared into life. I clawed at the mud and scrambled to my feet.

'So what? So bloody what?' The pressure surged in my head. 'For Christ's sake, *why* is it so important?' I kicked the bicycle hard.

For some minutes we were both still, the thick foliage pressing in expectantly, poised for his answer. But he said nothing more. With a massive effort, he lurched forward with his clogged bicycle. I waited, staring venomously at his back. I knew it would not be long before he was compelled to give in. Finally he stopped, his shoulders heaving. The silence fell like a curtain between us.

A brief flood of remorse chased my fury. This was Colum's dream and he was right: Livingstone *would* have done it somehow. He would have gone on even if at the end of the day he had only made ten metres and had run out of water. With God on his side, and with his unusual fortitude, he was indifferent to risk. Yet still I did not understand Livingstone. A seam of near-insanity ran through his optimism.

Anger with Colum returned as I faced our predicament. Apart from the immediate discomfort, the delay would mean hunger ahead as our supplies dwindled. But a more profound fear was seeping around the fringes of my thoughts. Unlike Colum, I was not obsessed with the authenticity of our expedition – it seemed to me that a little comfort would not impair, and might even enhance, the search for Livingstone's spirit. But I was terrified of complete failure. This was just the beginning of the rains. Were we going to spend every day of the next few months re-enacting the horror of the mud?

Without a word Colum laid his bicycle down. The panniers, glistening red, slithered over each other like bloated entrails. He pushed back the heavy folds of his poncho, and plunged his hand into the luggage.

'What are you doing?'

No reply. The heavily laden bike writhed as he undid the various straps.

'Colum…?'

'I'm unloading. We're going back.'

'But…'

His head snapped round and his eyes blazed for an instant. Then he shouldered a pannier and with slurping, ponderous movements, began retracing his steps. His bicycle remained – a carcass in the mud.

When I caught up with him he was standing still, his head cocked on one side.

'Do you hear something?' I strained to pick up a sound over the dripping silence. From deep among the trees came the light trilling of a child's laughter and the muffled thud of an axe. Colum plunged into the forest.

Ten minutes later, he exploded through the foliage back onto the track. 'Aisling, there's a small hut and a clearing. The farmer has said we can stay. Come on.' And he snatched up the pannier and was gone.

*   *   *

The forest thinned and soon we were overlooking a low valley planted with maize. A meandering line of trees marked the bed of a dry stream. There was serenity in the valley – no breath of wind, no stirring of animals. Just the stillness of grey sky, and the low murmur of voices.

Two walls of reeds thrown against each other formed the farmer's sleeping quarters. A hut made of rough branches was the living room. Outside was a bare open space and a log for sitting.

The man propped his axe against the log and stood, thin-bellied, rough trousers rolled up to his knees. 'Karibuni,' he said, welcoming us to his timeless homestead, to a campsite of flattened grass, to his water hole and to the fire that smoked in the depths of the hut. This was rescue. He extended a calloused hand to Colum. His skin was dry and cracked, stained with a lifetime's labour in the fields. A handful of people stared at us: a few boys gazing up the slopes from amongst the maize; shrunken old women at the eaves of the hut. Children cowered in crevices – all except a little girl who edged forward until her hand slipped into mine.

I closed my muddy fingers around hers and she led me down through the bushes to where a rude hole had been hewn in the ground. At the bottom there was a pool of cloudy water and soon she had scooped some into a bucket, swung it onto her head and was leading me back to our water bottles which we filled, one by one. We were friends.

Colum and the farmer were squatting beside one of the bicycles, absorbed in the detail of its mechanisms. The child tugged at me again and I followed her obediently, bending down to reach the hut's dim interior. Inside, a woman was feeding a baby and a toddler crawled around the smoking fireplace.

The woman looked up and smiled – and then she noticed my clothes. Boots, socks, trousers, shirt and hat – even my face – were streaked with mud. She raised her voice to a scolding tone, reaching out and clasping my sticky trousers. The mud was still wet and she beckoned me nearer to the smoky fire. The young girl drew up a smooth log and I settled myself close to the three smouldering branches. I watched the mother who gently rocked her suckling child and who stared back at me with fascination, and some disgust.

'But why are you going to the lake?' she asked suddenly in Swahili, her eyes widening. I was at a loss. She would never have heard of Livingstone.

'Well… we want to see it I suppose. And then we want to travel south to see Zambia.'

She shook her head and raised her voice, relaying the news to the women outside. I realised I should have said we were on business. In Swahili it was a marvellously broad term that meant simply that you supported yourself in a way more complex than peasant farming – trading soap or mending engines, for example – and your journey was essential to that purpose.

'How many children do you have?' she demanded.

'None,' I said.

'None!' she exclaimed loudly, for the benefit of the others. 'How old are you?'

'Thirty.'

'Thirty!'

'I'll have children later,' I assured her.

She raised her voice again and the women outside jabbered loudly, presumably discussing why – and how – I had postponed an event as inescapable as the rain.

Smoke curled through the hut, around the stack of branches that served as the bed and out through the bright doorway into the late afternoon. The woman's eyes never left me. The answers I had given her just didn't make sense: a woman of thirty, with no children, occupying herself by travelling to the lake for no other reason than a desire to see it? She shook her head and readjusted her child, which fed continuously from her withering bosom. She would have found Livingstone's motivation equally baffling. But then so did we.

*   *   *

A single idea would dominate Livingstone's every waking thought, his every deed. His obsession pushed him to extraordinary feats. He walked in a living dream that hung like a curtain around him, leaving him blind to any awkward truths that reality might present.

That is why, during his first journey to Africa, he missed the clues that suggested that his plan for the continent was fundamentally flawed. Those clues lay in the chatter of local people and in the readings of his geographical instruments, to both of which he was usually alert. Both revealed that, along a loop of the Zambezi River he had never seen, lay a gargantuan obstacle to his plans.

Livingstone had travelled to the coast from the Victoria Falls and, on the way, discovered a high and fertile plain which he at once identified as ideal for colonisation. He so passionately wanted the Zambezi to be a broad, calm highway stretching from the coast to his plateau that he ignored hearsay about furious rapids that lay along an eighty-kilometre loop he had skipped. He also failed to record the measurements that could have revealed to him a plunge he had not witnessed in the height of the river.

It was not until two years later, on his second trip to Africa at the head of the ill-fated Zambezi expedition, that he finally confronted the Kerabrasa rapids. With the roar of the fifty-kilometre-long cataract thundering in his ears, and to the amazement of his companions Livingstone sat down and wrote to the British Foreign Office: '*We are all of the opinion that a steamer of light draught would pass the rapids without difficulty when the river is in full flood.*'

Obsession. It pushed Livingstone further than self-discipline and faith alone ever could. And now, on the final journey, it was the Nile that lured him onwards despite the warning signs. His preoccupation with his own theory of its origin led him to dismiss the clues that the source might not be to the south-west of Lake Bangweulu. A more rational man would have heeded what local people said. They had claimed that the Lualaba, which Livingstone believed to be the upper reaches of the Nile, did not flow north to Egypt but made an abrupt turn and flowed west instead, towards the continent's west coast.

For the old man, tramping slowly southwards, the pursuit of the source of the Nile had become an act of obsessional faith, a mystical quest. He was inspired by those venerated authorities, the ancient Greeks. Images of the Nile drawn from Old Testament legend danced in his mind and he dreamed of following its course to uncover traces of the Biblical deeds said to have happened on its banks. '*If I could bring to light anything to confirm the Sacred Oracles, I should not grudge one whit all the labour expended,*' he wrote.

He knew that the origins of that river had tantalised humanity for thousands of years. From the Nile sprang the life of all Egypt. Without the great river's floods the people would have perished, for it watered their crops. The Egyptians fed on the fruits of the Nile. They dined on blossoms from the hearts of water lilies that grew in its shallows, and they baked the papyrus reeds that lined its banks.

Yet the sacred river was a mystery to its people. Why did its waters rise in the height of summer when other rivers declined? Where did it begin?

Herodotus, the father of history, travelled through Egypt in search of the river's origins but he found only one man who claimed to know – the scribe who kept the register of the treasures of Athene in the Egyptian city of Sais.

He told me that between Syene, near Thebes, and Elephantine there were two mountains of conical shape called Crophi and Mophi; and that the springs of the Nile, which were of fathomless depth, flowed out from between them. Half of the water flowed northwards towards Egypt and half southwards towards Ethiopia. The fact that the springs were bottomless he said had been proved by the Egyptian king Psammetichus, who had a rope made many thousands of fathoms long which he let down into the water without finding the bottom.

Centuries passed. Ptolemy was born in Egypt and grew up to become a geographer whose word would be revered for a thousand years. He left his own theory about the Nile. Far to the south, he said, near the Equator, lay the Mountains of the Moon and at their heart were two springs whose waters gushed down into two round lakes. It was there, he believed, that the Nile started its long journey north to the Mediterranean.

Seventeen hundred years later Livingstone was able to add his own evidence to the stories of the Ancients. Two years before he set off from Tabora he had met some Arab travellers in a village west of Lake Tanganyika. They told him that they had seen two springs far to the south. The springs rose to become a river with no name. The river flowed to the north. Close by were two more springs, whose waters flowed to the south. Surely, thought Livingstone, these four springs were the Fountains of Herodotus, the lakes of Ptolemy, the origins of the Nile.

This was the glorious idea which enchanted Livingstone. With just his religious conviction and his unrelenting will he might have lived and died a quirky citizen of Blantyre: God and fortitude were not enough to drive a man through the heat of the Kalahari, through endless malarial swamps and lands blasted by the slave trade. Obsession was necessary as well.

*   *   *

Across the smouldering hearth my companion suddenly stood up and held her baby aloft, like an offering – a gesture of compassion for my childlessness perhaps. Reluctantly I reached out to receive the baby and its fat limbs struggled to resist being deposited in my uncertain arms. I grasped it firmly and returned to my log, staring at my strangely silent bundle while its surprised brown eyes looked back at me. Outside, there were the peaceful end-of-day sounds of the men returning from the plantation and of the women preparing food.

Later, Colum and I squatted with the three men and scooped mounds of *ugalli* into our mouths, watched by the children who sat in a row under the eaves of the hut. When we had finished, they fell on the near-empty bowl to eat what was left. I never discovered when the women ate.

It was bedtime. First to retire were the chickens who, with great dexterity, climbed a ladder to reach their coop. Next our host clambered into his narrow shelter and pulled a straw door over the opening behind him. We took our cue and crawled into our damp and smelly tent clutching candles, journals and books. There had been no time to wash and, as usual, we fell asleep before the candles were lit or the books were opened.

9

From Sibwesa
by Colum

Your old men shall dream dreams, your young men shall see visions.
The Book of Joel, Chapter 2, Verse 20

WE PACKED away the tent, filled our bottles with filtered water, ate a breakfast of ground biscuit and powdered milk, and settled outside the hut to wait for the sun to dry the mud. Again our hostess was feeding her baby, her eyes never moving from Aisling, who was writing her journal.

Over the sound of morning bird song I heard a steady creaking. The woman glanced expectantly along the path that led up from the valley floor. At last our host appeared, his head bowed as he pushed a massive bicycle up the last stretch of path towards home. Draped over his handlebars was a bloody lump of meat so large that its tattered end brushed the spokes of the front wheel. He stopped in front of us, and the air was full of the raw, musky smell of still-warm flesh. He wiped his sweaty forehead with a bloodstained hand and grinned. His wife's gaze followed him as he wheeled his bicycle up to the hut to prop it beside ours, and there her eyes lingered. A puzzled frown passed across her face: 'But why do you not go to Zambia by bus?' Her question was no more than a murmur and I dropped my eyes to where the child's pudgy fingers were palpitating the skin of her breast.

'Authenticity' was the reason I had always given, but now it seemed a word too sterile to convey what I felt. And anyway, I did not know the Swahili.

'Kusikia Livingstone,' I said. It was the right word. *Kusikia* means more than to see; it also means to feel, to know. It was so simple all of a sudden.

We had come to follow Livingstone, but floundering in the mud had changed all that. Now I realised that I wanted to be more than just a camera, tracking with a cold, journalistic eye the man and the ripples that he made. I wanted to know him, I wanted to break through the uneasy taciturnity which enveloped him and kept me at arm's length, making me feel no more than a wide-eyed tourist. I wanted to measure his conviction and to feel his fortitude, to taste his obsession. I realised now that to see the world through Livingstone's eyes, we had to share his hardship.

Hardship changed Livingstone. It twisted more tightly the seasoned strands of his character as if they were the exposed roots of a sun-dried tree. By the end, his personality was so distorted that one historian has even labelled him mad.

'Kusikia Livingstone.' Now Aisling looked up. Her face was pale and streaked with mud, and her hair was matted and pulled untidily back. She smiled uncertainly. In two weeks of travelling, I had forgotten her smile. Hardship had changed her, too. She was more tentative now, and quieter than I had ever remembered her.

*   *   *

The heat grew stronger and the ground began to steam. Chickens strutted in and out of the hut's shade and lizards positioned themselves on the wooden eaves to soak up the sun. At last the light touched the valley floor, dispelling filaments of mist: shadows grew shorter, and the damp smells of night were deadened. We left by a small, overgrown path, lifting our bicycles through thick undergrowth and over the decaying trunks of fallen trees. On the track the air felt warm and stagnant.

We were returning to confront the mud that had defeated us the previous afternoon; the farmer had told us that a few hours of sunlight would be enough to harden the surface. After half an hour, we came to the place where we had been forced to dismount. The stretch of track looked less menacing now, without the grey sky and rain. But an exploratory attempt at pushing my bicycle forward showed that the slanting morning light had made little difference.

With mounting desperation, I laid the bicycle down. I could not believe that the expedition was going to be halted because of some mud. Aisling stood impassively by as I scanned the thick forest on either side. What would Livingstone have done? As I pondered the alternatives, a woman burst out of the vegetation on our left. Her path was no more than a worn place across the roots of trees, a narrow corridor of trampled vegetation, just wide enough for a bicycle. But it was enough, and we forced our way into the forest, barely daring to hope that there was a route that would take us past the mud.

By mid-morning the muddy track was no more than a bad memory, and we were winding up through the foothills of the mountains that border Tanganyika. The light was bright and hard, and once more we were surrounded by stillness and emptiness. The only sound was the dull creaking from my pedals, where some grit had penetrated the bearings.

We came to a small plateau and the trees thinned. Abruptly, my bicycle seized, its pedals locked. I dismounted, unhitched the panniers and swung the bike upside down so that it rested on its handlebars.

'What'll we do, then?'

'Well, I'll have to try and fix it.'

'Do you think you'll be able to?'

'Have you got any other suggestions?' I glanced up at her, instantly regretting the sarcasm in my voice. But she had drawn away.

To my great surprise, I felt elation. The waiting was over. The grey foreboding about bicycle mechanics had at last materialised into something so terrible that it was difficult to contemplate: we were stranded in the empty space between the lake and the Flat Forest with a broken bicycle, little food, and dwindling water: now there was nothing else to fear.

For some minutes, I stared at the pedal shaft, at the point where the spindle disappeared into a compact nest of concentric rings. I had to get inside there, to where grit was disrupting the intricate, tightly packed bearings and grease-clad surfaces. I spread out the tools, selected a spanner and engaged it on the pedal nut. As I leaned my weight on it, the bicycle sank into the sand. Finally I felt the nut yield and I unscrewed the pedal and shaft. A cloud of butterflies with wings of azure and lapis lazuli fluttered around my head. They landed on my sweat-streaked hands and uncoiled delicate probosci. One settled on the glimmering metal of the cog, another on the chain.

A new spanner for the naked pedal spindle. I pressed down with all my weight but there was no movement. The spanner slipped, and I fell heavily against the bicycle. There was an explosion of butterflies, a stinging pain to my hand, a thin line of blood. Aisling stirred in the shade under the tree: 'Are you OK?'

'Yup.'

The rumble of a vehicle: the first for two days. Aisling scrambled to her feet. 'Thank God for that...'

I watched her, an uneasy feeling creeping over me. She made her way to her bicycle and started unclipping the panniers.

'What are you doing, Ais?'

'I'm just getting these things ready...'

Now I could make out a small cloud of dust at the top of the preceding rise. The drone of the labouring engine grew stronger.

I turned back to the spindle and re-engaged the nut: 'I'll be staying here.'

I could feel her eyes on me. I leaned on the spanner again, and again it slipped.

'Colum…' She was standing next to me, close enough that I could hear her swallow, and her shallow, angry breathing. The dust cloud drew closer.

'I can fix it.'

'Looks to me like you're in trouble.' Her words were precise, hard-edged. They came too quickly.

'I'm staying. I'm going to fix it.'

She didn't understand.

The truck drew to a shuddering halt beside us and a man leaned from the window: 'Shida?'

'Hamna shida,' I answered. There was no problem. Nothing that Livingstone would not have taken in his stride anyway. The engine revved, and the truck heaved away.

The dust settled. Aisling was sitting at the trackside, her shoulders slumped. The noise of the engine receded to a dull drone, and she turned and moved slowly back towards a tree where she sank down in the shade: 'I hope you're satisfied…' Now she sat very still, gazing at the ground. There was an air of resignation about her.

'How much water have we got left?'

'Not very much. Less than four litres.' Her voice was flat.

I sniffed. It was going to be a thirsty day then. All sign of the morning's moisture had gone.

For three hours I fought with the bicycle. My body prickled with heat, and my eyes ached with the brightness. My fingernails were broken, the fingertips lacerated from pressing the spanner head to the nut. The tools became slippery with sweat and shone in the bitter light. The sun climbed the sky but time stood still: the point where the pedal spindle disappeared into the concentric bearing rings filled my world.

At last I felt the tiniest, grittiest movement. I was going to win. At once, I was flushed with a soaring, gloating feeling of vindication. Aisling was wrong, and perhaps Livingstone had been right after all: if you bend your will to something with enough commitment, anything can be achieved. Within ten minutes the damaged bearing was disassembled. I spread out my shirt on the ground and laid the parts down as the pedal mechanism offered them up, piece by piece. I brought out the new bearing and slipped it easily into place.

At last I was on my feet again, wiping my hands on my trousers, surveying my handiwork. The end of the new bearing shone behind the pedal shaft and I glanced down at the parts I had removed. After all my apprehension, they were just simple bits of metal. I decided to leave them there, arrayed neatly in a row in the sand.

*   *   *

We ate a handful of peanuts and continued up steeper hills and finally through a pass between the mountains.

'*Saw Tanganyika from a gentle hill. The land is rough, with angular fragments of quartz; the rocks of mica schist are tilted up as if away from the Lake's longer axis. Some are upright, and some have basalt melted into the layers, and crystallised in irregular polygons.*'

When I was much younger I was puzzled that roads did not appear in real life as the broad red ribbons which maps claimed them to be; nor were mountainsides scored with contour lines. Towards evening, we crested a final slope and some small child inside me smiled and was satisfied. Lake Tanganyika was, after all, as it should be: the smooth duck-egg blue that was shown on our map.

'*After a few hours climb we look down on the lake with its many bays. A sleepy glare floats over it...*'

We had made it through no-man's land and reached a new place where Europeans rarely come, where people's minds are crowded with a fear of the pale people whose blood has been drained. But here the torpor of the forest ends: at the lakeside there is vibrancy, ceaseless movement. From the lake, people draw their livelihoods. They fish, trade and gaze across the water to the towering mountains of Zaire, to fertile Burundi in the north and to Zambia in the south. It is to these places that they look, not inland, for their contact with the outside world. This is Lake Tanganyika, another of the great inland waterways that Livingstone had dreamed would allow the opening up of Africa.

10

In Karema

by Colum

'*REACH Karema district after 2³/₄ hours over black mud all deeply cracked, and many deep torrents now dry. We see Tanganyika but a range of low hills intervenes. A rumour of war tomorrow. Karema is a stockade.*'

Within a decade of his death, imperialists and missionaries inspired by Livingstone arrived at Karema. First to arrive was a detachment of Belgian soldiers, who built a fort to guard the eastern extremity of Leopold II's nascent Congo empire. In 1885 a group of missionaries also reached Karema, this time from the east. They had travelled through a land blighted by civil war and, as they approached the fort, they were praying that they had at last found sanctuary from the violence that had so far dogged their mission.

The feeble group that straggled over the muddy flood plain was a shadow of the expedition that had struck inland from the coast several years before. Then, there had been over 400 porters and armed *askaris* carrying a mountain of supplies and provisions. The ten White Fathers, resplendent in the long white robes of their Order, were setting out to begin work which had been assigned to them by Pope Leo XIII himself: to evangelise in the little-explored regions around Lakes Victoria and Tanganyika.

Although there was never any question about the religious mettle of the carefully chosen priests, the charismatic founder and leader of their Order had still taken pains to spell out to them what they were taking on, lest they should underestimate the enormity of their task. In a letter to the group before its departure Cardinal Lavigerie had written: 'I know well how much you have given up – your families, your country, your hopes of earthly success; and for what? To endure insults, privation, perhaps a cruel death. I have promised you nothing else.'

As they made their way into the interior, his melancholy pronouncement was to prove well justified. Unaccustomed to the heat and to the hardships of African travel, the European priests quickly weakened. They had not been journeying for many weeks before one of their number, Father Pascal, fell victim to fever. He insisted on struggling on until he could no longer balance on his donkey. Then his companions laid the sick man in a tent in the sweltering forest and looked on helplessly as he slipped in and out of delirium and cried out in his agony. Father Pascal took four days to die. The priests buried him and 'resigned themselves to the holy and adorable Will of God Who in His inscrutable designs had taken to Himself one of the most valued members of the expedition,' according to the Order's historian. They found consolation 'in the thought that their future missions would now have a powerful advocate before the throne of God'.

Gradually fever overtook most of the party and the caravan was reduced to a pace of two or three kilometres a day. Well before they reached Tanganyika their food ran out, and at the prospect of slow starvation in the forest, many of the *askaris* and porters quietly slipped away, taking with them what they were carrying. As the expedition crawled slowly westwards, the priests' problems were compounded by marauding refugees, the brutalised fragments of a society shattered by the slave trade.

At last a wealthy Arab rescued them, but it was many more months before two or three of the surviving missionaries at last set eyes on Tanganyika, and it was to be another few years before they would find somewhere to settle. In the meantime they were drawn into the slave trade's bloody wranglings. Their protection of the oppressed provoked a number of confrontations with Rumalisa, a powerful warlord. Finally, boiling with frustration at the attitude of the priests, he laid siege to their tentative mission station. As the priests fled, three of their number were impaled by arrows.

Scourged by hunger and disease, the remaining priests were at last offered protection by the Belgian soldiers at Karema. Their proud banner, the banner of the Sacred Heart, was filthy and tattered by now, but in the hearts of these men the missionary fire remained undimmed.

*   *   *

The White Fathers' conviction was worthy even of Livingstone: it had cost them dear, but the prize was to prove worthwhile. At Karema, the soldiers left and the priests staked their claim in the interior. Here, where an unprepossessing finger of land extends across the lakeside flood plain, they formed the nucleus of a Christian community. They built a mission and finally began their papal commission to evangelise the pagans.

Time was pressing. There were many souls to save in the vast new missionary fields opened up by Livingstone. The White Fathers were in the vanguard of an army of missionaries soon to descend on Africa, and whose activities had already goaded European governments into establishing spheres of influence in this virgin land. The drawing of lines on the empty map was a matter of great interest to the missionaries themselves – they were quick to see how notional borders could be used to deny access to the multitude of other European churches vying for the finite number of African souls.

During the closing decades of the nineteenth century, God's struggle for men's souls had therefore become intimately linked with men's struggles for colonial possessions. The evangelical zeal of the White Fathers coincided conveniently with contemporary ideas of imperial expansion. The priests and soldiers sharing the fort at Karema were the embodiment of this dual religious and colonial approach.

Since the White Fathers' arrival at Karema, two colonial administrations have arisen and disappeared in this part of East Africa. Now, as we pushed our bicycles along the crumbling causeway above the flood plain, I wondered what traces of the missionaries we would find.

*   *   *

An empty market place, a few mud houses, a dusty street. Yes, the mission was still standing; it was up the hill, an old man said. A steep road flagged with huge grey stones led us up between a jumble of huts clinging to the slope. We emerged in a wide space high above the plain and stood for a few minutes, bewildered. We had left the village behind and were on a boulevard that ran up the spine of the hill. On either side were neat houses of red and white brick, and the avenue was lined with perfectly spaced trees of solid maturity. We had stepped into an ordered, European world where the rhythmic spacings and angles suffocated the usual tumble of nature.

Behind us, at the point where the hill fell sharply away, a church was hidden amongst deep green trees. Its spire, surmounted by a cross, proclaimed itself high above the leafy crowns, all in faultless alignment with the avenue. To loiter in this place with no regard for the symmetry was to strike a discordant note. I shuffled my bicycle across to fall into line behind Aisling.

In front of us the avenue culminated at a gateway in a white wall. Imposing urns stood on the capitals of the red-brick gateposts, and beyond there began an extravagant spill of European architecture. Processions of steps gave way to grassy spaces, and spaces led to new staircases. The eye rose up the red and white confection, until at last there was a sweeping staircase up to a two-storey mansion, a perfectly-balanced vista of deep balconies shaded by red-tiled roofs, of arches and pillars and towering chimney stacks. This, then, was the monument to the White Fathers. It must have seemed impossible that the mission would do anything but thrive.

Slowly we wheeled our bicycles towards the palace gates, and now a second wave of incredulity settled on us: this Versailles in the wilderness was falling to bits. The houses that lined the boulevard were abandoned, their sad, dark windows shutterless. Red-tiled roofs sagged and walls crumbled away with an impertinent disregard for the architect's sense of symmetry. Beneath our feet the proud avenue had become host to a hundred vagrant tufts of grass. The wide boulevard was empty, except for the ghosts of the holy men, mourning the decay.

We walked through the gateway and stared upwards at the palace where Nature was gradually recovering her hold. The vegetation was rampant, thrusting out between bricks, from under tiles, and through empty window frames. Roofs had collapsed and lay broken-backed amongst the weeds that now covered the floors. Exotic, rust-coloured algae blotched the walls, and the white paint flaked.

We propped our bicycles by the gate and ascended the first flight of steps. On a pedestal at the end of each balustrade stood a battered and rusting tin: in one, there was a coarse green plant. In the other, a dry stick.

In the depths of shadow at the top of the stairs there was a flicker of movement. And then, to our astonishment, a figure appeared and tripped lightly down towards us. It was a slim Tanzanian wearing a crisp khaki suit and large square glasses. With a strangely stilted movement, Father Philemon Shabani stretched out his hand: 'Welcome,' he said.

Soon we were sitting in the shade of the balcony, the Father's dark face shifting in and out of the shadow as he rocked to and fro in his chair. He could have been any age; he had lost the elasticity of youth but his face did not show the passage of years. His arms hung inertly like those of a crumpled, wooden puppet.

'I am the diocesan priest for Karema.' His voice was without expression. He pivoted his head towards us, and I nodded at my reflection in the panes of his glasses. 'I minister to a large Christian community here...' As if tugged by an invisible string, his hands made an unrefined movement. I tried to relate it to the emphasis of his words, but there was no pattern. The limbs had a coarsely tuned life of their own.

'Just me and the other priest these days, in the old mission.' He fell silent.

It was the hottest, brightest part of the day, and the balcony was deliciously cool. Soft noises drifted up from the village, lapping around the hill like an untidy sea. Over a belt of green foliage, no more than a mile away, Tanganyika sparkled blue. I fought the desire to doze.

I was snapped alert by a loud chattering. A small monkey was sitting on the balustrade very close to my face. Its whole body was racked by a storm of passion: its wizened pink face was puckered, its mangey pelt bristled and its tail was arched into a stiff curl over its back. With small pink hands it slapped the stone. I glanced at Philemon. His face was wearing a stiff smile.

'My friend has come to greet you. You must excuse him though, he is not used to company.'

I raised my hand, and the monkey instantly became a spindly tumble of fright. It fled to the back of Philemon's rocking chair, where it hung, shouting shrill indignant insults.

'But you would like to wash, wouldn't you?' Philemon was addressing Aisling. 'You must wash and then I will show you where you can stay. You must stay here tonight and tomorrow,' and he got up, leaving the little monkey to ride out the frantic rocking of the chair. Aisling and I exchanged glances.

'Well that's very kind…'

'You must eat with me,' he added. Then, with an assertive nod: 'It is good to have an exchange of ideas.'

He showed us along the verandah towards a heavy wooden door. Inside, the cavernous bathroom was illuminated by a small, blindingly bright square of light: the window gleamed like a picture with the forest-green and tile-red of the sun-baked courtyard behind the palace. As my eyes adjusted, I saw that the room was dominated by a glorious porcelain bath standing on a low platform. It was narrow and deep, with knobbly taps still glittering through the tarnish of generations. Its feet were the regal claws of some heraldic beast.

Baths, then, had been one of the exceptions to Cardinal Lavigerie's rule that his priests should live as simply as their flock. Before the priests' departure the Cardinal had been explicit in his instructions:

'Follow the example of the great Apostle who said "I became all things to all men that I might save all". Adopt all the exterior customs of the natives, speak their language, wear the same kind of clothes, and eat the same food. Love the poor pagans; be kind to them; heal their wounds.'

Then, argued the perceptive Cardinal, the natives would 'give their affection first, then their confidence, and then at last their souls.'

It was a pragmatic if slightly disingenuous mechanism for winning converts. The truth was that nineteenth-century missionaries never intended to integrate with the Africans. Most of them would always remain aloof from the people they had come to change.

Reverently, I approached the bath and peered over its rim. With sudden disappointment, I found myself gazing through the empty plug hole at the dusty floor beneath. The grand bath stood in vain isolation. The pipes that had once supplied the taps now ended abruptly half way along the wall and had not carried a drop of water for decades.

Crestfallen, I glanced around the rest of the room. In one corner stood a comfortably dignified water closet with a water tank perched above it and a long chain, which I pulled. There was a dry, ineffectual clanking. The porcelain hand-basin, meanwhile, was cracked and useless. Of the White Fathers' ambitious bathroom facilities, the only one that still functioned was a drain in the floor. With a sigh, Aisling pulled out her flannel, which she had made one night by cutting a square from our only towel, and stooped over the two buckets brought in by the housekeeper. The water in them was still slopping.

*   *   *

Outside, the afternoon light gradually pushed the shadow towards the farthest recess of the balcony. Philemon and I moved our chairs, and settled again, and a slow conversation trickled between us.

'Yes,' he said, 'in those days, all this was owned by the Europeans, in theory at least. A Belgian man gave it to the White Fathers. All of it.' A rigid arm swung round like the mechanical arm of a crane, taking in the whole colourful, crumbling vista below us. 'His name is over there.' Philemon pointed to a tarnished plaque let into the wall. The name *J. Ramaeckers* was engraved on it.

'The White Fathers had such dreams, such big dreams, but…' His voice trailed off, and I saw a light frown on his forehead. All around, I felt the shades of the White Fathers stirring uneasily as the mild African priest left the reproach unvoiced.

I thought of the decayed grandeur of the bathroom, and of the European dream of grafting one civilisation onto another, religion, bath, architecture and all. And now, staring down the steps, I noticed that the walls and balustrades were no longer entirely symmetrical. The graft had slipped.

'Are there any European White Fathers still around?'

'Oh yes. I think there are three of them still alive. Old men now, retired really. They live about a hundred miles away, near Sumbawanga.' Idly, I wondered whether they missed their bath and pined for the old days of colonial religion. I wondered whether they had been assimilated in Africa, or remained quirky flotsam in a society that had changed beyond recognition.

'Are you the only priest here?' I asked, wishing I could see his eyes behind his glasses.

'No, there's another one. But we take it in turns to travel so whoever's here is always alone.'

'But don't you get lonely?' I regretted my question before I had finished it. Philemon paused.

'It's... OK,' he said. But there was little opportunity, I thought, for 'the exchange of ideas'.

'Where do you travel to?'

'We have a big diocese to cover. We minister to all the villages around. Sometimes we take the ferry up to the Mahale mountains in the north but usually we go on foot. I'm due to travel next just after Christmas. I'll spend two months walking from one village to another to hold services.'

I searched his face for signs of the zeal that had inspired Karema's other holy men. But Philemon's eyes were inaccessible and the rest of his face was blank.

*   *   *

In the late afternoon we joined Philemon for a dinner of boiled fish and rice which we ate beneath a picture of a blue-eyed, fair-haired Madonna. Philemon was quiet.

'I noticed light switches in the bathroom. Was there once electricity here?'

Philemon put down his knife and fork, and rested his hands on the table. 'Yes, they used Karema as a seminary until the late sixties, then they decided it was too full of disease – this is an unhealthy place – it is full of malaria. So they removed the boys to Sumbawanga.' He looked back down to the table and recovered his cutlery. We continued to eat in silence.

When the plates were almost empty, Philemon took a draught of water and cleared his throat.

'Tell me about mad cow disease.' There was a pause as Aisling and I exchanged surprised glances.

'How do you know about mad cow disease?'

He pointed to the corner of the room. 'I have a radio.'

With relief, I filled the silence by telling him everything I knew about the recent catastrophe in the British beef industry. Occasionally he nodded: ideas were being satisfactorily exchanged.

*   *   *

Philemon offered to show us to our room in the small hospital run by the Tanzanian White Sisters. We ambled back down the avenue where it was breezy and cool beneath the trees. The sun was low and long, mottled shadows stretched across the ground. The sky was deep, deep blue above the leafy mantle. Just before the church, Philemon led us down a small winding street paved with cracked flagstones, and in the brief dusk, we picked our way down steep broken steps.

On our left, the old White Sisters' convent reached high above us, solid and imposing. Nature was gradually working her magic on the robust stone walls here as well. On our right was the collapsing wall which ringed the entire mission. Straw-roofed huts huddled beneath it and straggled away amongst the trees, in the shadow of the great European bastion, and sheltered by it. On the rough street, we were treading the abrupt border between adjacent worlds.

The wall reflected the sharp divide that had existed between the educated European priests and the backward Africans since the moment that the white men had first arrived here. It was a division which had been perpetuated by the White Fathers' attitude towards their flock. In the words of Lavigerie, their sheep were 'simple, unprejudiced negroes, to whom the Fathers were to preach the Gospel plainly, dwelling on the miraculous proofs of Christianity, and speaking always with authority, without unnecessary arguments and explanations.'

Lavigerie's attitude was enshrined in the method of religious instruction, in which access to Christian knowledge was tightly controlled. For aspiring converts, diligence was rewarded by gradual initiation. At each level of Christian knowledge, examinations had to be taken, and years had to be spent demonstrating a model Christian lifestyle. Only then were sacred truths revealed, little by little. One day, far, far in the future, the White Fathers aimed to hand over their ministry to those they had taught.

Justification, if any was needed, for Lavigerie's paternalistic approach was the outstanding success of the Tanganyika missions. For decades, Karema and the other lake missions were overflowing, causing the Order's historian a degree of complacency: 'Every morning long before sunrise numerous neophytes from distant villages are found waiting for the door of the church to be opened. Some of them walk many miles to be present at Mass'. By 1927, the 'Apostolic Vicariate of Tanganyika' had fourteen mission stations around the shores of the lake. There were 303 schools and around 38,000 converts. Three years later, the historian was able to claim that Tanganyika was the 'White Fathers' Mediterranean'.

Within three decades of those words being written, however, a wind of change was blowing through the solid European architecture at Karema. No one could have foreseen that an establishment which had weathered two European colonial administrations and their world wars would not withstand a force from within – the rise of African nationalism. With the coming of Tanzanian independence Lavigerie's simple, unprejudiced negro had suddenly come of age, and the White Fathers stepped aside.

Darkness was smothering the cold ruin beside us. But down beyond the broken stone wall, the gloom was held back by the soft orange glow of cooking fires in front of a hundred huts. Figures moved to and fro around the hearths, their profiles fleetingly alive with the flickering light. The air was full of the murmur of their conversation, and occasional trills of laughter drifted up with the smoke. Somewhere, a baby cried.

As I listened, a strand of the low evening sounds resolved itself into distant singing – exquisite, haunting harmonies which fused and peeled away, rising and falling like the wind. The disembodied voices grew stronger, sometimes breaking into chatter and then gathering again into strange, beautiful song.

'That's our choir,' said Philemon. 'They've been rehearsing. Now they're going home.' Gradually, the voices receded, absorbed by the thickening darkness amongst the huts.

'Tomorrow they'll sing at the early morning service. It's always full to overflowing.' And he turned, and continued on down the broken steps.

Every day, then, villagers crossed the divide and filled the White Fathers' ruins with their own energetic brand of Christianity. As I gingerly followed Philemon, I felt pleased. Perhaps he was not the last lonely helmsman of a dying enterprise after all. With the voices still ringing in my ears, a conviction began to grow inside me that the decaying buildings really did not matter after all – they belonged to another, alien generation. The tumbledown mission was no more than an historical curiosity, too old and cold to house the vibrant Christianity that had sprung up at Karema, now that the Europeans had gone.

Log Book Extract

DAY 18 – Thursday 12th December

PHASE 2

FROM: Karema

TO: Kabwa

CAMP: Tent pitched in guest house room.

POSITION: 30°33'38" E
               7°4'1" S

TIME CYCLING: 10 hours 20 minutes

DISTANCE TRAVELLED: 32km

AVERAGE SPEED: 3.2km/hr

ROUTE: With guide along maze of paths across flat flood plain from Karema. Over steep hills, and then onto beach. After that, followed beach all day.

TRACK CONDITION: Reasonable path to begin with, but on the shore the sand was too thick to cycle. Mainly pushing bicycles.

BICYCLES – PERFORMANCE: Aisling's pedal bearing has started to make a grinding noise, as Colum's did after the mud near Sibwesa.

BICYCLES – MAINTENANCE: We have taken to sealing the exposed part of the pedal bearings in tape, as far as is possible. Checks on tyres, chains, cogs, spokes. Discovered many loose nuts on Col's back carrier.

WEATHER: Cloudy all morning. Sunshine in the afternoon. Refreshing breeze on shoreline. Midday shade temperature 28°C.

HEALTH: Took weekly malaria tablets. Col's knee packed in over last kilometre today. He has bandaged it tonight.

EQUIPMENT: We burnt a hole in the plastic top of the food box when using it as a candle stand. Now it is not watertight. Changed torch batteries for third time.

LANDSCAPE: Flood plain and then forest. Beach is thick white sand. Water of lake looks really attractive, though is reputedly rife with cholera. We continue to filter and sterilise our water.

EXPENDITURE: Dinner TSh1,800; Provisions TSh2,500; Guides TSh5,500

FLUID CONSUMPTION: 7 litres. The tops of two of the water bottles are leaking.

FOOD: During the day: *andazis* from Karema, as well as eggs, biscuits and mangoes.
Evening meal: goat stew, beans, rice and *andazis*

We managed to buy packets of spaghetti in Kabwa. How did they come here? Must make stock cubes last.

COMMENT: We saw the weekly ferry on the lake today, heading up towards Kigoma. They say that it is the boat scuttled by the Germans after the First War, then salvaged.

We have revised our estimate of the duration of this phase of the journey from 17 to 20 days, as it is mostly to be along the beach or on steep mountain paths – both are slow and difficult.

At Kabwa, we pitched the tent in the guest house room for protection against the mosquitoes – it was a bit of a crush.

Children, in particular, do not seem to have seen *wazungu* before in these parts.

LIVINGSTONE: He struck the coast at Mkombe (he called it 'Mukembe') in the 'district of Karema'. He is sticking to the mountain paths a mile or so away from the edge of the lake. Sensible man.

11

From Karema

by Aisling

*Dry, deep powdery sand: this clogs bicycle wheels and may force you to
walk or run, carrying your bike over one shoulder.*
Collins Gem Bike Book

WE LEFT Karema just after sunrise. Beyond low hills we came to a flood
plain of a greeny, dawn grey, perfectly flat. Single palm trees loomed in
the mist and among them a silent herd of cattle grazed, tended by
Wasukumu tribesmen, their long grey cloaks dusted with dew. They
seemed little more than shadows, melting back amongst their cattle as we
passed.

We had employed two guides on bicycles who were to take us on paths
that are separated from the lake by a low range of hills. Ultimately we would
cross the ridge, at its easiest point, and travel down the lakeside to Kabwa,
a substantial village about thirty-five kilometres from Karema.

Our guides were barely teenagers and they raced through the long, wet
grass. The speed was exhilarating at first. The air was cool, I was rested
and the tsetse forest was behind us forever: I had the unusual sense of being
equal to the task. But the feeling did not last for long. The path was not
difficult but it was strewn with stones, small craters and tough little bushes
which clamoured at passers by. I concentrated hard to keep my speed up
but then – snap – there was a thud behind me. The thorns of a bush had
pulled a pannier from my bicycle.

We all stopped and the grassland became silent except for the call of the
birds. One of the boys ran back and picked up the pannier. He fixed it on
with a smile and uttered some soothing words. I recognised 'mama', 'gumu
sana' and 'baiskeli' and realised he must have said: 'It's very hard for women
to ride bicycles'.

My calm was disappearing with the morning cool. We set off again: one
of the boys first, then Colum, then another boy and then me. Soon they
were racing madly along the twisting path and I strained to keep pace as
the ground became a blur beneath me. Once a thin, grey snake slithered

away just in time. Then, inevitably, I veered too close to a bush and the food box, tethered lightly to the back panniers, was pulled to the ground. I shuffled forward automatically to the nearest shade and waited while the box was fetched. The boy handed it to Colum and shrugged again, vindicated.

'Why do we have to go so fast?' I asked. 'We never normally go this fast.'

'Seems fine to me,' Colum said and turned away.

It was as if he had slapped me. I gazed at the man who was now pulling his hat over his eyes and unrolling his shirt sleeves – the morning ritual once the sun became strong. Colum had betrayed me. He was distant, very distant, and he had betrayed me, joined the boys so that now they were all against me. Colum set off again without another word and we returned to the same brutal pace. This time the path blurred even more as tears flooded my eyes at the realisation that Colum might well have been cycling deliberately slowly over the last few weeks just to humour me. I served no purpose at all on this expedition – nothing made me indispensable. I was, as I had foreseen light-heartedly in the train long ago, an encumbrance.

The sky was harshly blue. I wiped my tears away, smearing sweat and suncream into my stinging eyes, and began to pedal fiercely to catch up. Surprisingly, I reached the others quickly. They had come to a halt and, as I braked, I saw that Colum was retrieving a pannier from the ground and re-attaching it to his bicycle. This time the boys were silent – *mama* failed because of an inner flaw but *bwana* must have been the victim of external circumstances. Quickly Colum remounted his bike and the trio sped away.

I laid my heavy bike on its side – a procedure I usually avoided because pulling it upright again was such an awkward manoeuvre – and unclipped a water bottle from the frame. I had filtered the water the previous day and so it tasted good – flavoured only with heat and plastic. Then I searched for the suncream and reapplied it carefully, including the patches below my eyebrows which had a tendency to burn. I examined my hands – a week ago they had been covered in little red discs from tsetse bites. Now they were just a wizened brown.

I felt hungry but Colum had taken the food box – a battered plastic drum in which we placed whatever perishables we had hoarded: usually mangoes, bananas, boiled eggs and bread. Nevertheless, I decided, I was not going to move until I had eaten something. I knew that deep in one of my panniers, underneath the sleeping bag and the spare clothes bag and the books on cycle maintenance and Swahili and Livingstone, lay the medicine box. Inside it were packets of glucose tablets. Methodically I took every package out, laid each on the red earth and retired to a comfortable tree root to munch the sugar.

I gazed at the land which, so far that morning, there had not been time to appreciate. It was partially planted with the willowy stalks of maize and with the low, dark green leaves of ground-nut plants. I also discovered I was not alone. Roaming the vast plain were at least two herds of cattle and their elusive cowherds. Close by, the brown earth was alive with giant ants.

I was at a watershed, in a state of calm rebellion which sprang from a slender new shred of knowledge: that I had been right to claim that we were travelling unrealistically fast. Moreover my perfect companion, Dr Livingstone reincarnated, was also incapable of belting along tiny paths without scattering his luggage and, most importantly, he did not have the honesty to admit it. A stubborn surge of strength brought clarity to my thoughts. Perhaps it was female to be the first to complain – or even the first to suffer – but I was proud of being that way. I had my own virtues – having no fear of losing face was a prime one which allotted me a role comparable to a miner's canary, saving Colum from a witless death march into dehydration, hunger or exhaustion. I also had flaws, but from now on I would be ashamed of neither.

The men ahead would soon come to a grumbling halt, exchange knowing sighs and wait for me. In fact, as I peered ahead I thought I could distinguish them – a still cluster beside a grove of trees. I would catch them up but I would do so at my own, womanly, pace, exhibiting my slow, unappreciated toughness. I remembered now the first difference I had ever spotted between Colum and myself: he rips a plaster off while I coax it away, millimetre by millimetre.

I determined to get through this expedition the way I knew best – by plodding. It was the only way to survive. It would needle Colum, but I drew some satisfaction from the fact that he would not be able to complain: he could object to mutiny or foul-mouthed protestations, but not to the natural difference between our strengths. I stood up and brushed the red soil from the back of my trousers, repacked the pannier neatly and grasped the bicycle seat which had absorbed a sharp heat in the sun. Leaning my weight against it I hauled it upright, mounted and cycled on my way.

*   *   *

Some of the entries Livingstone made in his journal as he progressed down the shores of Tanganyika were too sensational, too bitter, to grace the published edition – or so thought Horace Waller, who duly excised them. The thoughts he deleted reveal a sinister side to Livingstone's obsessional nature – darker broodings that distorted his view of the world and led to his pathological inability to trust other people.

He dwelled incessantly on the injustices that he believed he had suffered back in Britain and fantasised often about the wrongs that people might be doing him at that very moment, when he was helpless in central Africa.

Perhaps he wrote ferociously during the exhaustion of hot afternoons when he could foresee nothing but days of illness and hunger stretching ahead of him. Or perhaps he scribbled at night by the light of a candle, when he was lonely. Maybe it was then that unacknowledged fears pressed most at his mind: was he strong enough to complete his task? would enemies from Britain cut him off, find the Four Fountains before him? In his solitude he even questioned the motives of his most loyal friend, John Kirk, the man who had been the most forbearing member of Livingstone's Zambezi expedition, and the only one to emerge from it on cordial terms with his leader. Kirk had subsequently become the acting British Consul in Zanzibar, despatching caravans of supplies for Livingstone into the interior – and ignorant of the fact that they never made it through to Tabora. Livingstone, mulling over those missing supplies, became convinced that Kirk wanted to set up his own expedition and find the Four Fountains himself.

'*Mr Kirk's public recommendation to me to retire and leave the rest to others is ominous,*' he wrote in his notebook. '*The other plan to which govt. looked points to a private offer of himself* [Kirk] *and his advice to* [another] *expedition... the strong urging* [to me] *to go home may not be less than the extreme greed of low villainy.*'

This accusation against Kirk was not merely a single lapse in a moment of despair. Livingstone believed that, because the missing supplies were stolen, Kirk was guilty of '*culpable negligence*' and told '*half truths*' to the British government to escape blame. When Kirk expressed opinions about the geography of Lake Bangweulu, Livingstone dismissed his ideas as '*a sally of audacious ignorance*'.

Invective filled the pages of his notebook: he ranted at other explorers, against the British government, against the Royal Geographical Society. His fears were partly the distorted speculations of a mind isolated from fellow countrymen, who might have been able to guide it back to the paths of reason. But they were also the last sparks of a flame that had singed his relationships with most of his acquaintances and friends. Livingstone's first fear when he met a man was whether he might deliberately undermine his projects. His second fear was whether he would undermine them through ineptitude. The result of such mistrust was often disaster.

He quarrelled with almost every colleague when he was working as a conventional missionary during his first time in Africa. On his second journey, when he had power over other men, his treatment of Europeans was profoundly disturbing. On his ill-fated mission up the Zambezi his team was six-strong: he dismissed three of the men; relations with another sank so low that the man refused to board the boat unless it was essential; he had raging quarrels with another. Eventually, two of the six asked for permission to leave.

Livingstone's paranoia extended to interpreting people's deaths as deliberate attempts to scupper his plans. The best a missionary or expedition colleague could hope for as an epitaph was the claim that their death was the consequence of gross negligence rather than deliberate calculation.

On the Zambezi expedition one able young man in his early twenties died of fever: Livingstone pronounced that '*folly killed him*'. His verdict on the brave Bishop Mackenzie was even more astounding. The Bishop led the Oxford and Cambridge Universities Mission to Africa following an appeal led by Livingstone. But instead of reaching the peaceful and healthy lands Livingstone had promised them, the missionaries soon found themselves embroiled in a guerilla war with local tribes. Within a year Mackenzie had died from a fever caught in unhealthy swamplands through which he had been forced to wander. Livingstone's angry verdict was that this most respected of men was guilty of '*coarse living and rash exposure*'.

The most painful example of his misperception of motives was the fate of two missionary families who travelled to southern Africa at about the time of the Zambezi expedition. They went in response to an appeal by Livingstone and they arrived to find the local tribes unexpectedly hostile and Livingstone absent, both circumstances contrary to what they had been led to expect. Within two months, three of the four adults and five of the seven children had died miserable deaths. Livingstone expressed no regret afterwards, publicly or in his journal, and he blamed the missionaries themselves for the disaster.

Yet there were times during his life when Livingstone's selfishness and lack of compassion vanished. It was when he travelled with Africans that he revealed he was capable of humanity and his behaviour became the antithesis of his behaviour with Europeans. He was patient, he cared for them when they were sick, he forgave them when they betrayed him – and he thus inspired tremendous loyalty in many of his followers. When he wrote of them in his journal he began from a standpoint of sympathy rather than suspicion. Of a dangerously disruptive woman in his party he wrote: '*she is somebody's bairn never the less – a tall strapping woman – must have been the pride of her parents*'. And of a cold, wet child discovered in the grass he recorded: '*I ordered a man to carry her, and we gave her to one of the childless women; she is about four years old*'.

When Livingstone was among Africans he was in the role of benefactor and employer, and that is the heart of the reason why he worked well with them. Britain defined him – it was where status and reputation were built. So amongst Britons his life was complicated by the need to angle for power and influence. With Africans those concerns vanished and relationships could be simple and harmonious.

Exceptional human beings can be excused their imperfections. Many of Livingstone's flaws had gradually been revealed to us as inevitable consequences of his strengths – his obsessional nature, his stoicism and his religious faith. Yet one blemish remained, exposed in those ugly writings that were hidden from public view for over a century. Livingstone was guilty of inhumanity. Even worse was his refusal to admit that guilt.

12
To Kipili
by Aisling

We left a broad valley with a sand river in it, where we have been two days, and climbed a range of hills parallel to Tanganyika, of mica schist and gneiss, tilted away from the Lake. We met a buffalo on the top of one ridge, it was shot into and lay down, but we lost it. Course SW to brink of Tanganyika water.

Up a steep ridge and into a wood sprinkled with yellow and purple flowers and littered with shards of rose quartz. One of the boys hauled my bicycle up for me – an appropriate gesture, I now felt, because he was the stronger one. Here the air was full of the smell of vegetation and the forest was pleasantly cool. I called a stop after an hour for mangoes and biscuits.

Over the ridge we descended through vegetation and then emerged, abruptly, at the side of the lake. The sand burned with crystalline brightness and there was the dry smell of hot rock. Beyond, a hot breeze blew white cusps into the blue water and hurried a dhow with a patched white sail. I was too encumbered with boots and long clothing to plunge into its seductive coolness, so instead I crouched down and wafted my hands through the shifting waves.

In the shade of a shack near the water's edge were three men, torn-clothed and barefoot, talking excitedly in voices that fragmented in the breeze. Soon one was delegated to approach, a short man truncated further as his feet sank into the soft sand.

After greeting us he fell silent. He had sullen eyes. At last he reached into his pocket, pulled out a small glass jar and, with great care, unscrewed the top. We all leaned closer, trying to see what was inside. Then he tipped the jar and poured a chaos of glinting green shapes into the palm of his hand: gemstones.

'Tourmaline,' Colum said. The treasure hunter nodded. He seemed surly.

'Where did you find them?' Colum asked in Swahili.

His eyes never leaving Colum's face, the man swept a wide arc that took in the hills through which we had come. He was not going to tell us exactly where he had found them – he was a treasure hunter, and they guard their secrets.

We had met treasure hunters before. In villages they form clandestine groups bound by oaths of secrecy. They make sorties into the forest to search for hoards of gold or gemstones by looking for signs in the rock and omens in the bends of trees. They dredge stories from the past to support their theories. They dig for years, young men jealously guarding the secret of their hole in the ground. When the rains come they stop for a while and sometimes their holes collapse and their scratchings in the forest are swept away.

They sustain themselves with dreams of their future wealth, with modest plans to become 'businessmen' or to send their children to school. Now, on the shores of the lake, we had found a man who, by incredible chance, had found something other than gravel and sand. I could see why he was sullen: his find had not catapulted him into immediate riches. On the remote shores of Lake Tanganyika there was no one to buy his stones.

'How much?' he asked Colum.

Colum played with the pieces, tipping them between his cupped palms in fascination. 'You know I shouldn't think they're worth much. They're too small.' Carefully, he funnelled the fragments back into the jar and handed it back: 'Sorry'.

The man's face fell, but then brightened: 'I have another stone – a big red one'.

'Bring it to us,' Colum said. 'We'll be staying at Kabwa.' We could just make out the lakeside village on a spur of land farther south. The man carefully replaced the lid and returned to the shelter. We never saw him again.

On our distant left the hills gained in height and grandeur, and started their oblique march in towards the lake. Small bays sheltered clusters of huts that cowered from the sun among massive, smooth boulders. Fishing boats dried out on the beach or bobbed on the water.

But Lake Tanganyika is hell as well as paradise. The waves that crumble onto its shore are not tidal and so nothing cleanses the sand. The people have fish to eat but little else. In the tiny village of Mkombe we peered into the shop: on the sand floor lay an emaciated child with a huge head, a bowl of a stomach and puppet's limbs.

We retreated and sat outside the shop in a sliver of midday shade, our backs to the water, and gazed inland. Mkombe was where Livingstone reached the lake. We scanned the ridge to see where his passing place might have been, and then forced our way up the sandy beach into the centre of the village. A woman clanged at a water pump but there were few people around.

'We might have come here yesterday, but were too tired. Mukembe... is ruled by chief Kariaria... The chief Kariaria is civil.'

Where there was no path the soft, thick sand collapsed under our weight so that every step was a strain. Only at the water's edge did the foaming wavelets give rigidity to the surface. There, amongst the smooth driftwood and fantastically crenellated shells we were able to push the bicycles. But my muscles burned and sweat trickled down my back. The pedals knocked the backs of my legs, nurturing slow bruises. I kept going – slowly and taking rests.

'This heat makes me useless, and constrains me to lie like a log. Inwardly I feel tired too.'

A duck and her brood halted us on their expedition to the water. A water snake reared its head in anger but I walked past oblivious to the danger – and then turned to see four little boys clubbing it to death.

'At sunset the red glare on the surface made the water look like a sea of reddish gold...'

It was a moonless night and Kabwa was alive with comfortable evening sounds and smells: the hum of a generator; the scent of oil burning in home-made lamps. Even in the darkness a throng of children followed us, murmuring like night shadows. We found a *hoteli* and dined well on rice and beans and goat stew. Later, in a small room in the dilapidated guest-house, the mattresses smelt stale and we fell asleep to the sound of cockroaches clattering across the concrete floor.

*   *   *

The next day we left our guides and continued down the lakeside. Men trudged along the shore with hoes on their shoulders, off to the fields. Fishermen brought in the night's catch of small, silver fish and scattered them like splashes of raindrops onto the beach to dry. A woman glided towards us balancing a bowl on her head that flashed in the sun and out of which protruded the fantastic forked tail of a giant fish.

Under a viciously clear sky men washed, naked, in the lake, their vigorous bodies glittering behind the white soap. Women squatted at the water's edge to scrub heaps of clothes or dishes with sand.

The people grow cassava in the hills and the floodplains. When it is ripe they cut it into shards and soak it in pools by the lake. They dry it in the sunshine and it smells of sour milk. Then they pound it, or take it by boat down the lake where it is milled into coarse flour.

A very great deal of cotton cultivated all along the shores of Lake Tanganyika; it is the Pernambuco kind, with the seeds clinging together, but of good and long fibre, and the trees are left standing all the year to enable them to become large; grain and ground-nuts are cultivated between them. The cotton is manufactured into coarse cloth, which is the general clothing of all.

In the rainy season great rivers rush down between the hills to the lake. But now the river beds were empty chasms into which we had to lower the bicycles, manhandling each one back up the other side. One village was split in two by such a gorge. When the rains come, I wondered, do the two communities say goodbye to each other for a while? Does the river divide families and dampen love affairs?

Though we suffer much from the heat by travelling at this season, we escape a vast number of running and often muddy rills, also muddy paths which would soon knock the donkey up.

We scared the lake people. Three singing women screamed when they discovered us and ran, skirts streaming behind them, parcels clutched to their heads, babies bouncing on their backs.

All are very tired, and in coming to a stockade we were refused admittance, because Malongwana had attacked them lately, and we might seize them when in this stronghold. Very true; so we sit outside in the shade of a single palm (Borassus)...

We slipped through one village almost unnoticed. At its far end we toiled up a steep hill and at the summit I turned. Below us a crowd of children had gathered. They stood quietly, watching us – small, wide-eyed things, big tummies only half concealed by their rags. I felt a pang as if, somehow, we had cheated them.

Late that afternoon we camped unseen in a wood at the side of the lake and watched through the trees as a lone fisherman, standing in the stern of his canoe, turned to a silhouette in the sunset.

Crossed two deep gullies with sluggish water in them and one surrounding an old stockade. Camp on a knoll, overlooking modern stockade and Tanganyika very pleasantly.

Colum made supper as usual, but this time he pulled from his bag a tiny packet of peppercorns. He counted some out, and poured them into my palm.

'Would you mind grinding them?'

'What with?'

'Oh, I don't know... two stones?'

I found a dented stone and another, rounded one and scrambled away from the trees down to the beach where there was still some light. I opened my hand: there were ten precious little black beads.

Carefully I tipped them into the shallow dimple of my rock. Three escaped and bounced into crevices between the boulders. Seven left. Slowly, I brought the other stone down and pressed it on a single peppercorn: it shot away into the undergrowth. I tried another, it did the same. I ground the remaining five peppercorns and scraped what I could of the fragments into my palm. As I stood up with my precious powder I lost my footing. The fragments scattered.

'I've dropped all the pepper...' I did not apologise.

'Oh... well it doesn't really matter.' But I knew it did.

At night, we heard the sound of drumming from the lake, and deep singing, and the rush of water past the hulls of canoes. In the tent, I felt Colum's hand groping till it reached mine. I held it.

*   *   *

Rest, and kill an ox. The dry heat is distressing and all feel it sorely. I am right glad of the rest, but keep on as constantly as I can. By giving dura and maize to the donkeys, and riding on alternate days, they hold on; but I feel the sun more than if walking.

The next day the path dwindled and at times was nothing more than a deep drainage channel a foot wide. Often it became narrower than the pedal-span so we would climb out of it and bump through the plantations. Sometimes there was an easy track high above the lake, winding through plots of deep green cassava and ground-nut.

'*... two lions growled savagely as we passed. Game is swarming here, but my men cannot shoot except to make a noise.*'

In fields beyond the lake we found mushrooms and filled our hats with them. We would cook them later. It was the end of the dry season, and there was little but the promise of food.

'*We got a water-buck and a large buffalo, and remained during the forenoon to cut up the meat, and started at 2pm...*'

The rain began as we crossed a green floodplain behind the shore. It fell straight, and with such intensity that distant green became grey.

Went on South... till we came down, by a little westing, to the Lake again, where

there were some large villages, well-stockaded, with a deep gully half round them...
Food dear, because Simba made a raid lately. The country is Kirando.

The village of Kirando was Karema's small and ghostly twin, an old mission, now almost abandoned. Its church was tall and circular, built of brick and bright stained glass. Bats swooped in the steel lattice work of its roof.

After Kirando we reached a mud road, one of the few that strike inland from the lake. We sped inland for a while relishing the smooth surface – it was the best track since Tabora and it swept across an open plain. Mountains ringed the horizon and clouds stacked precariously at a distant edge of the sky. After an hour we turned south-west, slipped back between the hills to the lake and reached Kipili by dusk.

13

In Kipili
by Aisling

Africa was a tabula rasa.
African scholar Crawford Young

DUSK drops over Kipili like a cloth of grey silk, hiding the sordid bother of human affairs. In the stillness of the evening, men sit and smoke under straw eaves, and women pound cassava with the steady thud that comforts village evenings across the continent. Boys perform their last outlandish tricks of the day on outsize iron bicycles. In the bay, fishermen in long canoes are reduced to flawless silhouettes. And above them all, on the northern hill, a small white church watches in benign presidency.

When morning comes, it will reveal the village's mundane imperfections, and also its peculiarity. For Kipili is an exception among lakeside villages. Village life has been interrupted, and has readjusted to the presence of two families of Europeans. One group is a Danish missionary family, envoys from the Moravian Church which first arrived in sub-Saharan African more than 250 years ago. The Danes live beside the little church.

The other is an Austrian couple. The Austrians live on the opposite side of the bay, half an hour's walk away. They are also following a white tradition in Africa, although it is a very different one. For them Africa is a toy. It is the continent that Theodore Roosevelt described as '… an ideal playground alike for sportsmen and for travellers who wish to live in health and comfort and yet to see what is beautiful and unusual…'.

The sun has set. The sapphire lake has turned to black. Up the steep hillside at the Moravian mission the Danes are saying their prayers before dinner. Paul Jansen, a man with a kind and mournful face and a slow gait, helps his twin twelve-year-olds to their food. His wife, Ulrikka, is tossing in bed with malaria, her skin the colour of white marble. During the night her delirious cries will disturb sleepers all down the hillside. There are rooms in the mission where the mosquitoes crowd so thickly in the corners that their tiny whinings combine into a hiss. Paul feels a little strange himself. He fears that he, too, is developing fever. Not again, he thinks wearily.

The family eats by the light of candles. Electricity disappeared one day when the solar panel broke. No one can fix it. Water is scarce too. There is a tank which collects rainwater but it is running low. Lake water is dirty and infested with disease, and someone must carry it up the steep hill.

But the beleaguered Danes did not come to Kipili to seek an easy living. Nor did they come for the beauty of the view, although they thank God for that every day. They are here to minister, and so they overcome life's frustrations through self-discipline and prayer.

A violent crackle stutters through the air. Soon a message ripples across the village: 'It's Fritz. He's shot a hippo. Before it killed someone.' On the other side of the lake the orange-tanned Austrian returns in satisfaction from the lakeside to his octagonal bungalow where he puts his gun away.

He strolls across his property. Once it was ten acres of bush and rock but he has tamed it and now it stretches from the foot of the hill to the lake shore. His land is dotted with neat circular buildings that he built himself and painted gleaming white. Their architecture resonates with the simple design of the village huts, but Fritz has equipped them with running water, concrete floors, electricity from his generator, and thatch as thick as that of an English cottage.

Fritz passes through his garden where his wife has planted an exotic fury of vegetables, types that have never been seen before in Kipili, and reaches his bar and open-sided dining room. There he settles with a cold Austrian beer and cuts into a plate of roebuck, the most succulent meat ever tasted, in a cream and pepper sauce. He shot it yesterday. Tomorrow they will feast on hippo. It is a fitting reward for protecting the local population from their most dangerous foe.

He is pleased with himself. He relishes Africa as his predecessors have. He is the latest in a long line of adventurers and game-hunters who have delighted in Africa, and have made strange bedfellows for missionaries. Even Livingstone, on some of his early explorations, had at his side the wealthy game-hunter William Cotton Oswell. Indeed without him he could not have afforded to travel.

Fritz arrived here twenty years ago in search of tropical fish to sell back in Austria. Felastino, the village chief, liked him so much that he gave him some land. Ever since, Fritz and his thin and silent wife have spent six months of the year in Austria running their hotel and six months in Kipili, where she sunbathes and cooks and he hunts.

He delves into a chest of Austrian luxuries and produces a fine wine, handing it to his wife to uncork.

'You see,' he explains in his heavily accented English, 'in Europe I could not even afford one square metre of lakeside property. But here...', and he makes a wide, circling gesture as if the whole of Kipili is his.

He explains that his spread of houses and tents and shelters is an embryonic hotel. He and his wife have been building it for twenty years, but so far they have invited no guests. 'I am not ready,' he declares. 'I don't want our Austrian friends to come until this place is perfect.'

*   *   *

The plastic bag drips blood and bulges with the grey hippopotamus meat. 'That's kind of Fritz,' says Paul. He gazes across the bay towards his neighbour and says with uncertainty: 'He is a good man'. Then, more resolutely: 'He has always helped us when we've had a problem'.

He drops the bag in the kitchen sink, returns to the sitting room and sits down heavily in a wooden chair. He is tired because today he has been exorcising. 'There is a lot of demonic possession here,' he says, his voice mild, like an echo. 'Take Michael, for example. He was a drunkard who lived down the hill. Then he asked me to help him. He told me he was possessed; by spirits, he said. So I exorcised him. He's been sober ever since.' There is a quiet satisfaction.

'I have exorcised many houses too,' he continues quietly, 'Sometimes they have belonged in the past to Christians who then... well... drifted....' Paul's eyes are thoughtful. They are focussed far away, towards where the sun is dipping towards the horizon. '... into Satanism. I blot out the evil, after they have left.'

He pauses, leans forward, his voice a whisper. 'Sometimes there will be a room where Satan has appeared in a vision. We hold Communion there. At that moment there is such a sense of victory, such an overwhelming sense of serenity...' He sighs, and gazes out at the golden brilliance of the bay.

*   *   *

In the bright midday light Fritz's face is as contoured as leather, except for his nose where the top layer has burned away to reveal tender pink skin. He is relaxing in his dining room. His wife, chain-smoking, is preparing the meal. He empties a cold beer down his throat.

'See that?' He jabs a finger at a row of banana trees just above the shoreline and thumps his empty glass onto the table. 'When I came here the first thing I did, the very first thing I did, was to plant those trees in a straight line.

Look at them: dead straight.' He is triumphant. 'I said: this will show these villagers that we Europeans are straight people. We think in straight lines.' He calls for his wife to bring another beer.

'Then, and only then, did I call some men to cut me a road out here. Within a few days they came to me and said they had finished. I didn't believe them. I went down there to see with my own eyes. The road was like a snake – it went round every tree and rock. Africans are not straight, you see. They do not understand straight lines.' His voice grows louder.

'I said: You think we Europeans are snakes? That we are happy to travel in curves and bends? No, we Europeans are straight, straight. And I took them down to the banana trees. See, I said, everything must be in a straight line for Europeans. So they returned to the road and they cut it straight, just like the banana trees. It took a lot of effort I tell you, uprooting bushes and moving boulders.' He pauses ruminatively. 'They learned a lesson that time. But there are some things you can never teach an African.'

Fritz shakes his head and helps himself to some of the exquisite food his wife has brought to the table. 'I have never met an African who can use a tap properly. Never. They twist them and twist them in one direction until they break. I tell them: no, this is how a tap works. You turn it one way to open it and the other to close it. But they never learn. I have had to replace my taps so many times that I have lost count.

'You see, you can do nothing to help these people. But they are not unhappy. They should just be left alone. I've said that to the aid workers who come down here trying to help. Help! Christ! They have wasted so much money on their useless projects. It is madness, madness.' His face is flushed with excitement.

'From my seat here I can point to two failed aid projects and I can tell you of five more down the bay – that makes seven. Seven!' He chuckles. 'Madness.'

'Over there, just look.' Suddenly he is standing, clutching his serviette to his waist. He is pointing to a distant spit of land where there are some low grey structures. 'Do you see those buildings? Do you know what they are?'

He pauses for effect: 'They are a Swiss fish factory'. He sits down. 'The Swiss came here; they built it; and then they left. And since then not a single fish has been processed. Too expensive to keep it all cool, you see.

'It's just the same with the other empty buildings to the south. They were built by German aid workers. You won't believe what they came to build. Try and guess…' He looks searchingly from my face to Colum's. 'It was a bloody kindergarten project. I met them when they first arrived. They told me – *they* told *me* – that all the problems of the village could be solved if only mothers did not have to look after their children all day. So they built their beautiful German kindergarten.'

His bleached blue eyes grow wilder; he is almost shouting his punchline: 'But the mothers did not want a kindergarten. They wanted their children at home where they could keep watch on them as they worked. Kindergarten! In Kipili! Christ! It did not operate for one day.' His wife puts his coffee on the table and clears away the dishes. He lights a cigarette, inhales and sighs in contentment.

'But I am saving you the best story for last,' he says. He leans forward, fist on the table. 'They decided the water here must be purified – well so it should be; today we have a case of cholera in a family that lives by the lake. So the Swiss came back, this time with a solar water heater. It was a complicated machine with a large handpump to drive water up through the solar panels.' New levels of scorn enter his voice.

'It was exhausting to pump it. Such hard work. And it could not provide nearly enough water for the whole village. So...' He pauses for a deep and beery guffaw.

'Soon, the twenty-litre jerry cans thoughtfully provided to every family for collecting the water were being used to store kerosene for lamps. No one used the water purification system at all.' Fritz is bursting with glee: 'Thank you. Thank you very, very much, clever Europeans'. He claps the table with the flat of his hand, making the cutlery dance. 'You can't change these people you see. It's mad to try.' He tilts his head up at the Moravian Mission. 'They, at least, should know that by now. More to drink?'

His wife sits down at the table and lights herself another cigarette. She begins to speak but Fritz interrupts: 'Sometimes I think I am the only one who is neither stupid nor mad around here. And the arrival of you two has not changed that. Cycling down the lakeside is crazy. You'll never finish it. There are no paths. You'll never do it.' He stops to drink, and I feel uneasy. 'We've managed it so far,' says Colum, his voice edged with irritation. 'Hmmph,' replies Fritz.

All day I have watched Colum asking people from the village about the next leg of the journey; all day I have watched people shaking their heads, shrugging their shoulders. It's a different reaction now from the one we encountered farther north. There, people were incredulous – they knew how foolhardy we were, because they knew the route we were taking. But now they look at us blankly – to do what we are suggesting is outside their experience. Very few people do that journey, and it cannot be done by bicycle. From a distance, I watch them mouth the words 'kali sana'. The route ahead is very fierce, very difficult, very rocky, very steep. All diminish to the same phrase in our limited vocabulary.

Colum is worried. I know because he no longer talks to me about the journey. Failure is too hard to contemplate, and pride too stiff. My heart sinks. But I have to know. 'Fritz, can we really get no farther?'

Colum starts to say something but I scowl at him. The Austrian's reply is vague, his hand-movements expansive: 'It's too far... it's never been done before... there are cliffs down to the water's edge. What you need is a motor boat.' He pauses, rotating his beer glass so that the liquid catches the light like amber. 'I don't have one but the Danes do. It's a missionary boat, they go up and down the lake with it to do their visiting.'

'We're not going by boat.' Colum's voice is quiet. 'When he came through here, Livingstone was walking.'

Fritz shakes his head impatiently. We fall further in his estimation. Then Colum says slowly: 'I know...'. Something in his voice makes me look up. '... we could load just our bicycles onto the boat...' His tone rises. '... then, we could ask someone to set off from Kipili with the boat in a few days' time.'

'And we walk?'

'Exactly...'

'... well'. I consider for a moment. I find I have no fear of a long walk: it is just one step followed by another after all. 'I suppose it would be easier to walk an impossible path than to cycle it,' I say. But Colum is no longer listening. He has already pulled the map from its battered case and is looking for a point beyond the mountainous stretch of coastline where the bicycles can be landed.

His eyes are hard. It seems he can make anything happen – anything – when he is in this mood. I fluctuate. Part of me can see only complications: both Paul and Ulrikka are in bed with malaria, so how do we negotiate such a delicate request? Who will take the boat down the lake for us? What will happen if we, or they, are delayed?

Fritz has lost interest. He has begun a rambling story about how he and his wife built themselves a raft, floated it on the Congo and drifted downstream through the Heart of Darkness to the river's mouth on the west coast. It is an astonishing tale, particularly from one who has defined himself as a gem of sanity in a crazy world. But we are itching to leave. It is early evening. By morning we could be gone.

*   *   *

It was always so important to be gone. There were perpetual reasons for moving on – impending rain or diminishing food supplies or the great distance to the next village. Whatever the reason, we always had a meticulous schedule. Colum continued to travel with a passionate urgency. He had become consumed by the journey, and now this man, whom I had never known to be ill, was starting to show signs of stress. He had begun to suffer from pains which gripped his stomach nearly every day.

He saw that we needed always to be alert, looking ahead, foreseeing the insurmountable and running towards it as if to beat it through sheer momentum. It is not possible to alternate between that mood and the vulnerability that comes with relaxation and temporary disengagement. This was Livingstone's mode of travel as well – constant negotiating, searching for food and water, coping with the unpredictable through force of personality. Without his maniacal sense of purpose he would never have penetrated so far.

We could have spent two weeks in Kipili waiting for the Danes' malaria to subside, searching for a guide and buying provisions. Instead Colum negotiated with Paul that very evening, when he emerged from his bedroom for supper. He agreed a fee for the use of the boat, two men and petrol. Felastino found us a guide and we bought the only provisions we could find: peanuts and biscuits.

By the light of a candle I packed essentials into two panniers: we wanted to carry as little as possible. Jon, one of Paul's twelve-year-old sons, came to watch Colum preparing the bicycles. The two of them had developed a rapport over a few days of swapping tools and adjusting brake cables.

Tonight Jon seemed puzzled about something. He persisted in asking us about our visit to Fritz, which had been lengthy. Had we drunk beer there? Had we liked him? Finally he said: 'Colum?'

'Yes?'

'Are you a Christian?'

Colum paused. 'No,' he said. 'No, I am not a Christian.'

'Do you get drunk?'

Again Colum waited, trying to understand how his reply would be processed. Finally he said: 'No, I drink beer but I don't get drunk.'

'And you don't use bad words, do you?'

'No.' said Colum. 'I never use bad words.'

After that, Jon was silent. Soon he said goodnight and left us, his black and white twelve-year-old world having become an uncomfortable shade of grey.

Log Book Extract

DAY 22 – Monday 16th December

PHASE 2

FROM: Kipili

TO: Kaseri near Ninde (Livingstone's 'Linde'), by foot.

CAMP: On sandy shore of lake.

POSITION: 30°43'22" E
            7°41'24" S

TIME WALKING: 11 hours

DISTANCE TRAVELLED: 35km

AVERAGE SPEED: 3.1km/hr (WALKING)

ROUTE: Avoided coast walking by striking inland a little, skirting
   behind lakeside ranges.

PATH CONDITION: Small path as far as Mtosi. Then returned to
   coast and scrambled across steep hillsides as far as Ninde.

BICYCLES: Sent on ahead by boat.

WEATHER: Bright and sunny with patches of cloud all day. Hot.
   Midday shade temperature 32°C.

HEALTH: Both have very stiff leg muscles and severe foot blisters. Col
   has stiff hip.

EQUIPMENT: We carry with us only a basic medical kit, some food,
   our notes, the camera and the machete. The rest has been sent on by
   boat.

LANDSCAPE: Low forest and cultivated land, steep hills around us.

EXPENDITURE: Tea and *andazis* TSh500; Biscuits Tsh2,250; Supper
   Tsh750; Guide (Otto) TSh5,500.

FLUID CONSUMPTION: 8 litres approx.

FOOD: Breakfast: bananas
      During the day: nuts and biscuits, black sweet tea and *andazis*
      Evening meal: *ugalli* and fish, cold water with cocoa powder on
      beach before bed.

We discovered that we have dropped a bag of nuts on today's journey. This is bad news. Food is difficult enough to find here without this.

COMMENT: As we were warned in Kipili, we could not have got the bicycles across the steep hillsides here. Today is Monday; we have to be in Wampembe by Wednesday to meet the bikes from the missionaries' boat.

LIVINGSTONE: He is sticking to the mountain paths, and grumbles about the steepness of the hillsides near Ninde.

14

From Kipili to Mvimwa
by Aisling

I sent a doti to the headman of the village to ask for a guide to take us straight south...

'AH, YOU are taking Otto with you,' boomed Fritz. 'He will be a good guide.' He slapped him on the shoulder. 'Otto is the biggest hunter in Tanzania.' Wiry Otto grinned at the praise as we strode out of Kipili, its white church, frail in the morning sun, swiftly disappearing behind a hill. Otto loped ahead in sandals made from worn tyres, one of our bicycle panniers on his shoulder. Swiftly we reached hidden paths that wove through the woods behind the lakeside hills. The ground was peppered with brilliant waxy flowers that had popped straight from the earth without stalks or leaves.

Otto — resilient, animated, mischievous — knew every twist of the landscape. At a fork in the thin, sandy path he knew instantly which direction to take. He led us away from the water into the depths of the forest, back into bays at the lakeside and then deep inland again.

'*The sides of the Tanganyika Lake are a succession of rounded bays, answering to the valleys which trend down to the shore between the numerous ranges of hills...*'

Sometimes he would freeze, his hard body bent, and scan the trees for the trace of a fleeing animal. He would pause over a pawprint to tell us which animal had trodden there and when.

Otto had a hundred hunter's tales to tell. A leopard had attacked him once and now he re-enacted the fight. Suddenly he was the leopard, swaying in fearsome confusion; then he was brave Otto with his hunter's cry, tantalising the beast. Then he was the leopard again, his face contorted into ferocity as he hurled himself across the path. As the leopard pounced Otto dodged it. It pounced again, and as it hurled itself past him Otto pinched its bottom. He continued to perform for us, jumping back and forth, snarling, clutching his arm in mock agony.

'*The people brought in a leopard in great triumph. Its mouth and all its claws were bound with grass and bands of bark, as if to make it quite safe, and its tail was curled round: drumming and lullilooing in plenty...*'

Otto trod onwards. We stopped him every hour for rest and a swig of water, to gobble nuts and let the blood drain from hot, pounding feet. We had told him to bring his own food but he did not, so he ate ours. He also brought no water, so he drank ours.

We reached a bay: a few huts, a pig. Children, women and old men gathered to sit on the ground around us while Otto told our tale. Who knows what he said. All day he explained us to the people we met and each time he finished with: 'Mama tired' and a shake of the head. Outrageous to take Mama on such a trip, they all agreed.

'I'm not that tired,' I would protest, rising resolutely onto my swollen, aching feet.

On. Out of the forest shade. Into the sucking heat. As we threaded past the cultivation outside a village Otto spotted a woman standing silent in the vegetation.

'Why aren't you on the path?' He cackled. 'She's afraid of you. She has not seen *wazungu* before.' All day children would flee from us, toddlers would cry, women would rush from the path at the sight of us and then be subjected to Otto's taunts. Once he thumped the heavy pannier, now on his head. 'They think this bag is full of African blood,' he chuckled enigmatically.

Blister. A deep blister was growing in the ball of my foot. Every step was a dull pain apart from the pressure on the blister, which was a sharpness. Then, after eleven hours, we rounded a difficult cliff and arrived at Kaseri, with its neighbouring village of Ninde, on a sandy fractal sticking into the lake.

'*We rested two hours in a deep, shady dell, and then came along a very slippery mountain side to a village in a stockade. It is very hot today and the first thunderstorm away in the east. The name of this village is Linde.*'

I sank onto the beach and gazed at our precious lake, open as a sea. Colum and Otto went to find the chief. Then the children came – hordes of them, rushing to see the *mzungu* mama. They stood round my collapsed form, chattering, shouting, laughing, pointing, sniggering. I leaned back against a rock, my view of the lake blocked by a crescent of threatening village life which I unwillingly drew towards me until there was just a little box of space in which I could move. As they laughed I willed Colum back. But he did not come. And then, after an hour, he rescued me: 'Children, watoto,' he cried. 'Mnataka nini? What do you want?'

'We want to shake hands,' they chorused.

'Well, we are very tired and we need to sleep,' Colum said. 'We will make an agreement. I will shake everybody's hand and then you will all go home.'

'Yes,' they replied.

Sixty curious hands, some grasping, some tentative, thrust forward and Colum shook every one of them. Then they were gone.

Ninde has no roads, electricity or running water. But it has a bylaw: no one may sleep on the beach during the rainy season. It was, in theory, the rainy season, but the rain had not yet come. Should the *wazungu* be allowed to camp on the beach? It had taken an hour of discussion amongst the village administrative hierarchy before the chief made the decision that we could do so.

In the warm dark we stripped and washed in the silky water of the lake. Revived, we discussed our plan. It was Tuesday night and we hoped to reach the village of Wampembe farther down the lake by the following evening. The motor boat was due to arrive there at midday on Thursday. All we needed was more food. This, however, was a growing problem.

I had thought that finding food would be easier by the lake; after all, there was plenty of fishing. The reason that we spent much of our time hungry was that the villagers had no reason to catch more than they needed – there was no market to support in these villages.

'... *the lake folk are poor, except in fish...*'

With great difficulty, and for a high price, we persuaded a woman to prepare a meal of boiled fish for us.

'... *Remained to buy food, which is very dear. We slaughtered a tired cow to exchange for provisions...*'

*   *   *

Otto was late. We had already been walking for an hour in the morning cool before I spotted his skinny form hurrying after us along the beach. He was limping.

'Panya,' he explained, and pointed to two neat puncture marks in his toe. Then he launched into an animated soliloquy. Colum turned to me: 'A rat got him during the night, and he was so badly upset that he thought he would sleep a little longer.'

Otto quickly strode in front of us: 'Mama is very tired.'

'We're both tired,' I retaliated.

I remember nothing from that walk but the monotonous path, the endless sand path between the hills. My blister felt like a broken toe; my feet were swollen. The heat baked my mouth into a grimace. I thought only of how many minutes there were until the next appointed stop. At noon, we shuffled into the outskirts of a village and I sank to the ground.

'Come on,' said Colum, but his voice was kind. 'We'll just get into the village.'

Msambo is a small, untidy place where we found a straw awning beside the lake. 'I'm really sorry,' I said. 'I can't go any farther. I don't even know if I'll be able to walk tomorrow.' I had to say it, though it satisfied Otto. Colum was limping too though he would say only that he had a sore hip.

'Mokassa, a Moganda boy, has a swelling of the ankle, which prevents his walking. We went one hour to find wood to make a litter for him.'

The children were gathering. Colum bellowed at them in Swahili which made them dart away for a little before sliding back. We retreated from their oppressive curiosity into the dark alcove of a walled compound, where a family brewed us sugary tea and boiled us a bucket of sweet potatoes. But we had to get to Wampembe by midday the next day or our bicycles would probably be lost. We had no wheels; we effectively had no feet; there was only one form of transport left.

That night we slept for four hours in the open, huddled together against the mosquitoes while wavelets chuckled on the shore. At two we rose, joined a couple of young fishermen and slipped down to the waterside where their small wooden boat was waiting.

There was a slight breeze in the darkness which I fancied had raced eighty kilometres across Tanganyika from the troubled wastes of Zaire. Fear brushed my stomach as we climbed on board and I untied my boots in case of capsize. Then we swished away from the shore and into the nothingness. Colum seized an oar and paddled at the back while I sat in the bows behind Ernest, one of the fishermen. He threw off his shirt and grasped his paddle, holding it threateningly above the black water. Then he stabbed downwards, plunging the oar through the water and back up towards him until he had drawn himself to a high poise above the lake again. For a fraction of a second he was absolutely still, like a killer relishing the imminent drive of the dagger home. Then he lunged again. It was a precise, aggressive, bewitching repetition echoed by his companion who sat behind Colum in the stern.

I dozed lightly, and then snapped awake at a disturbing thought: was this a compromise? It seemed much easier to be sitting in a boat at night than flogging along the shore during the heat of the day. I comforted myself with the thought that, if there had been no alternative, Livingstone also would have taken to canoes. But still it troubled me. I turned round to Colum, but my question died on my lips.

By the light of the thin moon I could see rivulets of sweat on his brow, and large dark patches on his shirt. He grimaced with each stroke and I could hear his breath rasping. For him, at least, this was not the soft option.

We sped through the warm water close to the coast while the thin moon watched us. In the distance disembodied yellow lights bobbed on the night-fishermen's boats. By sunrise we were racing before a gathering storm and struck the coast some distance from Wampembe, walking through a downpour towards the village.

In the muddy space at the centre of the settlement the village idiot, bony and wild-eyed, was approaching. He muttered at us. Then he muttered again. A few locals bawled with laughter and shouted for their friends as the man approached us, all the time repeating his incomprehensible sentence faster and faster. The audience whooped: men, women, children gathered for the spectacle, forming a wide circle.

'Just don't catch his eye,' said Colum. 'Don't encourage him but don't annoy him.' The swift, idiot Swahili began to turn to gibberish as the madman clutched at his rags and began to shudder. He was shouting now as the crowd screamed in hilarity at his utterings. Foam bubbled from his lips and down his chin.

The chief, sitting in a windowless, bare office, was uninterested in our plight. He inscribed our names in his book, locked his office and left us to the crowds.

Down the muddy street the *hoteli* was shut. 'Kwisha,' said the landlord pointing to the empty cooking pot. When food is finished in Tanzania it is well and truly gone until the woman has fetched new firewood, collected water and boiled a beany brew for hours. The crowds gasped as we backed out of the dark café and into the ring they had formed around the little building. They parted to let us walk towards the stall next door which sold onions and peanuts. As we bought them a deranged old woman joined the idiot in haranguing us. He waved his arms up and down while she led the army which was now following us wherever we went. As we wandered hungry through the streets searching for a place of sanctuary, the women started a raucous singing.

On the beach we escaped onto a huge boulder where we could watch for the motor boat. The crowds stood some distance away and we hoped that if we did nothing they would grow bored. What was it about this dusty village that had turned its occupants sour? The people had nothing to do and nothing to sell, but their lives appeared no different from those of many other villagers we had met along the lake. 'Hostile' was the wrong word for them. Perhaps 'tribal' was better. They were utterly lacking in empathy. It was beyond them to imagine that we, too, were human.

Ponsian, a local man, spoke some English so Colum addressed him accusingly: 'Your people are behaving very badly. Is this how you treat visitors? Don't you say welcome? We have been to many villages but never have we been treated like this.' Reluctantly Ponsian let us into his home where we sat inside and ate our peanuts while he paid the price for his hospitality – his yard filled in to overflowing outside.

Ponsian explained that southwards, where we wanted to go, there was a choice between a steep mountain path that was almost impossible even to walk or a coastal scramble over rocks and along sand. 'You cannot do it by bicycle,' he said unequivocally. 'You will have to take the road inland.'

'*The mountains now close in on Tanganyika so there is no path but one, over which luggage cannot be carried. The stage after this is six hours up hill before we come to water...*'

'But there isn't a road inland,' Colum protested. There was no road on our maps. 'Yes there is,' said Ponsian. 'But it is rough.'

'*The large donkey is very ill, and unable to climb the high mountain in our front. I left men to coax him on, and they did it very well. I then sent some to find a path out from the Lake mountains, for they will kill us all.*'

Defeated by the Tanganyika mountains, Livingstone too had turned inland to loop round them and re-emerge on the southern tip of the lake.

*   *   *

The motor boat was only two hours late. The moment it appeared around the headland Colum ran to the shore in excitement. Long before it was near he was in the water up to his waist. A huge crowd gathered to watch the spectacle. At last the launch drew into the shallows, and a few minutes later Colum emerged from the water, his thin body streaming, with a bicycle held high above his head. A forest of hands reached out to him but he growled and people shrank back. I, too, felt unforgiveably triumphant. There was one thing we could do that these infernal villagers could not – escape from Wampembe – and our means of doing so had just arrived.

One by one we carried the bikes up to the comparative seclusion of Ponsian's house. Colum disappeared into the cool gloom inside while the villagers again thronged the yard. Colum didn't hear me as I came in. He was squatting beside my bicycle flicking the gear lever to and fro, intently watching the small, precise movement of the derailleur. At each tiny click he gave an almost imperceptible nod. Then he ran light fingertips along the chain, and plucked three of the rear spokes. There was a small, unexpected smile on his face.

We were hungry and mentally exhausted. The most sensible decision would be to sleep at Ponsian's and embark on the journey the next day. But we hated Wampembe with venom. By half past four we were gone and Ponsian, on foot, was with us.

'It is a rough road,' pointed out Ponsian each time I stumbled. 'There is lots of sand,' he said each time I teetered to a halt in the middle of it. The track followed the lakeside north for a little until it reached a gap where it could creep into the mountains.

Sad Ponsian walked barefoot and carried a few possessions in a plastic bag. He was a mournful representative of Wampembe. He told us that when he was younger, in the days of Tanzanian socialism, it had been government policy to shuffle students around the country to promote national harmony. But after his secondary school education near Arusha he had not been able to find a job so he was forced to return, doomed to live in Wampembe or starve.

Like most others in Wampembe he was a peasant, cajoling sticks of cassava to burst into life in earth he had ploughed by hand.

'Are people in Wampembe happy?' I asked.

'The farmers are not happy,' he said. 'They work very hard, they have no animals or machines to do the work for them.' Most of the farmers, he claimed, longed to be fishermen – the only other occupation in the village. But that required a capital outlay on boats and nets. And perhaps there were other barriers, that I could not discern, to such an exchange of lifestyle. The commercial life of the village was almost non-existent as nobody had anything to sell. There was just the single shop providing the usual long, yellow bars of soap, little bags of sugar, and jars of petroleum jelly. How these goods reached the village was a mystery.

I watched Ponsian. He walked slightly ahead of me, his eyes always on the ground. I felt a pang for him, doomed by his dislike of farming and fishing to a life of eternal dissatisfaction. I caught up with him: 'So what can you do about it?' Ponsian's answer was immediate, the product of years of brooding which must have always led him to the same conclusion.

The road. The road was the answer, he said. If only the road could be improved then life would get better. He would be able to take his surplus produce out to the bigger world and sell it for cash with which he could solve his numerous problems – he could, for example, send his children to school.

The road, Ponsian said, had been cut in 1994, but already it was impassable. In the last twelve months only one vehicle had reached Wampembe along it. As we followed it through the gap between the mountains it was in places little more than rock face – so steep that the three of us carried each bicycle up one by one. To our left was a deep gully down which water cascaded. Great green trees hung overhead and behind us the lake dwindled to a patch of silver, until finally the mountains shut it away.

Ponsian was obsessed with his road, and today, by being our guide, he had been given a rare excuse to work some sympathetic magic, tread his rough road and escape briefly to the wider world.

I imagined his excitement when he heard that the road was being cut; when over months, or perhaps even years, he knew that a man with a grader was ploughing towards Wampembe from the outside world. When Ponsian wasn't growing his cassava he would have climbed through the mountains to see how his unlikely saviour was progressing, watched him blasting through the rocks with sticks of dynamite. Soon, Ponsian would have thought, his modest dreams of business would come true.

And then Ponsian would gradually have realised that the project had failed. The road was no good. The long winding track, forty-five kilometres, was a shambles. It descended the steepest of screes; it cut across sheer rock; its camber was always in the wrong direction. It was such an appalling ruin of a road that it served only those on foot.

'The highest parts of the mountains are from 500 feet to 700 feet higher than the passes, say from 1300 feet to 1500 feet above the Lake. A very rough march today; one cow fell and was disabled.'

There is a straw-topped village, almost indistinguishable from the earth on which it was built, which lies an hour into the mountains. It was once a collective village, built in the early 1970s by the socialist government, a focal point to which people were enticed to move from disparate homes. They were promised clean water, a school and a dispensary. In return they had to live a lifestyle compatible with African socialism – tilling communal fields and sharing the fruits of communal labour.

Its gregarious chief let us camp in the shell of a building that was the school. I was soon pitching the tent while Colum tinkered with the bicycles. Then I filtered the water while dusk fell and Colum cooked dinner. We were tired but we had reached a comforting rhythm in the evenings. I almost enjoyed the monotonous pumping, the row of bottles full of clean water when I was finished. And Colum looked forward to the excitement of cooking dinner – the fight with the flames, the juggling of the four tiny cooking pots, the flair required to turn rice and onions into an original dish.

We devoured our dinner. Now all that remained of our food supplies were twenty biscuits and a little packet of peanuts.

'I had to punish two useless men this morning for calling out "Posho! posho! posho!" (rations) as soon as I came near. One is a confirmed bange-smoker…

'… we killed a cow today and found peculiar flat worms in the substance of the liver, and some that were rounded.'

*   *   *

We woke weary, longing for a place to stop for a while where the living was easier. Soon after the three of us had rejoined the road, Ponsian resumed his complaints. 'This is a poor country. We are the third poorest country in the world.'

I was irritable: 'Yes but at least you have peace. Isn't it better to live here than in a richer country like Zaire where there is so much violence?'

His face turned sullen. Peace is the supreme treasure yet it is transparent to all but those at war. In Tanzania, the socialist state achieved peace through social engineering. Tribal power was broken, government officials were plucked from their villages and sent to other parts of the country so they would understand their distant compatriots. But the price of peace through socialism was the economic failure that now touched Ponsian so acutely.

In silence we pushed our bicycles up the track which remained a secret even from the cartographer. Deserted, it wound upwards and inwards, deep into layers of mountains and among tall forest, taking us back through the buffer zone between the lake and the inland people. It climbed and climbed. Frequently a twist would reveal another forty-five degree scree – we numbly inched up, and went ön.

After hours the track emerged, suddenly, on a shoulder. Ahead was a plateau, a vast open country without a single tree. To either side and below us were forest-clad mountains, and deeper still were valleys into which storms broke. The surface was hard now and we could ride again, cycling at intoxicating speed.

Then a storm, higher than the ones we had seen in the valleys, erupted over us. Immense roars of thunder set the air shuddering and left us in terror. There was nowhere to shelter, not a tree under which to hide. The thunder cracked downwards – deafening, dominating the beating of the heart. We could do nothing but tear hopelessly onwards.

'Thunder all the morning, and a few drops of rain fell. It will ease the men's feet when it does fall. They call out earnestly for it, "Come, come with hail" and prepare their huts for it.'

The havoc subsided, the storm passed. We descended from the plateau into the land below and still there was no sign of human life. Ponsian, who lived without a clock, had estimated that the day's journey would take four hours: so far it had taken eleven and the last biscuit had been finished long before.

Then the miracle happened. We reached a junction, turned right, and found ourselves in rolling countryside planted with banana, cassava and maize. A few kilometres farther on the road finished at a pair of gates. We rolled through them into another civilisation.

15

In Mvimwa

by Colum

The spirit of Missions is the spirit of our Master: the very genius of His religion. A diffusive philanthropy is Christianity itself. It requires perpetual propagation to attest its genuineness.
David Livingstone, November 1872

SATURDAY night. A soft shuffling of feet and the low beat of pop music reached us through the floor above our bedroom. The noviciates were relaxing. They must have shed their white monastic habits to pad around in time to the music. White and coloured light pulsed from the upstairs window, competing with the lightning on the horizon.

After two days at Mvimwa Monastery, we had grown used to the strangeness. Here, in one of the remotest corners of Tanzania, we had stumbled on a band of African Benedictine monks absorbed in the creation of a small oasis of civilisation in the wilderness. Their campaign to subdue nature relied heavily on imported technological ideas. From the rocky mountain towering over the monastery, a clear stream fed a small reservoir contained by a dam which the monks had constructed in a deep ravine. Water from the reservoir was piped downhill to drive a hydro-electric plant, its power supplemented by ranks of shining solar panels lining the monastery roofs.

Technology had made Mvimwa a haven of material luxury in which we revelled. On our arrival, a solemn young noviciate showed us to a small, airy room. With a deferential bow and downcast eyes he then quietly withdrew. Just over the threshold, we stood, speechless, gazing about us.

White sunlight flooded across the floor, and particles of dust drifted slowly in the bright air. Against one whitewashed wall stood a huge hospital bed, made up with crisp cotton sheets. I had a strong presentiment of the sensuous pleasure to be derived from slipping in between them. A sink gleamed in one corner. Gingerly, Aisling approached and tried a tap. When water flowed, she gave a yelp of delight, and when, after a few more seconds she was shrouded in clouds of steam, she beamed rapturously.

No aspect of the room was too insignificant to be overlooked, but our tour of inspection was interrupted by a light knock on the door. It was the Deacon, who had earlier welcomed us at the monastery gates. Now he handed me a heavy tray, neatly draped with a white cloth. I looked at his face and saw something that might have been a mischievous smile.

'A small present from the Prior,' he said, and then he was gone. Under the cloth lay three bottles of beer.

On that first morning at the monastery I noticed with dismay how Aisling's face showed traces of the hardship we had experienced over the last four weeks. In spite of the sun her skin was pallid, her cheeks hollow with hunger. Now, in this gentle interlude at the monastery, we had time to recover. We filled our hours easily: we ate, we slept, we washed. Time was measured only by the slipping of shadows, and the slow turning of morning into sunny afternoon.

In this environment, the care of the bicycles became to me a source of fulfilment. Gone now were the anxious moments when I glared at the mechanisms, not understanding them. Instead, my senses were filled with the slick movement of the gearshift, the smell and taste of graphite oil, dull light glancing from the chain, and the smooth sound of a new cog engaging. Surrounded by ball bearings and other, more esoteric components from a disassembled rear wheel axle, I started to see that, after all, a bicycle is no more than a collection of outlandishly shaped pieces. The miracle was that, assembled correctly, the components became alive, a symphony of swift, uniform noises, a glimmering blur of regularity and synchronicity.

In principle, I knew how the discrete mechanisms worked, yet there remained something mystical about the complex beauty of the entire machine, almost as if it was sustained by my belief in it. There, in the quiet of the monastery, bicycle maintenance became more than the lip service described in our travel-worn manual. It became an act of faith.

As I recuperated I grew aware of the steady rhythm of monastic life flowing around us. The Benedictines' is an uncompromising life, dedicated to hard work and prayer, their days marked out by the periodic ringing of the chapel bell. It began very early in the morning, the clear repetitive sound only half-noticed as I skirted the ragged edges of sleep. Once, I raised my head from the pillow and glimpsed white-clad figures flitting towards the chapel through the half-light before dawn.

At midday, with the plain below the monastery awash with sunlight and flecked by cloud-shadow, the bell summoned the monks from the fields. Once more during the afternoon, and then at dusk, which is no more than a short, breathless pause between day and night, they flocked up the chapel stairs again. At last, just before retiring to bed, with the dull chirruping of the cicadas a white noise in the background, the monks gathered to pray one final time.

Three times each day we were summoned by the Deacon to eat, and our worlds touched. In the refectory, three long trestle tables stretched out from below a raised area. At a high table on the dais sat the fathers, the Deacon, and the Prior, a stout man with a ready smile and a low chuckle. He looked out on the world from beneath lowered eyelids, and presided at the table with an easy grace.

At the monks' table, the food was plenteous and delicious. Aisling's eyes widened as the dishes were uncovered before us at our first meal. There was meat: succulent pork, lamb and beef. We ate eggs, and hard white cheese, and honey the colour of heavy oil, smelling of sunshine on hardwood. There was rice, beans, potatoes and other vegetables, the produce of the monastery farm.

One late afternoon, the Deacon led us by a winding path to where a large silvered cross stood on top of the craggy hill. The plain stretched out below us, thin bush turning into open grasslands, then giving way to the blue mountains in the west, the mountains through which we had cycled. Thin veils of rain chased each other out of the deep passes and drifted over the flat savannah, occasionally catching a slanting bar of sunlight. Directly at our feet was the farm.

It appeared as a small, vivid patchwork of vegetation at the point where the mountain merged with the plain. Squares of dense green banana plantation alternated with the light green of cassava, and with the bright yellow of sunflowers and the dull gold of wheat. A cleared area of pasture was dotted with the solid, dark shapes of cattle. As I watched, hens issued like a burst of dust from a farm outhouse.

It was a tranquil scene, a scene of agrarian order. It could not have presented a starker contrast to the barren wilderness through which we had come. Over the weeks we had passed through a chaotic natural landscape in which order imposed by humans consisted of nothing more than the shallow scratchings of farmers with hoes. These were soon eroded by the elements, or lost in the riot of the forest.

Then we had stumbled on Mvimwa. It was a chance comment by an old man on the track from Wampembe which had alerted us to its existence. Our maps showed nothing but a grid square heavily scored with contours, and with a small note saying that broken rock made local relief uncertain. The Benedictines had tamed this wilderness: they had moved the rocks and coaxed the fertile soil into production.

A bell tolled in the monastery below, summoning us for the evening meal, and we began our return from the mountain. A septic blister had turned my foot an angry, throbbing red, and I picked my way carefully. I was grateful that the path was wide and smooth, cutting a formidable course through thick bush on precipitous slopes.

I asked the Deacon how recently the path had been completed.

'Oh, just last week,' he replied, his English perfect. 'It has been the project of Father Michael. It has taken him and the noviciates a year and a half.'

We continued in silence, and the sun slipped behind the mountains, leaving tatters of cloud crusted with orange and gold.

'And why did he do it?' I asked.

'So people could reach the cross,' he replied.

Later, when it was dark, Aisling and I returned a short way up the same path to where the monks were building an ambitious terraced garden on the mountainside. It was awash with the heavy night-scents of exotic flowers, and alive with the sound of a stream diverted along the terraces from the reservoir above. We sat in a small, open-sided shelter, perched high on a massive boulder.

Mvimwa was unlike anything we had seen in rural Tanzania. The path to the Cross and the garden were elaborate projects undertaken by people who could be concerned with more than the problems of mere survival. Mvimwa was, for us, a place of material luxury. But now I started to see that the monks had gone further than that. They had created a place where ideas could be nurtured. They had created a place where a dream could grow.

*　　　*　　　*

The old man had insisted. He wanted to give me his name so that I would remember him. Now he was writing slowly and with great concentration. His quivering hand was like a dried lizard. He had told me he was seventy-nine and had been working as a caretaker at the monastery since its foundation, eighteen years ago. When he had finished writing, he folded the paper with the slow deliberation of age, ran a broken thumbnail along the crease, then tore off the ragged edge. He raised his head from where he had been stooping over the table and blinked, as if the afternoon light in our room was too strong.

He smiled a slow, childish smile, and offered me the slip of paper. His eyes were milky and moist.

'Thank you.' I glanced down. He had only written three words, but they were a small work of art. His hand was copperplate, his letters perfectly formed in smooth billowing curves. Each word had soft rhythm and fluidity, and each capital letter was embellished with a delicate flourish.

'Mission school?'

He nodded slowly, glad that I knew.

His must have been a boyhood full of optimism. The white men had arrived in his parents' generation with unimaginable wealth. They had brought fabulous magic and had taught him and his generation to read, so that they could understand the Bible.

But for many, the teachings of the missionaries had also awakened a brooding dissatisfaction. The Bible taught that all men were equal in the eyes of God, and yet many Africans found themselves excluded when they aspired to progress in the white man's church. Having rejected their own traditions in favour of the attractions of Christianity, these people felt themselves to be strangers in their own land, and began casting about for a new identity.

At first there had been a resurgence in witchcraft as the normal checks and balances in society were disrupted, but gradually disenchantment with Western Christianity started to manifest itself in the formation of independent churches. These were often a dismal parody of the strict mission environment from which they had derived their inspiration, and were ruthless in their rejection of all that was African.

Confronted with the cold intransigence of the missionary movement, many others sustained themselves with the belief that a golden spiritual age was just round the corner: the existing order would soon be overthrown and the oppressed would inherit the earth. Acting as a focus for those who were repressed spiritually and culturally, some African churches became a vehicle for those attempting to realise a nationalist dream. And so it was that nationalism and spirituality grew together, a heady mixture in the twilight years of the colonial era. A prayer used by one congregation expressed the sentiments of many:

'Oh God the Father forgive us and feel pity for us. The foreigners brought us the new missions which made us leave our traditional customs which are now lost. We are asking you to bless and give us freedom.'

A way of life which had been unchanging for hundreds of years was convulsing under the pressures imposed by the white man's religion. Even within the lifetime of this old man, the old order had been turned upside down.

I looked back to where he was standing, fragile, and with head bowed. As I watched, he shuffled away from the table and disappeared into the brightness through the door. I glanced again at the slip of paper.

'John Mambo,' it read.

On the line underneath, he had written 'peasant', as if describing his profession. It puzzled me at first, and then I realised its implication: this

old man, the carefully cultivated product of a mission school, had been part
of an early experiment in African socialism.

In 1961 Julius Nyerere became the first Prime Minister of Tanganyika,
later to become Tanzania. Nyerere was a visionary. He decided that his
country, which was in the forefront of those liberated from colonial power,
was to be a model for African nationhood. In the short term however, he
recognised that economic backwardness threatened the new country's very
existence. Within a few months of taking office he declared war on rural
mass poverty and chose for his foot soldiers the poorest of the rural farmers.
John Mambo would have been proud to have joined the ranks and fight in
the socialist revolution.

In spite of the frugality and hard work which Nyerere demanded of
every true patriot, there were, at first, spontaneous nationwide
demonstrations in support of Nyerere's crusade. He had mobilised the
masses and the peasantry were imbued with a new dignity. Rural villages
were to become the focus of a reorientated economy. Peasant communities
would take responsibility for their own development, and change would
be driven by their desire for social justice. This would replace the entirely
unsuitable drift towards small-scale capitalism that the colonial
government had encouraged. Agricultural collectivisation would allow
economy of scale and would permit the benefits of modern farming practice
to be more easily targeted.

Socialism, he argued, was nothing new in Africa. Traditional African
society was based on the unit of the extended family structure, in which
the emphasis had always been on living together, working together and on
sharing equitably the fruits of the community's labour. For the coming
together of peasants into rural collectives, Nyerere used the Swahili word
Ujamaa, which loosely translates as family communalism, and which carried
the cultural connotations on which Nyerere wanted to build his new
society:

'We need to emphasise certain characteristics of our traditional
organisation, and extend them so that they can embrace the possibilities of
modern technology and enable us to meet the challenge of life in the
twentieth century world.'

Nyerere's plans were ambitious. After a decade in power his regime came
to realise that to make *Ujamaa* happen on a significant scale, villagisation
would have to become compulsory. Only then would Nyerere be able to
realise his dream for Tanzania.

*   *   *

Uncomfortably embedded amongst the monastery's new farm buildings there was an old mud house. The heavy thatch was fraying and had fallen in at one end. The windows were empty and dark. A blackened cooking pot stood just outside the door, cracked and half-buried in the earth. The Prior followed my gaze: 'That's where the old farmer used to live. He had to move in the great villagisation that came after Ujamaa.'

One dry season at the start of the 1970s, the farmer was one of many who had been directed to pack up his farm implements and leave with his cattle and family and their few pieces of clothing. It was not worth taking the broken cooking pot, and so it remained, a quiet testament to the cycles of life and death that this dwelling had seen.

They were heading for a new life, a small knot in the tide of several million who were making a great migration. They came out of the vast empty places to converge on one of the government's many *Ujamaa* villages and, all through the long hot dry season, the nation anxiously watched the skies to see if they would be settled before the rains came.

The farmer, too, must have been anxious. He was being compelled to give up the work of a lifetime to start all over again on untried ground. But at least there was the promise of government help and encouragement, a school for the children, and even a hospital. Above all, Nyerere would have pointed out, he would find himself a part of a supportive community.

'Were they really forced to go?' I asked.

The Prior smiled at me. 'Let's put it this way,' he replied, 'those that looked as if they might stay were finally encouraged to move by the army.' He walked out across the empty white sunlight towards one of the monastery's new buildings. It was remarkable because of its regularity – the straightness of its edges, the uniformity of its greyness, the squareness of its windows – all strangers in this world of crooked lines and the chaos of nature.

Outside, a dog lay asleep in the shade of a dismembered tractor. The Prior threw open some large doors to reveal a well-equipped workshop: 'This is where the young people from the villages come to learn about machinery.

'When the monastery was founded at the end of the seventies, they were scared of cars, and any sort of machinery in fact. They didn't even wear clothes.' He paused, and then continued, half to himself: 'There was a lot of ignorance in those days... And such poverty, you would just not have believed it.' He shook his head and sighed.

We turned down a track towards the farmyard. The sky was high and clear, and the light had gained the peculiar intensity – almost a flintiness – that I had come to associate with impending rain. It was a searing brightness that made you avert your eyes. To blink became a small luxury, like breathing when you are out of breath. One of the old monks had told me that it was because it had already started raining high, high up, and that made the air like washed crystal.

'Since arriving, we have been able to improve the strain of farm stock. And our work here has provided many jobs, and we can train the people.' The Prior kept looking across at us as we walked beside him, his sweat-beaded face serious. It was important that we understood his work. 'We have been able to introduce many new crops to this region... maize, bananas, and these sunflowers.'

In the two fields which flanked the rough road a legion of yellow-maned sunflower heads were locked onto the sun as it tracked across the wide arch of the sky. Surrounded by such boundless colour and brightness, the Prior's cassock seemed to be the blackest thing I had ever seen. His hands were clasped behind his back: he was a large, benevolent crow pacing along the dusty track. 'More than anything, we need monks with education if our community is to prosper. It is education that is the lifeblood of a monastery like ours. It allows the monks to train new monks, and that will ensure our future.'

His voice was animated. 'Soon, we will build a school for the surrounding villages.' He pointed towards the proposed site – a low hill which rose out of the plain some kilometres off. The Prior pointed out where the monks had already built a causeway: the school would be accessible even when the rains made the intervening grassland into a desolate inland sea.

The farmyard was an open square of low concrete buildings. Through the door of the first building, we walked down an aisle between pigsties. It was feeding time and two or three of the noviciates were pushing bundles of greenery into each food trough, pausing occasionally to pat a hairy pink hide, or scratch behind a scaly ear. In the end sty there was a large litter of piebald piglets, and an exhausted mother lying on one flank, her udders distended and limp. She was smaller than the other pigs, and had the mottled grey-brown colour of the forest. Her hair was coarse, like stiff wire.

'This is our experiment in improving the line.' The Prior's hands moved expansively, released, at last, from behind his back. 'We bought the mother in a village. She is Tanzanian. The piglets are Tanzanian-Tamworth crosses.'

The cattleshed was separated from the piggery by a chasm of hard sunlight across which we dashed. As we plunged through the door into the sweet-smelling half-light, the Prior's gait took on a new urgency. He strode on ahead, speaking rapidly over his shoulder, his hands working furiously, driven by the tempo of his speech. 'And just over there...' – we found ourselves ducking down to look between slatted barriers and the legs of cows – '… you can see the outlet pipe…', and then he was pacing out of the byre, still talking: '… power for the whole community…' and '… valves to control the back pressure…'

Around the back of the building was an area strewn with bricks and timber, and other detritus of building work. Amidst all this were four brick vessels, half-buried and incomplete: jagged, brick-lined cavities in the earth. In a few more months these would be a biogas generator. The Prior paused impressively, and then went on to describe the system. Slurry, piped from the nearby cowshed, would be allowed to ferment in these vessels, forcing enough methane gas through a series of pipes and valves to provide heat and light for the entire monastery.

The Prior's enthusiasm was contagious, and soon the workmen were striking poses for the visitors like children at a party. We asked to take photographs. The backdrop was carefully selected to include the most-nearly completed vessel, and the craftsmen collected their tools, and arranged them to best advantage. They adjusted their hats to jaunty angles. Through the lens, the Prior's smile seemed a little uncertain now. Perhaps it was the light.

                    *   *   *

It was the Sunday before Christmas and I went to a service in the monastery's church, squeezing in behind a packed congregation. It was a light and airy building, soon filled with heavy wreaths of incense laced with the resinous tang of the hot, still forests.

I defocussed my eyes. The officiants became the butterflies that gather at puddles after rain. Their surplices were vivid fragments of colour that settled and then drifted on, gliding up and down the altar steps, pausing momentarily to bow before spiralling past each other. Over the low Swahili incantation the soft tinkling of a bell hung in the scented air, then faded.

Perhaps I had been expecting some sort of incongruity: this was a religion which had, within not much more than two lifetimes, been grafted onto an alien culture. But at Mvimwa, Christ was not the white, emaciated Caucasian stretched out on the crucifixes of European churches, his face and body blue-shadowed with hair. At Mvimwa, Christ was a Tanzanian farmer.

                    *   *   *

'The problem is the communion wine.' We were sitting at dinner, and the

Prior was describing the mapping of Catholic symbolism onto the African way of life. The other fathers listened attentively.

'It is not just a question of finding something that looks like red wine. We need to find an African equivalent that reflects the symbolism of the vine – its fertility… its many branches…'

'Cassava?' I ventured.

A murmur rippled down the table. The fathers looked at each other, gauging each other's opinion. Some nodded, others conferred quietly.

'Or mango?' I said, encouraged by the reaction. 'After all, the mango tree has many branches, and produces huge amounts of fruit.'

'Yes, it is a good idea,' the Prior said thoughtfully. His elbows were on the table, his hands clasped together. 'But we think we may have found an answer.' The fathers fell silent, their eyes fixed on him. He lifted a piece of fruit from a bowl, and regarded it gravely: 'It is the banana.'

Each evening after dinner, Aisling and I were ushered into a large room scattered with low chairs.

'Now we have a period of recreation,' the Prior had announced on our first evening in Mvimwa, as he guided us towards a couch behind a long coffee table. The six or seven fathers from the high table had settled themselves on other chairs, and were regarding us expectantly.

'Tell us about your travels,' the Prior had said.

Over the following two or three nights, we painted a picture of our journey so far, and showed them our maps, and the copy of Livingstone's journal and of the contemporary map which we had brought with us. This, in particular, was a source of great interest. The fathers pored over the old map, curious to see if Livingstone had known of their own home villages, and wistful as they remembered families they had left there.

At the end of the second evening the other fathers drifted off to prepare for their prayers. Only Father Hector remained. He was quieter than the others. I asked him where his parents lived, and he leaned over the map which was still draped over the coffee table, and pointed to a large empty area to the north-east of Lake Malawi – not an area which Livingstone had penetrated. I unfolded a modern map, and he was able to show me the corresponding blank space, traversed now by a thin, uncertain red line.

'That is the main road: it is two days' walk from my village.' He looked up and engaged me with clear, intelligent eyes. 'It is very remote.'

'More remote than around Mvimwa?'

'Yes. There is very little in the Ruvuma region.' And he folded the map up, and handed it to me.

There was a moment's silence as I fiddled with the map case. He gazed ruminatively at the window, where the warm, sticky night was pressing against the glass.

'I have heard that there are many witchdoctors there,' I said.

'It is true, there are many. There are many in my village.'

He had settled back into his chair, placing the tips of his fingers together. His face betrayed nothing, and I felt hesitant.

'Is there much bad magic in your village?' He shifted in his seat, and, for a moment, our eyes met. His gaze was calm.

'Yes, there are bad things. And there are good things as well.'

'When you say bad things, do you mean demons?' I spoke the words carefully, but they still came out in a rush. There was a pause, and his brow wrinkled.

'You in the West are more advanced than we are here.' In the silence, I tried to read his face. Then his fingertips became unstuck, and one hand moved dismissively. 'Those that Africans call "demon-possessed" simply have a psychiatric disease.' And his face broke into a smile.

Father Hector missed evening prayers that night. For the next hour, he spoke at length about the work that the monastery was doing in rural areas. He described how conveniently Catholicism fitted onto traditional African culture, the ease with which the Catholic saints could be identified with the ancestors who were at the heart of the local religion. There was even a model for the Resurrection, he explained, as it is believed that ancestral spirits are reborn in today's generation. Finally, with what might have been the hint of a triumphant smile, he told me that behind the ancestors, the local people believe that there is an Omniscient Power. 'They call Him "Mpanga",' he said. 'It means the "Great Arranger".'

*   *   *

On our last night in Mvimwa the weather broke. The rain fell with such fury that the paths and tracks around the monastery became rivers, their surfaces torn by the pelting water. The dining room was a storm-embattled ship with nothing but wild blackness beyond the rain-creased windows.

After dinner, the Prior made a short speech to bid us farewell and I was filled with admiration for these kind men. They had wrested their identity from a turbulent past, and had achieved what Nyerere had dreamed of: they had formed a community which was heavily rooted in the African way of life, but which had taken the best that the West had to offer. Most obviously, they had drawn on Western technology. More fundamentally, they had built their dream on Christianity, introduced from the West by Livingstone.

Before we left for our room I took a photograph of the monks, with the Prior in the centre, an easy, comfortable smile on his face. It showed the confidence of a man who knows that he is part of something greater, part of a monastic tradition that stretches back almost two thousand years, and which remains substantially untouched by a changing world.

The rain had stopped, and before retiring to bed I walked out in front of the monastery. The air moved around me like the sea after a gale and was fresh with the smell and taste of rain. The night was filled with the noise of a thousand new streams. At last I turned back towards our room. As I went through the door, a large brown rat scurried past me on his way back outside after the storm.

Log Book Extracts

DAY 28 – Sunday 22nd December

SECOND REST DAY AT END OF PHASE 2
  Staying in Mvimwa Monastery.

POSITION: 31°7'11" E
          7°48'38" S

DISTANCE TRAVELLED: None

BICYCLES: Complete overhaul of both, replacing worn-out tyres on
  Colum's bicycle, and brake blocks on both. Gave old tyres to one of
  the monks, who was delighted.

WEATHER: Overcast all day. Rain in evening.

HEALTH: Aisling very tired. Aisling has diarrhoea. Colum has started
  a course of antibiotics for septic blister.

EQUIPMENT: Inventory and cleaning of all equipment. Losses so far:
  our towel, Colum's T-shirt, Aisling's penknife. The monks washed all
  our clothes for us.

EXPENDITURE: None

FOOD: Lots – proper breakfast, lunch, afternoon tea and dinner.

COMMENT: Planned Phase 3, which will take us from Mvimwa to
  Nsombo, at the northern end of Zambia's Lake Bangweulu. We have
  lost some faith in our maps, as some of the Lake Tanganyika villages
  are shown in completely the wrong place.
     The track condition is the big unknown in Zambia – we have
  attempted to classify the tracks into six categories (ranging from
  metalled surface through to almost uncyclable) to work out how
  long the journey will take. Colum estimates 25 days, including rest
  days. We have covered approximately half the total distance to
  Livingstone's grave.

*　　　*　　　*

DAY 29 – Monday 23rd December

PHASE 3

FROM: Mvimwa

TO: Matanga

CAMP: Tent pitched in headmistress's office in village school.

POSITION: 31°30'48" E
                8°1'5" S

TIME CYCLING: 8 hours 30 minutes

DISTANCE TRAVELLED: 56km

AVERAGE SPEED: 7km/hr

ROUTE: Took track for Kate from monastery, then right at next village and right at Kasenge.

TRACK CONDITION: Track generally good. A few hills.

BICYCLES – PERFORMANCE: Rain has aggravated the creaking in Aisling's pedal bearing. Aisling's back tyre valve appeared to be leaking and needed replacing shortly after we set out. Colum's back tyre difficult to pump up. Colum's back carrier snapped – now held together with jubilee clip.

BICYCLES – MAINTENANCE: Checked tyres, chains, brakes.

WEATHER: Heavy rain clouds. Midday shade temperature 22°C.

HEALTH: Aisling and Colum both have stomach problems; Aisling's left knee hurt all day, although both of us are well-rested and in buoyant mood.

EQUIPMENT: Aisling has badly ripped her shirt, but has repaired it.

LANDSCAPE: Marsh at first, then around the edge of a massive fertile plain ringed with hills. Treeless and barren towards the end.

EXPENDITURE: Biscuits TSh1,200; Kerosene TSh330;
In Matanga: Onions, tomatoes, bananas TSh120; Soap TSh100;
Sugar TSh530.

FLUID CONSUMPTION: 6 litres

FOOD: Breakfast: tea, bread and eggs at monastery before leaving.
        During day: *andazis* and bread, biscuits
        Evening meal: beans and rice in small *hoteli*.

COMMENT: We are very heavily laden with food – we think the extra weight snapped Colum's back carrier.

LIVINGSTONE: He strikes inland slightly farther south on a detour to avoid the mountains.

16

From Mvimwa to Kasanga
by Colum

My map of Africa lies in Europe...
Otto von Bismarck, the Iron Chancellor

WE LEFT Mvimwa with reluctance early the following morning, our panniers bursting with newly baked bread and *andazis* which the monks had prepared for us. The air was fresh and cool after the overnight rain and thin mist floated over the marshy ground beside the raised track. By lunchtime we were skirting the edge of a rolling plain ringed by mountains – an undulating treeless land, black and fertile.

Ahead of us a team of oxen paced the skyline, and a woman breasted the hill, a curved vessel on her head. For a moment her silhouette was framed against swirling white clouds and then she dropped out of sight. I looked back across the amphitheatre formed by the distant mountain ring where a massive drama was unfolding. Patches of sunlight and shadow chased each other over the floor, lightning flickered and clouds massed and broke up; grey striations of rain swept across the plain. The people working in the fields seemed like ants, indifferent or impervious to the turmoil in the sky.

In a small village called Matanga we camped in the office of the headmistress, and the following day we turned westwards back to the lake, the detour that had begun in Wampembe nearly over. We branched off the main road to Zambia onto a smaller track leading to the lakeside village of Kasanga. It was Christmas Eve and in several villages men were gathered on the trackside around the collapsed and bleeding form of a cow slaughtered for tomorrow's feast.

Towards evening we glimpsed Tanganyika – a wide bar of opalescence below the rainy sunset. At the next village there was a festive, expectant mood, the smell of roasting meat, loud shouts of laughter and the flickering of fires. People sauntered amongst the puddles – women in extravagant billowing dresses, men in crisp shirts, excited children.

We coasted through, feeling remote from festivity. Night came and behind me, a sudden clattering jarred the darkness. I turned to see Aisling's ghostly form sprawled on the ground.

'This is stupid. We've got to stop.'

She was angry. With the small ball of her fist, she thumped her pannier. Inside my head, I heard a sarcastic laugh. Outside my head, someone spoke.

'Are you OK? What's the problem?'

'The problem is that I've fallen because I can't see the track.' I had moved very close – close enough to see her face. Our eyes locked, but I felt as if I was watching the episode from the outside, watching two people enveloped in darkness and silence, on a remote African track on Christmas Eve. It would have been ridiculous, except that I had become aware of a smooth hard object, a cold incandescent thing, that was growing inside me, and which I knew to be anger.

I heard my voice speaking again: 'Get up, and for God's sake pull yourself together.' There was silence, then the scraping of loose stones. Slowly she got to her feet. The edge of the moon broke the horizon and I started to make her out more clearly. Her eyes were on the ground, her shoulders were sagging: an object of pity? No. Because I knew her. She could go on if she wanted: she was being deliberately stubborn. The idea had been growing in my mind for some time but I had dismissed it. Until now. Now it seemed clear to me that a small part of her did not care for Livingstone, or for this journey. A small part of her was trying to undermine what we were doing.

'We're going on.' And I turned away and continued slowly down the slope, my ears straining for any sound that she might be following.

'No, Colum ... you don't understand, I really am staying...' Her voice was milder now, and firm.

We camped nearby at the edge of a cassava field, beside large smooth boulders that still threw off the day's heat. Below us in a low valley a few fires winked. I cooked a peanut curry beside the warm stones, and afterwards we sat in silence and looked out across the strange, moonlit forest. Low drums pulsed from the village, an ancient, pagan sound heralding the arrival of another Christmas.

At dawn the festivities were still going but the noises seemed frail, as if the revellers were trying to eke out the darkness. When we rejoined the track, the remnants of the party were trailing home like an ebbing tide. Amongst them another tide flowed: the spruce early folk, rejoicing in Christmas Day.

*   *   *

It was only twelve kilometres to Kasanga but the descent through the mountains became steeper until we were reduced to a crawl, walking our bikes and scrabbling for footholds on the loose surface to prevent them careering into the forest. At last we inched our way around a precipitous bend and Tanganyika was spread out below us.

At its fringe, where the mountains met the water, there were glimpses of white buildings between the thick crowns of palm trees. I could see the old mission and a larger building which had to be the church. At the water's edge there was a long crescent of yellow sand littered with fishing boats and flanked by a rocky promontory, with a pier and a large, jagged ruin above. A river snaked lazily across the sand into the glittering blue beyond. As we paused, enjoying the cool of the mountain's shadow, a bell rang out. The Christmas Day service in Kasanga was about to begin.

We stumbled down the last rocky stretch of track. The doors of the Moravian Church were wide open and people were flowing in, the women in richly coloured dresses and matching head-wraps, the men in ill-fitting suits. People cast us curious glances. Aisling's clothes were filthy. Her shirt was ripped and stained, and there was a smear of dried blood on her cheek. As I looked at her, she pulled off her dirty sun hat and clawed ineffectually at her hair with grimy finger nails. I ran a hand over my chin – I only got to shave on rest days. With horror, I realised that I must have looked even worse than Aisling.

As we stood uncertainly outside the door a cloaked figure fluttered like a giant bat across the brightness: 'Good morning . . . you're just in time. Come on, come on.' And we followed the vicar as he swirled up the steps of the church, leaving his flock eddying in his wake. He whisked us to the front and insisted that we sit by the lectern, facing the congregation. From there we could survey the church, which was decorated with bunches of banana leaves and vivid orange flame tree blossom. The windows cast oblongs of light across the people as they crowded onto the benches.

Soon the building was packed and seething with excitement. It grew hotter. At last, the vicar mounted the altar steps and turned to face his flock. A hush fell and the air tightened with expectancy. The vicar raised his arms: 'Hallelujah.' There was a sigh and the women broke into loud warbling. The service had begun.

For three hours, fine discordant harmonies filled the church and spilled through the pointed Moravian windows into the stifling brightness outside. Different choirs took it in turns to lead the singing and the old women, dressed in their finest colours, sang until it seemed their hearts would burst. Between anthems each word of the minister elicited an ever more passionate response until the women could contain themselves no longer and they broke into escalating ululations. Then the people would rise from their benches and sway and gyrate in the aisles, and the minister would dance. If any form of Christianity was indisputably African, this was it.

*   *   *

Across a dusty open space, opposite the door of the Moravian Church, there is a small, derelict building. Its roof has partly caved in and its windows are dark. The old church of the London Missionary Society has long since been deconsecrated in favour of the Moravian Church nearby.

It was in the decade after Livingstone that the London Missionary Society arrived in Kasanga and built its mission. As a sheltered harbour so close to the southern tip of the lake, Kasanga was a geographical pivot – an obvious place for them to consolidate their hold as they surveyed the central African wilderness to the west. Later, the imperialist nations that inevitably followed in the missionaries' wake, with their sweeping plans for East Africa, also incorporated this village in their schemes. At Kasanga, the Germans built a fort to secure their western border in East Africa.

But the German fort, like the LMS church, is forgotten now. On the afternoon of Christmas Day, we walked amongst its ruins. The high arches, solid walls and stately courtyard were imposing reminders of a confident imperialism with which Livingstone would have identified. Nowadays, they call it the Bismarck. They say that Kaiser Wilhelm himself visited here. In the village, the oldest man's father remembered him coming, or so they say.

It was in 1890 that German and British colonial officials drew lines on maps and determined that Tanganyika should be a German sphere of influence. But German tenure was short and turbulent. Over the first decade, one tribe and then another was quelled. In obscure corners of the territory proud chieftains perished before the devastating modern weaponry of the colonialists, or took their own lives in an ultimate act of defiance.

In the end the Germans subdued a vast area stretching from the Indian Ocean to Lake Tanganyika, and from Lake Victoria to Lake Malawi. The wilderness that they had conquered soon proved itself capable of producing wheat in abundance, coffee, honey and hides. And then there was the promise of more exotic prizes: the Rift Valley and surrounding areas were yielding rubies and sapphires, tourmaline and opals. In some places, gold could be picked from amongst the debris of shattered quartz.

But the Germans never had the opportunity to exploit fully all that the region offered. The European war came and ultimately they were forced to abandon their fort on Tanganyika along with the rest of their East African possessions. When they left their fort crumbled, like a secular Karema.

Nowadays, Kasanga still retains some importance. It is here that the first track for hundreds of kilometres emerges at the shore. Kasanga is firmly tied by this umbilical cord to Tanzania, but the village looks outwards across the water. A new pier has been built, and the ferry which calls at Zambia and Burundi stops here once a week.

It calls at night. For several hours beforehand the pier and the shore are crowded with people, patiently awaiting its appearance around the headland. When it comes, it shines with fabulous lights, gliding above many more in its shimmering reflection. It brings people, it brings news, it brings a touch with other villages, other countries, parts of the diverse community bordering the central African lakes. It docks for a few brief hours, and then it is away again – but even so, canoes skim out to it for almost as long as it is visible, anything to prolong the contact with the world beyond.

Kasanga is a border town. On Boxing Day, we walked along the beach to the Immigration Office, where we roused an official. She stamped our passports, and then drank beer with us in the shade of a palm tree.

Log Book Extract

DAY 33 – Friday 27th December

PHASE 3

FROM: Kasanga

TO: Chongo (Zambia)

CAMP: In tent beside village headman's hut.

POSITION: 31°14'18" E
            8°36'58" S

TIME CYCLING: 7 hours 45 minutes

DISTANCE TRAVELLED: 20km

AVERAGE SPEED: 3km/hr

ROUTE: Lousy steep hill from Kasanga to Kawala, then pleasant track through shady woods (villages: Mpombwe, Kaposi) to Kalambo River, which we forded.

TRACK CONDITION: parts reasonable, but very variable.

BICYCLES – PERFORMANCE: Col had puncture in back tyre. Stopped to replace.

BICYCLES – MAINTENANCE: Checked tyres, all nuts, chains. Repaired inner tube.

WEATHER: No rain. Stayed bright.

HEALTH: Aisling has a sore inside her nose – very painful.

EQUIPMENT: Thermometer is broken.

LANDSCAPE: Steep hill from lakeside, then rolling forested hills and descent to the Kalambo.

EXPENDITURE: Kw1,000 on guides; Kw8,000 on food. Food very expensive – we are concerned about money. Cost of living is about twice what it is in Tanzania.
£1 = Tsh1,000 = Kw2,000

FLUID CONSUMPTION: Can't remember, but water is not a problem.

FOOD: Breakfast: ground biscuits and nuts with powdered milk
During day: coconut, mangoes, biscuits, nuts
Dinner: banana, mango, peanut and onion curry with rice

COMMENT: The Kalambo River marks the Tanzanian-Zambian border.

LIVINGSTONE: Food scarce, and Livingstone in poor health, although donkey has temporarily recovered and has started to eat again.

17

From Kasanga to Mbala
by Aisling

WITH a twist in the steep scree road out of Kasanga, Lake Tanganyika disappeared for the last time. Our journey south continued among the inner lakeside hills. At midday we arrived in a comatose village where we rested on the steps of a church. As usual, villagers drifted out of their midday lethargy to gather around us. One man whispered urgently in Swahili: 'Get Phineas'. Then he turned to us: 'You must wait here for Phineas'.

An old man came limping through the dust. He was thin, as brittle as a dry stick. His trousers were bunched around his waist with a piece of string and his face was withered.

'You are most welcome, you are most welcome,' he cried as he hurried towards us. His English was perfect, formal. One hand clutched his baggy trousers, the other gesticulated, half to get our attention and half to keep his balance.

'Where have you come from?' he gasped as he reached us. Then, without waiting for a reply: 'It is so good to talk in your language. I learned it when I was a little boy at mission school many years ago. I love the British.' He sighed deeply, grasped Colum's shirt and peered up at him. The yellowy whites of his eyes were blurring into the uncertain edge of his brown irises.

He took us to the *hoteli*, which was shut, and roused its unwilling owner into brewing tea. We sat down at the single wooden table. Young men had followed us into the café and squashed in round us. Children gathered at the window and stared inside.

'Why are you here?'

As I explained, his eyes stretched wide and his old hands squeezed the edge of the table. He paused when I had finished and then, softly: 'David Livingstone?'.

I nodded.

'David Livingstone.' He repeated the name with triumph and leaned towards us, preparing to say something of significance. 'Everything that I know,' he said slowly. 'Every little thing that I know, I know because of Livingstone.' He searched our faces. 'He was a great man,' he added with feeling.

A few years after Livingstone marched down Lake Tanganyika, London Missionary Society preachers converted Phineas' father. He became an evangelist, preaching in and around this village, Mpombwe. Phineas attended missionary school where he learned about Livingstone's life in detail. He remembers it all today.

He was beaming now, but his eyes were wet. When Livingstone had passed this way he had brought with him the spirit of another, more confident world. Phineas had imbibed that spirit through Livingstone's successors. He had drunk deeply – until the local drink seemed tasteless in comparison. Mission teachers made him British: then they abandoned him and disappeared back to Britain. A lifetime later, the only trace that remained in Mpombwe was an elderly Anglophile.

'You British are different from us Africans. You make big plans and you work at them and you know that one day they will be finished, even if it is after your death.' Phineas clutched my arm. 'When you die, someone else will take over until it is done.'

The young men stirred restlessly. They were bored with this foreign chatter which they did not understand. Finally they could contain their curiosity no longer, and out poured the usual questions, but Phineas cut across their Swahili with his clear, deliberate English: 'Does David Livingstone have any living descendants in Britain?'

I smiled. 'Yes, at least one. His great grandson. We spoke to him before we came here.'

'You spoke to him…' Phineas was incredulous. He was silent for a little, thoughtful. Then his eyes widened as an idea came to him. 'I could write him a letter and you could take it back for me.' His voice was husky with excitement.

I presented him with a fresh page in the tatty exercise book I used as a journal. He bent his head and began to write. Everyone watched: the pale-eyed whites; the doggy-eyed children; the impatient young men. When he had finished his inscription, he returned the book. He had written:

Phineas Sulambo
Moravian Church
Sumbawanga
Tanzania

I remember Livingstone with admiration and adoration. He will never escape my memory. To hear that you are one of his offspring pleases me beyond consideration.

With a little more ceremony than usual I replaced the flimsy book in my bag. Colum stood up: 'We must go'. Outside, the heat had baked the village into stillness. Life bubbled from the little *hoteli* like a hot spring into the desert. The tide of children drew back from the door and started chanting 'Mama, Mama', and Phineas looked at me indulgently: 'They want to see Mama riding her bicycle.'

Not for the first time, I was amused that of all the novelty we presented to villagers the combination of Mama plus bicycle was the most entertaining. And, not for the first time, I also found it irritating.

'Tanzanian women should be able to cycle. They are very strong because they spend all day fetching water.'

His reply was instant: 'You Europeans think we treat our women like animals'.

I was taken aback at his directness. I had been ready for a little skirting of the gender issue, trying to pick up the odd hint about the lives of women. I searched his face for meaning and decided he was embarrassed, but I could have been wrong.

'Perhaps it's a cultural difference,' I said.

'Yes, a cultural difference.'

*   *   *

All that afternoon, as we cycled through sunlit forest, the memory of Phineas troubled me. His gratitude towards Livingstone was vexatiously simple compared with our own feelings. He adored the missionary explorer while we grieved over his inconsistencies, unable to forgive him despite our eagerness to be in sympathy with him. I wondered whether Phineas would have thought any differently of Livingstone if we had told him some of the unsavoury tales from his life – and I decided the answer was no. He would have dismissed the accounts of obsession and cruelty as mere details. Perhaps it was Phineas who had the clarity of vision.

Livingstone: selfless moral crusader or heartless egotist? We had searched the central strands of his character for an answer, but all we had found was contradiction. His religious fervour certainly inspired him to look outwards, to see suffering in the world and to try to banish it. Yet it also convinced him that as God's Instrument he was superior to other men. His stoicism was admirable. He would endure any pain in pursuit of his cause. But that same quality made him careless of others – sometimes fatally careless. His obsessional nature was what transformed him into a campaigner of superhuman stature. Yet it, too, had its dark side. Paranoia haunted him, led him to denounce anyone – old friend or innocent participant – in order to promote himself.

'*The Nile sources are valuable only as a means of enabling me to open my mouth with power among men.*' Phineas would have been pleased with that, the justification that Livingstone gave before leaving for Africa for the last time. But I wondered whether his words really did sum up the simple agenda of a deeply committed Christian explorer, or whether they were the self-delusion of an extraordinarily vain man. Cycling through the serenity of the cool and shady wood, I turned the words over in my head, and slowly, a realisation dawned.

I began to see that, having lived with Livingstone the stranger for so long, I was at last moving closer to understanding his character. In that single sentence justifying his hunt for the Nile's source, Livingstone fused his personal success with the success of the wider moral campaign – with evangelism, the annexation of East Africa, the abolition of the slave trade. To find the source would bring him personal glory which, he argued, he would exploit to further his humanitarian campaign against the slave trade.

Like a tree and its symbiont his success as a person and the success of his missions had twisted together, feeding on each other for better or worse. Livingstone's own advancement at the expense of others was the same thing as the advancement of his moral crusade. He would not – and later could not – distinguish between them. And so Livingstone could think the unthinkable about his peers and say the unsayable about them. If men insulted him, or beat him to a prize, or unwittingly foiled his plans, they undermined his '*power among men*' and thus committed the worst crime of all – they corrupted God's work.

In the shade ahead Colum had stopped and was looking at the map. I paused some distance behind him. Absolute silence. The track was flanked with deep forest shadows of bluey-green, splashed with pools of yellow-green light. I felt overwhelming relief. It was as if, after months, Livingstone had emerged from the broken light amongst the trees, and was now standing with his character illuminated by the sun's full glare. His flaws pained me still but they seemed easier to bear. From now, I knew that our understanding of him could only mature as we followed his decline.

'Are you coming?' Colum was looking at me enquiringly, puzzled at my stillness.

'Yes…' As I remounted my bike I realised that what I now felt towards Livingstone amounted to affection. The final impediments to sympathy had fallen away. And while I would never share Phineas' adulation, I no longer felt uneasy about admiring the legacy that Livingstone had left and which we had come to understand on our journey through Tanzania.

From that first meeting with missionaries in Mpanda to the Christmas

Day celebrations in Kasanga we had watched the gradual reconciliation between Christianity and African belief. It was all, directly or indirectly, part of the religious chain of events started by Livingstone.

Yet I felt that the picture was only half drawn. His legacy was alive, but his spirit remained elusive. He was, above all, a man who burned with a deep humanitarian conscience. We had found no one yet who was alight with the same passion as Livingstone about the welfare of Africans in this world. Could people with the same confidence, the same sweeping agendas, exist late in the twentieth century?

*　　　*　　　*

There must have been two hundred children this time, roaring and whooping in crescendos that only diminished when we shouted at them. They were taking us along a bush path that they insisted led to the Kalambo Falls, where the river that marks the border between Tanzania and Zambia plunges 200 metres before it reaches the lake.

The track narrowed and the forest thickened. Then, without any warning, the path fell away below our feet and was quickly engulfed by the forest canopy. We slipped and slid along as it twitched back and forth down the cliff and finally we emerged on a ledge of rock at the lip of a deep chasm.

The shrieking children fell silent. We were at the end of the world. At our feet, a smooth sheet of water scrolled off the ledge into the emptiness beyond and broke apart into a thousand beads of light. Way, way below, so far away as to be silent, the water plunged into a pool which glinted like an eye. Beyond, the valley floor was spread out like a map; the river was a thin silver ribbon amongst massive clumps of trees no bigger than patches of moss.

'*Over gently undulating country, with many old gardens and watch-houses, some of great height, we reached the River Kalambo, which I know as falling into Tanganyika...*'

We scrambled back up the bank and retraced our steps. Somewhere near here, a few kilometres upstream of the falls, Livingstone must have crossed:

'*... the Kalambo is shallow, and say twenty yards wide, but it spreads out a good deal.*'

The other bank was in Zambia. Ready with our passports, we came to the place where the path peters out at the river's edge. With sinking hearts we looked out across the eddying water in front of us. The children had gone: there was only an old man on the other side who waded waist-deep across the river, warned us of thieves, and then passed on his way. We returned our passports to the document case – no one was interested in them after all – and began the slow, wet business of carrying each piece of baggage, and then the bicycles, to the other side.

Once over, we dragged the bicycles up a slippery path and emerged on a rough track. We were resting when a small black shape appeared on the crest of the hill. As it drew nearer we made out a boy on a bicycle. Strapped to his back carrier was a heavy wooden table that would have seated eight. On top of the table was an even longer bench.

The boy cycled slowly, eyes fixed on the lively undulations of the surface. Then he glanced up. He looked surprised to see us. Colum waved and shouted a greeting and the boy raised an arm in return. It was his last intentional movement for some time. His unwieldy load lurched and he tipped himself to one side to counteract it. It followed him back; he shifted his weight the other way. Soon he had set up a great oscillation in which the bicycle danced from side to side as it hurtled down the track, the boy fighting with the table and bench for control. The battle raged to and fro until the furniture appeared to win an indisputable victory and the bicycle plunged into the ditch. We cringed in readiness for the devastating crash.

Then we watched, amazed, as the boy emerged from the undergrowth, still astride the bicycle and with cargo in place. With consummate piloting skill he steered the speeding bike back onto the track and on down the hill. Gradually the bucking furniture subsided, and the boy settled back into his saddle.

'How rude not to reply,' said Colum.

It was different in Zambia. Even so close to the border our Swahili greetings elicited blank stares. Here the people were Bemba and had no understanding of the language which Nyerere had artificially propagated throughout Tanzania. There were other differences as well. The houses had a feeling of greater permanence – more care was taken over their appearance. Some were painted in ochre patterns, others had flowers lining the walls beneath the eaves of the carefully groomed thatch. Most were surrounded by the household crops. These were homesteads which had not been subject to the sort of political whim which, in Tanzania, had separated the farmers from their land. These were houses that had been lived in for generations; scattered haphazardly through the forest with a freedom that Nyerere's villagisation had banished.

We camped at the heart of a small village under the watchful eye of a very old man. With great reverence, he showed us two smooth pebbles which, he alleged in very rusty English, Livingstone had carried in his pocket throughout his last journey. Then he offered to sell them to us.

*　　*　　*

The following day at about lunchtime we arrived in Mbala. In its heyday some eighty years ago this town was called Abercorn and was the centre of a thriving community of Britons who found in the high, temperate place fertile farming land not unlike that of their homeland. But even Mbala's most dedicated inhabitants now said it was a town in decline. The history books mention it only in relation to one event – in 1918 the German commander von Lettow-Vorbeck surrendered here.

Now a fraying tarmac road runs through it, lined with solid buildings that house its banks, post office and shops. To us the shops were like treasure-houses. They stocked biscuits and bread and chocolate, and, inexplicably, rows and rows of tins of pilchards and corned beef. Away from the main street we followed a red mud road into a tatty market where we traded dollars for Zambian Kwacha with a sharp group of youths. Beyond the market Mbala's corrugated iron and rough cement suburbia began.

Anyone lifting their eyes above Mbala's shanty horizon can see a building that is quite unlike its neighbours, both in architecture and in enormity. It squats a little distance down an incline from the main street as if it is trying to hide its bulk – but its efforts are in vain.

On New Year's Eve, just before sunset, if a passer-by had raised their eyes a little higher to the sweeping curve of the cathedral's remarkable saddle roof, they would have noticed a man. He was standing still at its highest point, hundreds of feet above the dusty ground. Gradually he raised his arms until they were stretched above his head. There he remained, not moving, as if waiting for the right moment to dive.

'Go on Aisling, take the damn thing…' Colum waited, immobilised by vertigo, turning gold in the setting sun. Below him the roof swept down and rose again towards its other, lower peak. There I crouched as close to the slippery roof as possible, trying to capture Colum on film.

Finally I stood up and we both gazed at the sprawl of Mbala. Then we crept back, scrambled down a ladder past the cathedral's rich stained-glass walls and jumped to the ground.

Hans, the White Father in charge of Mbala Cathedral, had recommended the trip to the roof. He also took us inside, where there was a dim, cool, European silence. Saints watched us from the expensive, multi-coloured windows. Wooden characters in a triptych imported from Germany interpreted Biblical stories in a serious Teutonic way. A leaflet praised the selflessness of all who had laboured to transport steel and glass from another continent to build the cathedral here. It also explained the engineering achievement of creating a vast concrete saddle roof that was only supported around the edges.

Hans led us past a wall hung with large black and white photographs. They showed the consecration of the cathedral. I paused and gazed at one. The event had been an elaborate affair with plenty of European dignitaries.

'What a party!' I said.

'It's cultural imperialism,' sniffed Hans to my surprise. He was a man of about sixty, outspoken and grumpy.

'Were you there?' I asked him, peering at the figures.

'Yes, I had to be...' He spoke quickly. With his strong German accent he was hard to understand.

'... but I didn't want to be. I protested against its construction, in writing. Many missionaries did. I said we should spend the money on a printing works so we could distribute the Word of God much more widely. But Germany was paying and Germany wanted to see a cathedral in Mbala.' And now, after thirty years in Zambia, Hans was in charge of the very white elephant he had tried to strangle at birth. He dismissed my sympathy with a mutter of German and a more comprehensible wave of his hand.

A handful of other priests lived in the cloisters, overlooking a quadrangle where sleepy tortoises lumbered across the grass. I followed Hans to the dining room. I was a little afraid of him, but he was amusing as well as acutely intelligent, so I sat beside him at dinner. Opposite me was a Zambian nun who was deeply shy. I could think of nothing to say to her and she ventured nothing herself. On my left sat a more relaxed Irishman whose fair skin had turned a painful pink. He was training to be a priest and had just arrived in Mbala. There was also a Tanzanian noviciate and a lay Englishman who said he had come out 'to help' for a year.

I tackled Hans again: 'Why did they go ahead with the cathedral?'

'Ah, it was a time of optimism,' he said with a shrug. 'Macmillan said the wind of change was blowing in Africa. Countries were gaining their independence. We thought that congregations could only grow.' Forty years later, in an age whose imperative was to disinfect Christianity of its European origins, the cathedral was a monstrous irrelevance. Christianity vibrated from tiny, mud-brick churches instead. When Hans leaves Mbala, I thought, its cathedral will begin to decay. Its demise is a certainty. The concrete will crumble; bats will discover its lofty corners. In fifty years it will be another Karema.

Yet Hans defied compassion. He obviously dreaded the handover of the cathedral to Zambian priests, but I suspected he had sufficient inner resources to cope.

'If you could do anything you wanted with the cathedral, what would you do?' I asked.

'I would pack it out with marriage seminars. I would fill it with couples.'

He turned to me: 'So many problems here arise because the men and the women do not communicate with each other'.

I was surprised at the alacrity with which he gave his answer. In the numerous villages through which we had travelled the men's friends were men; the women's friends were women. There was little socialising between the sexes. Even on Christmas Day, in Kasanga, the men had gathered under the shade of a mango tree for the afternoon and the women – well – I didn't find out where they went.

I helped myself to another plateful of food. I knew I would feel sick later, but after so many hungry weeks I could not prevent myself gorging. For Hans to perceive that dialogue between the sexes was integral to a better life was refreshingly subtle. We had talked to several development workers in Dar es Salaam and Tabora before we began our journey. They were advocates of the theory that the roots of poverty lie in the helplessness of the women. Yet their talk was almost militant, of a battle for power. Apparently their projects could not support the female without confronting the male.

'In fact, you two could probably do with a marriage seminar. This journey will be changing your relationship.'

'Yes, you're probably right.' Instinctively I wanted to confide in him about my paralysis earlier in the journey; the way I had taken to hiding behind Colum when there was something difficult to do; my fear that the expedition could be eroding my confidence rather than building it. And then I wanted to blurt out about the change I was seeing in Colum, his coldness, his withdrawal. Yes, he was probably a good marriage counsellor.

He was dour though. He was as morose about development projects as he was about the future of his church. Like Fritz, who had chuckled about many a development disaster over his beer in Kipili, Hans had depressing stories to tell. Each story followed the same pattern. First, he would describe some local problem; then he would tell of the faultless solution invented by some foreigner. People were thirsty so outsiders decided to build wells for them; new-born babies were dying so they began to train the midwives. Then, Hans would tell of how a project was implemented, apparently successfully, and its perpetrators, usually from Europe or America, returned home content.

But all Hans' stories had unhappy endings. The new wells were unused because women who fetch water prefer to socialise in the privacy of a distant river; the superior midwives were sacked because they wanted pay rises. The reason for the failure was always, with hindsight, utterly obvious.

I thought of my revelation about Livingstone a few days before, and of my resolve before the expedition began to seek his spirit among the people

I would meet on our journey. I would like to have known Hans before the layers of cynicism settled on him – when he was an intelligent young man dedicating his life to God and to Africa. He would have been like Livingstone, perhaps – determined, bent on self-sacrifice – though not as concerned about his reputation back home. I tried another tack: 'So what really makes a successful development project?'

Again, the answer was instant: 'The preparation should take twice as long as the execution. But people have bosses to please back home in Europe so they do not prepare properly.'

Hans finished his meal. Propriety had demanded that I stop eating and satiety had stopped everyone else. Because it was New Year's Eve the young trainee priests persuaded us to go to a bar just outside Mbala and meet up with some local development workers. Hans came too.

The three girls at the bar seemed very young – agricultural graduates from America, drab and plump with flowery skirts and beaming smiles. They enthused about their work.

'The idea is that over three years we work ourselves out of a job,' said one. She sounded as if she was reciting. 'We don't tell them what to do of course. We come out here with all our "great Western ideas"' – and she spoke the phrase with disparagement – 'and they listen to them and decide whether to accept our advice or not. We gradually hand the work over to them.

'In fact,' she said admiringly, 'they're already taking over and the project is only four months in.' I glanced at Hans. He was staring at his hands. I knew what he was thinking. Earlier he had told me of his ideal community: it should be a balance between the illusions of the young and the disillusions of the old.

18

From Mbala
by Colum

THE FOLLOWING morning, in the dining room of the Grasshopper Inn, the New Year's Eve party was in its closing stages. At a table covered in beer bottles two men were arguing, their Bantu sentences flowing and mingling like oblivious streams of bubbles. A third man sat opposite them, taking each bottle in turn and holding it up like a telescope to his eye.

A drunken Christmas tree was propped in a corner. The toilet paper which draped it was tattered and awry, and gave it an air of shambolic undress. We picked our way over the party wreckage strewn on the floor – the upturned chairs, the empty bottles, a solitary shoe – and took our places at a table. There was no sign of breakfast.

Abruptly, there was silence. One of the men who had been arguing had slumped forward, his nose pressed against the table. He was snoring gently. His antagonist got up and, with a hurt expression, weaved towards the door. The third reveller finished his inspection of the bottles and came unsteadily over to our table, where he sat down heavily.

He started speaking with a passion that suggested he was taking up the discussion where his colleagues had left off. His English was fluent, if slurred.

'We Zambians are hungry. The people must rise up and seize *true* democracy for themselves.'

I nodded. Encouraged, he put his face close to mine. His breath was gassy from a long night of warm beer. It was the only way for the people to avoid starvation, he murmured, and belched loudly. Then he slumped back into his chair. I looked round for a waitress.

He did not seem to notice when we got up to leave. Outside, we mounted our bicycles and set off. As we passed through the gates, I fancied that I could hear him still, addressing his sleeping friend perhaps, or remonstrating with the tired Christmas tree.

Beyond Mbala, we hurried along on an empty tarmac road for two hours and then struck west on a small track that meandered through the bush. The path was good and there was a pleasant breeze, but before long we were compelled to stop.

For some weeks now I had been sleeping fitfully. A hollow gnawing in my stomach had been waking me in the darkness like the dismal night-howl of a dog. By the morning, the discomfort always seemed to have no more substance than a half-remembered dream. But over the last few days it had entered my waking consciousness, and now I was curled up on the ground like a bent old man, confronting a pain that clawed angrily if I dared to move.

At last a woman and child appeared round the corner. Catching sight of us they stopped uncertainly, the woman putting a hand up to steady the jar of water on her head. They hovered on the brink of flight, but then the woman seemed to find extra resolve: taking the load from her head, she cautiously approached.

She showed us to a smaller path which wound away through the forest. The grinding pain forced me to stoop as I pushed my bicycle. Between the trees I caught glimpses of square huts, some painted with white and black designs. Flame trees and vermilion jacaranda grew beside their carefully swept paths. Curious eyes watched us as we weaved through the forest, our progress heralded by people darting from hut to hut. Before long, we had gathered a retinue of children and dogs.

We emerged in a dusty open space. This was the heart of the village – a few empty market stalls and a rusting hulk that had once been a generator, where children now played. A large building gleamed with new paint; its brightness hurt my eyes. I felt myself swaying, and Aisling raised a hand to steady me.

Our following of children erupted towards the new building and plunged through the open doorways, shrieking wildly. After a few moments, a white man appeared at one of the doors, the children swarming around him. For a few seconds he regarded us from the shade of the overhanging tin roof, and then with long, rapid strides he was crossing the bright open space towards us, his khaki shorts flapping around his knees.

'Good heavens – foreigners! What the devil brings you here?'

He was grinning broadly, a tall man, gaunt, and with a few days of stubble. He was deeply tanned, his thinning hair bleached pale gold. It was speckled with white paint; he still held a paint brush in his hand.

That was how we met Malcolm. He led us down a broad track towards what he called 'our camp'. No sooner had Aisling mentioned that I was ill than he had snatched away my bicycle, and insisted on pushing it. Bereft of support, I stumbled along beside him, doubled up with pain.

He took a long, searching look at me: 'You look as if you could do with a good rest'.

As we walked he talked excitedly, his words tumbling over each other and his paintbrush describing circles in the air. He was the engineer working with a small group of British volunteers to build a dispensary here. The volunteers had raised the money and then come to Zambia to help the villagers with the construction. And why were we here?

'Oh, we're on the David Livingstone heritage trail,' said Aisling.

At last we turned off the track into a large compound, walled off from the bush and the rest of the village by a thick grass fence. At the entrance he turned on the crowd of children.

'Right, sod off you lot,' he barked. The children scattered, squeaking with delighted laughter.

'Sodding kids. Early on we had to make a rule – otherwise they'd overrun the place.'

The camp was an open area dominated by a huge mango tree. In its shade stood a large canvas and bamboo structure. Two European women emerged from inside when they heard Malcolm's voice. They were also tanned, and wore large coloured wraps like the local women.

'Judy, Fi, we have visitors. Come and meet Colum and Aisling.'

We sat at a long table in the shade of the mango tree, and sipped tea with milk and ate scones covered in honey. 'We certainly don't do too badly here – we take it in turns to spend a day doing the cooking. That lets the others get on with the dispensary.' Malcolm's eyes roved over the little camp. 'Yes, it's a good life here. The charity looks after us well…' I looked around. Beside the tree a circle of rocks had been placed around a fireplace. Beyond that, a barrel of water stood beside a small grass barrier, forming a rudimentary bathroom. A washing line was stretched between two trees. Against one fence was another large bamboo shelter, a tarpaulin stretched over a jumble of brightly coloured sleeping bags and rucksacks.

The other volunteers drifted into the compound in ones and twos, young people, partly Africanised by the few months camping in the bush. One arrived on the back carrier of a large, black bicycle ridden by a Zambian. On dismounting, the two immediately started a close inspection of our bicycles, exchanging comments in the local dialect.

In the early afternoon, we rested in the sleeping area. The tea and scones seemed to have acted as a balm for my pain, which had shrunk now to a small hard ball in the pit of my stomach. By the time we stirred ourselves, the brittle midday sunlight had softened. We went back to the dispensary with Malcolm.

A long line of women was gliding across the space where we had arrived that morning, each carrying on her head a bucket of water. They wore yellow and turquoise, emerald and the deepest indigo: quiet tongues of flame against the white-washed wall of the dispensary. They swayed forward with the muted grace of a line of ships under full sail.

'That's the women doing their part. Community effort, this work,' said Malcolm. In silence, we watched as each woman paused, arched over, and directed a bright arc of water into a large tank. When the first woman saw us I saw her lips move and as one, they turned bovine eyes in our direction. Malcolm half-raised his hand in greeting and one of the women gave an imperceptible nod, and then they were moving away without a backward glance, but talking now, in low voices.

He disappeared into one of the dark doorways, paintbrush in hand, and Aisling and I walked on into the village.

'You are the British with badness in the stomach?'

A small man had fallen into step with us. His English was confident, his accent unusual. He peered round into my face.

'Maybe,' I said.

'I know it is you. I can give you medicine to make you strong again.' And he flitted away from us.

A group of children led us to his home: two large huts, a chicken-coop on stilts, an open-sided rondavel which was the living-room. He emerged from under the low thatch as we approached.

'You are welcome to my home.' He extended a bony hand. He had more delicate features than the other villagers. His hair was tufty and unkempt, giving him a wild look, but his eyes were intelligent and steady. They did not smile. They appraised us. He led us towards a small hut.

'This is my consulting room.' We ducked through the low doorway. It was hot and gloomy inside and there was a sharp, aromatic smell. Some small creature rustled in the low thatch.

He gestured us to two low, rough stools with polished seats, then took his place opposite us, cross-legged on the floor. To his right, a series of jars was arrayed on a smooth animal hide. To his left was a carving in black wood. It was about a metre high: a bulky lattice-work pyramid. It was only after I had been staring at it for some time that I realised it was made up of contorted human forms, carved so exquisitely that I could make out the tortured expressions on each face: the grimaces, the scowls, and the faces with mouths wide open, frozen in endless, silent screams.

'You have badness?'

I nodded.

'Then I must get help. British are difficult.'

I moved my legs, expecting him to go out and summon a fellow witchdoctor, but when I looked at him, his eyes were tightly closed. He started shaking a small rattle and inserted the handle of a teaspoon in his ear. The teaspoon was tethered loosely to the black-wood carving by a cord strung with beads. After three or four tight turns, the cord ran down to a small wooden manikin which stood in front of him on the floor, its crudely painted face towards us.

After some concerted rattling, he made an impatient clicking noise with his tongue and withdrew the teaspoon. He briefly examined the end, gave it a sharp knock with the rattle, then re-adjusted it in his ear. Almost immediately, he started speaking.

'Allo, allo. Trois, sept, huit.' He paused, looking down, fiddling with the cord.

'Trois, sept, huit, Oui, oui.' Another pause, longer this time. Then: 'Mais bien sûr, bien sûr.' His shoulders hunched with frustration and his voice rose. 'Trois, sept... Non, non, attends: trois, sept, huit. Huit, je dis huit. D'accord.'

He waited, idly tapping a blunt finger on his knee. Then he snatched up his rattle, and started a vigorous shaking over the manikin. He stopped abruptly, frowned, and twisted the teaspoon: 'Allo, allo...'

Now his face lit up, and he began a long conversation in French, interspersed with fragments of another language that I did not recognise. At one point, he drew a stubby pencil from amongst the tufts of his wiry hair and scribbled some notes on a shred of newspaper. Gradually, the pace of the conversation slowed.

Finally he said: 'D'accord – ciao', and unlooped the teaspoon from the beaded cord and slipped it into his pocket.

'Who was that?'

'It was my teacher.' He was winding the loose cord tightly round the manikin.

'Where is this teacher?'

'In Zaire.' He carefully replaced the manikin, took up the scrap of newspaper and studied his scribblings intently.

'How do you speak to him?' I asked. I thought he had not heard me. His lips moved as he continued to read through what he had written.

'It is the spirits.' He glanced up now. 'They connect me.'

'From here to Zaire?'

'From here to Zaire. Many miles from here. In the country's centre. My home is there.' There was silence as he busied himself with his little bottles.

'Now I can give you medicine,' he said, and selected a jar which held something like fine, grey sand. From his pocket he drew a small, clear vial with a screw top, and very carefully poured some of the powder into it. He passed it to me. 'Take it with water at sunrise, when you eat, and at sunset.'

I slipped the bottle into my pocket.

'Wait. Take this also,' and he pressed something into my hand: two small pieces of wood the thickness of a pencil. Each was notched, like a rudimentary key.

'When you feel the badness coming in your stomach, fit these pieces of wood together, and hold them tight in your hand. The badness will go away. This will also protect you from lightning.'

Now he settled back and fixed me with his cold, steady eyes. There was a moment's silence. Payment.

'Sport,' he said.

'Sport?'

He mimed smoking a cigarette. Sport cigarettes.

'Just as a present,' he explained, and his mouth grinned.

'OK,' I replied. 'I'll have to come back later.' He nodded. Treatment on credit was fine.

Now he moved the manikin reverently to one side, and started rearranging his bottles. 'Do you mind me asking how your medicine works?' I ventured, wondering if he was bound by a professional code of secrecy.

'It is the power of Satan. I use it to cure people.' He didn't look up. Aisling and I regarded each other. The witchdoctor was polishing the end of his teaspoon with the hem of his tee-shirt.

'So how exactly does Satan help?' asked Aisling. He continued polishing.

'He sends spirits to come and help me. They do as I command.' He nodded towards a dark corner of the room. 'I control the spirits using that.' For the first time, I noticed something hanging from the rafters. As my eyes accustomed to the gloom, I saw that it was an animal pelt, roughly fashioned into a garment. It was hung with strings of brightly coloured beads, and glinting at its centre was a polished rectangle of tin. 'I can see many things in that mirror.'

'But to use Satan is evil.' It sounded naive, and I half expected him to laugh. But he spread his hands, and wrinkled his brow with what looked like frankness.

'No, I just use his power – and only for good.'

'So how are you protected from Satan?'

At the threshold, a crowd of children had gathered and were regarding us in silent wonder. The witchdoctor addressed them with a few curt words, and they fled and light spilled across the floor again. He pulled his shirt sleeve up, and with one finger he pressed on the outside of his arm. Just back from where his bicep stood out like a band of taut ribbon, something moved under the skin.

With light fingertips I felt a small hard ridge like a matchstick lying under silk. He pressed again and the matchstick moved. 'What is it?'

'It is protection. It is from the spirits.'

He pulled up his trouser leg, and there, on the side of his shin, was another object. This one felt like a small disc.

'And how did they get there?'

'I drank medicine, and I asked the spirits for them.'

'And they just appeared?'

He nodded. I took his arm. There must be a scar here somewhere. But I could see nothing, just the same glossy skin, with the pliancy of a new leaf which you crumple, and which then springs back.

We got up to leave.

'Do you want to speak to my teacher in Zaire?' – he passed me the teaspoon which he had again attached to the string of beads. As I turned it over, light played along the handle. It was an ordinary teaspoon. But then, I thought to myself, a telephone receiver is an ordinary piece of plastic. The beads made a faint clicking noise as they fell against each other. I looked at him. His irises were very large, and tawny brown. His pupils were the tiniest pinpricks, which was surprising, I thought, in this semi-darkness. His gaze was level and steady, the faintest trace of a smile still lingering around his mouth.

'No,' I said, passing back the teaspoon. 'It would be bad to disturb him again…'

The witchdoctor nodded, and we emerged into the glaring brightness. Away from his hut, I took the vial from my pocket. The grey powder inside looked like ash. Embossed on the metal, screw-top lid were the initials UNICEF.

*   *   *

After dinner we sat around the fire beneath the arched roof of the mango tree. Outside the ring of light, the campsite was flooded with bright moonlight. I told Malcolm about our visit to the witchdoctor.

He gave a slight shake of his head and took a mouthful of coffee. 'Yes, I know a lot of it goes on round here. I try to ignore it as much as possible. Some of it is a bit, well, sinister.'

'What do you mean?' I asked.

'Well, we've seen some funny things. One night a few of the volunteers stumbled on a group of the villagers chanting round a fire – they seemed to be in some kind of trance. Nobody saw the volunteers and they were able to watch as the people slaughtered a chicken. Blood spurting all over the place.' Malcolm threw his coffee dregs into the flames. There was a sharp hiss.

He turned to me. 'The witchdoctor you saw was the traditional village community health care. The episode with the chicken was the more colourful side of the same service.' He fell silent. Beside him, someone picked at the strings of a guitar. Then he spoke again. 'I suppose there's no harm in killing a chicken. People in the UK do it every day, although not for medical or spiritual reasons...' His voice trailed off and he sighed.

'There's such a lot we can only guess at, or just do not understand at all.'

Someone handed me a mug of something warm and fizzy, and faintly redolent of honey.

'Who knows, perhaps chicken therapy works after all. We tend to come in assuming that we know the answer to everything, but sometimes I suspect we do more harm than good.'

'What do you mean?' asked Aisling.

Malcolm had drawn a battered cigar case from his pocket, and was extracting from it an equally battered cigar.

'Well, take what we are doing here. It makes me very uneasy. Our emphasis is on using the villagers' initiative to get a scheme going. The idea is that they are the driving force behind the work, and we are here just to "facilitate", and to provide some labour.' Carefully, he lifted a glowing log from the fire and pressed it against the end of the cigar. 'The reality, unhappily, is not like that.'

He settled back against his rock, and offered me the cigar: 'I keep it for special occasions,' he explained.

Slowly I drew the smoke into my mouth, and my vision blurred with tears. 'So what, exactly, is the reality like?'

'Well...' and he paused, '... we come here with such good intentions – to show the Africans how to help themselves, and then to step aside so that they learn self-reliance. But it's just not realistic.'

'Why not?'

'It's not the charity's fault, of course, but it's just not the way we're made.' He dragged his gaze away from the fire and regarded me seriously. 'From the day you were born, you've been taught that if you want something done, the best thing to do is to go out and do it yourself.' There was a small shower of sparks as he knocked ash from the glowing tobacco.

'So, after all the careful preparation that is done in a village like this – our people come along to gauge the villagers' motivation before we arrive – we come in at the last minute and grab the initiative back from the very people we were sent here to kickstart.'

He swept his eyes around the volunteers sitting at the fire. 'They're so absolutely brimming with energy. They've got nothing else to do but build this dispensary. And me, well, I'm in my early thirties, I want to succeed as an engineer in development. This is my big chance...'

He looked around at me as if for understanding. I nodded.

'I've really pushed this project. I've called meetings, I've pleaded with the village chief for more workers, I've tried hard to inspire the volunteers. The villagers have just loped along behind.'

'So what should you be doing?'

He shook his head and raked the embers with a stick. 'Well, ideally, I should let them go at their own pace... the dispensary would take years to build but at least they would feel it was theirs...' He paused. When he continued, his voice was far off. 'You see, we're all here because it's a marvellous chance to do things we would never do at home... Africa is a fantasy world.'

Most of the volunteers were sitting at the fire. Some nursed cups of coffee, one smoked a cigarette, another was reading a dog-eared letter. A few sun-burned faces were turned towards the glow, eyes held by the small flames dancing around the crumbled logs. None of them seemed to be listening to what Malcolm was saying or, if they were, they gave no indication.

'We Europeans come here and impose our ideas. We think we know best... we think we have the key to reform African society from its backward ways.' Malcolm's voice was calming. He was talking to no one in particular; his was a soliloquy that we just happened to be hearing. He was thwarted somehow, and now he was working through the facts to find out why.

'In this village, the charity has established a women's group. It is meant to be the point of contact between the charity and those who will benefit most from the dispensary. Sounds good, doesn't it?' He drew on the cigar, then held it vertically between his fingers.

'But it by-passes the traditional village hierarchy which is entirely made up of men. You see, women have never had any voice, any say over resources. We aim to help, but sometimes I wonder whether we are changing a society just to suit today's fashionable idea of development. That would just be vandalism.' He was silent for a moment, then continued, his voice almost a murmur: 'If I speak to the women's group, I insult the village leaders... but I'm not toeing the modern line if I ignore the women.'

The embers collapsed with a light crack. The fire had diminished to brilliant, blue-orange dereliction. My mind was slipping away, lulled by the soft orange glow that wrapped us round, and by the dull murmur of the last of the flames.

'I just can't win.' His words hung in the air. And then at last, he drew out a penknife from his pocket and nipped off the burning cigar-tip. He inspected the severed stump, then slipped it back into the battered case.

Drowsily, I reflected that there was little of Livingstone here. Malcolm was probably a decade older than the breathless girls in Mbala and two decades younger than Hans. He had only had a few months' direct experience as an ethical adventurer in Africa, but already his freshness was corrupted. He stood up and paused for a moment, gazing at the fire. The soft glow illuminated his face, which seemed careworn now. He was too aware of his own footprints, too introspective and uncertain, to be from any era but the late twentieth century.

Later, we stretched our sleeping bag out on the ground. It was a night of light and movement. The constellations swung overhead, and from time to time shooting stars arced from horizon's rim to horizon's rim. The moonlight was alive with the movement of small, scuttling animals, and with large moths with gleaming eyes and wings like darker fragments of darkness. There was drumming in the village, the slow blood-pulse that had haunted the missionaries in Mpanda. My dreams were filled with the death of a chicken, the blood spilling from its quivering neck and covering the ground like silver lace.

*　　*　　*

At dawn Aisling and I walked through the village to the well. As we moved between the round huts and along broad paths of beaten earth, the rising sun flushed the shadowy spaces with diffuse orange light. Women were out in front of their huts using bundles of twigs to sweep overlapping curves in the dust. On a patch of neglected ground, two toddlers fed handfuls of grass onto a small fire, its flame a splash of hard brightness.

The well was a deep wide hole with crumbling sides where women were taking it in turns to throw a battered bucket down on the end of a frayed rope. There was a dull clunk as the bucket reached the bottom and lay in the small pool of milky water, which was just a few inches deep. Without a word, a woman drew the bucket up time and time again and poured the hard-won water into our bottles.

We returned slowly through the village until we emerged in front of the dispensary where women were working to level the ground. A mound of cut grass had been set alight, and billows of smoke rolled across the open space. It was very bright, so bright that the colour seemed to have drained from the day.

I only caught glimpses of the women in the smoke. Slowly, they moved abreast of where we stood, and fleetingly, as the swirling smoke cleared, I was looking down a line of swaying black silhouettes, mattocks wheeling like the arms of a continuously spinning machine. Above the roaring of the fire I felt, rather than heard, the dull bite of the blunt tools as they rained down on the hard ground. Then all was lost again as the greyness enveloped the black forms and I could see nothing but the sullen gleam of the corrugated iron roof through the smoke's bright curtain.

The men formed untidy groups around the fire. The flames were insubstantial in the brightness, but made the air quiver like a ringing bell. They chatted, some sitting, others leaning on hoes in studied poses. Malcolm strode amongst them, exhorting, remonstrating. For a few minutes, he took up a pick and joined the line of women. But it was to no avail. Manual work had always been the domain of the women, and of the women alone. One foreigner with different ideas was not going to change the legacy of generations.

Then I saw him talking to a short man who wore a construction hat. It was the village chief. Malcolm pointed, and counted things off on his fingers – his mouth was moving but I could make out nothing above the crackling of the flames. The chief nodded, and his hands formed an apology in the air. Then his shoulders sagged. Malcolm shook his head and turned away.

*   *   *

'So what will happen?'

'He will die.'

We were in the old dispensary. There was silence as we both regarded the child. He looked like a lump of raw meat lying on the ground, except that his head rolled slowly from side to side, and he emitted a continuous low moan.

'Sixty percent burns.'

I nodded.

'He was wearing a nylon shirt. You can see where the material was not touching his skin.' Malcolm indicated an isolated patch around the child's navel, and the area around his groin where there was a frayed area of glossy brown skin. Flies buzzed lazily, attempting to settle at the crusty tideline where the skin and the rawness met. A woman sat close by, her hand waving slowly over the child's body.

The air was heavy with a sweet smell that I did not know and that I did not like. I wanted to get out into the bright sterility of the sunlight. But Malcolm had not moved. His eyes were locked onto the red glistening mass that was the child. A muscle at the corner of his eye twitched.

'Yes, he will die. No sterile water, so he will die. No saline drip, so he will die.' He was speaking very softly, as if I was not there.

'Not even a fucking bed. So he will die.' He jerked his head round, and his look was fierce. 'Whatever I said to you last night – whenever I have doubts about white men meddling in Africa – I just come in here. And I always go away knowing why I am doing what I am doing.'

Log Book Extract

DAY 39 – Thursday 2nd January

PHASE 3

FROM: Malcolm's village

TO: Kapatu Mission

CAMP: In school beside mission.

POSITION: 30°44'20" E
                    9°43'9" S

TIME CYCLING: 10 hours

DISTANCE TRAVELLED: 79km

AVERAGE SPEED: 7.9km/hr

ROUTE: Heading west-south-west through undulating forest. Through
    tiny villages all day.

TRACK CONDITION: Rough track through bush. Adequate surface,
    with some rocks and standing water.

BICYCLES – PERFORMANCE: Front derailleur playing up on
    Aisling's bicycle – trouble engaging middle front cog. Bottom
    brackets grating severely on Aisling's bicycle. Bikes heavily
    encrusted with mud.

BICYCLES – MAINTENANCE: Some mud removed.

WEATHER: Started bright and sunny, but then continuous, cold, heavy
    rain from mid-morning onwards. Our equipment all wet through.

HEALTH: Aisling has developed a rash on her chest – though no
    irritation. She has a blocked nose and a sore throat. Colum has
    recurring stomach pains, and is moody. Took weekly malaria tablets.

EQUIPMENT: Fuel we bought in Mbala seems dodgy and sends two-
    foot flames out of the camping stove. It makes cooking difficult.

LANDSCAPE: Low forest, low hills, neat settlements with maize and
    cassava cultivation – though crops seem very scrawny.

EXPENDITURE: Kw300 on biscuits, coconut.

FLUID CONSUMPTION: 8 litres

FOOD: Food is scarce – some biscuits available in Malcolm's village and coconut. Hungry all day.

Breakfast: none

During day: coconut, three biscuits each

Evening: last of rice. Curry powder all wet, so had to be discarded. Some garlic, though peppercorns finished.

COMMENT: New Year celebrations still continue. Many drunk Zambians still staggering around. We must try not to run so low on food. It is difficult here, because the locals have none to sell to us. They speak only Bemba. Colum killed a snake on the path, and notched the machete.

LIVINGSTONE: Some 20km north of us in the Malembe Hills where he found a nutmeg tree in full bearing.

19

To Mporokoso
by Colum

NOT FAR from modern Mbala, Livingstone called a halt for a few days, and set his party preparing for the next phase of the journey.

The men turn to stringing beads for future use, and to all except defaulters I give a present of 2 dotis, and a handful of beads each. I have diminished the loads considerably, which pleases them much. We now have 3¹/₂ loads of calico and 120 bags of beads. Several go idle, but have to do any odd work, such as helping the sick or anything they are ordered to do. I gave the two Nassickers who lost the cow and calf only 1 doti, they were worth 14 dotis.

It was a time for his men to recuperate, and for Livingstone to take stock. From here, he was to turn west, heading out across the low rolling hills of what is now north-eastern Zambia. Before long he would break away from the territory which he knew from previous visits into new areas devastated by the slave trade.

After four days, Livingstone was ready to be off again. By now, the rains had begun in earnest, and his party, which until a week previously had been suffering from inflamed feet from the scorching earth, began moving forward across cold, waterlogged terrain: '*Very heavy rain and high gusts of wind, which wet us all.*'

To make matters worse, one of Livingstone's donkeys had died a few days before. '*Its death was evidently caused by tsetse bite and bad usage by one of the men, who kept it forty-eight hours without water. The rain, no doubt, helped it to a fatal end; it is a great loss to me.*'

The rain and the death of his donkey were the first of a series of minor setbacks to befall Livingstone. He would barely have noticed any one of these in isolation, but together they constituted a change in his fortunes. Over the next few months reversals were to stack up against him and were to push him into the slow decline towards death.

*　　　*　　　*

A dark sheet of cloud reared up from the horizon and before long, the deluge began. Again, pain gripped my stomach and we were forced to stop. Leaden pain beneath a leaden sky. We were soaked through, and Aisling was shivering. She draped a poncho over me, and delved into the musty depths of a pannier.

At last she drew out a coconut. In spite of the sharp ache, my mouth filled with saliva. I watched her weighing it in her hand. It was small, but I could see that it was gratifyingly heavy. She punctured it, and we drank the sweet milk and the pain subsided. And then Aisling drew the machete and swung at the shell. The blade glanced off and she whimpered and clutched her jarred wrist. The coconut had skittered across the track. The pain rose again in my stomach, and I drew the clammy waterproof around my neck. I began to shiver.

She picked her way slowly between the puddles. Her second blow embedded the coconut deep in the mud. My anger was so sudden, so all-consuming that a part of me was left watching, a small, dispassionate eye, as I jerked to my feet. As I lunged across the track towards the coconut, my pain felt like a freshly healed wound bursting apart.

I pushed past Aisling and she shrank back, pale and open-mouthed, the blade limp in her hand. Now I saw myself snatching the coconut out of the mud. With a movement that wracked my whole body, I hurled it against the smooth grey trunk of a tree. There was a hollow crack, and a man exploded out of the undergrowth. He was close enough for me to glimpse his rain-streaked face, his eyes wide with fear. The noise of him crashing through the forest receded like a dying echo, and the dripping silence rolled back.

I looked at Aisling. Wet coils of hair plastered her forehead and her cheeks. Her face betrayed nothing. She raised a hand as if to lay it on my shoulder, but then hesitated, and it dropped again to her side. Instead, she turned away and bent down to retrieve the shards of coconut from the mud. I sank back down against a tree, and started shivering violently. The pain stirred angrily and I felt dizzy.

At length the rain abated, leaving the air alive with moisture and the sky blanketed with low grey cloud. We set off again. There was silence, except for the light hissing of our wheels through the mud. The forest around us was a monochrome photograph relieved only by the muted gleam of the leaves.

After a few hours our track shrank to a path, and gradually the wet forest pressed in until we were forced to walk, brushed by wet undergrowth and leaves. Then the cloud lightened and we arrived at a clearing on a low hill. There was a small village huddled around a broken school building. We pitched our tent in a classroom by the light of a rain-rinsed sunset.

*   *   *

The following morning we breakfasted on mangoes from a nearby tree. We cycled all morning along a broad sandy track, and by noon our remaining food had dwindled to four biscuits. We came at last to a few buildings, a broken tractor, an illegible signpost.

Across one doorway there was a rudimentary counter. I peered into the gloom inside, and someone stirred. There was a flash of white teeth, and a skinny boy came forward. I looked past him at shelves stacked with nothing but small bags of salt and jars of vaseline. I turned away. A tall man in a cassock was standing behind me, his hands clasped behind his back. He was gently shaking his head.

'We have no food to sell. There is nothing.' He opened his hands, palms upwards, and shrugged his shoulders. His face was creased with anguish.

'The price of fertiliser has increased three-fold since last year. So people cannot afford it. They did not plant this year.'

'So what will happen?'

He remained quiet, the wrinkles fixed on his brow. His eyes were on my face, but he was looking through me. In silence, we wheeled our bicycles back onto the track, and prepared to remount. And then I saw that he was hurrying over towards us, rummaging in the folds of his cassock.

'Take this – a present...' A brief smile, and he pressed a small bag into my hand. We cycled away.

Out of sight, we stopped, and I opened the bag. A handful of peanuts. I looked up but Aisling had turned her face away.

'Let's go on,' she said.

*   *   *

Even the end of a good year normally brings little food surplus for barter, but in 1872 the slave trade had shattered normality. No crops had been planted or harvested, and many villages were deserted. The people that remained were traumatised and half-starved. '*No food to be got on account of M'toka's and Tipo Tipo's raids... Here there is none for either love or money.*' The hunger of the local people sharpened their distrust: '*Those who were sent to find food return without anything – they were directed falsely by the country people, where nought could be bought.*'

The provisioning of his party constantly exercised Livingstone's mind. On some days there was a note of triumph that he had managed to barter successfully with a chief for flour and a fowl, or a sheep – '*a welcome present, for I was out of flesh for four days*'. On another day he noted, without comment, that his men were hungry, and that four of them were sick. On 5th December, he observed simply : '*The people eat mushrooms and leaves.*'

Later, our food was finished, and we bought mushrooms. Each was the size of a large dinner-plate and we had to break them to stow them on our bicycles. The flesh was pale and spongy and had the ancient smell of rain on dry earth.

On 13th December, Livingstone's writing was erratic. No two words looked the same. It was as if each had been drawn from him with some effort: '*Westward about by south, and crossed a river, Mokobwe, thirty-five yards. Ill, and after going S.W. camped in a deserted village. S.W. travelling five hours. River Mekanda 2nd. Menomba 3, where we camp.*'

*   *   *

Livingstone was ill with such regularity in Africa that it was usually only in passing that he mentioned it in his journal. Illness, like rain and hunger, was an African tribulation to which his will had simply not submitted in the past. To look at now, he was not very different from the man who had strode out so purposefully from Kwihara one bright hopeful day many weeks before. Certainly he was weather-beaten and travel-stained, and the skin of his face was sunken a little; but then Aisling's face had also grown hollow.

The difference was that Livingstone no longer had the recuperative powers of a younger man. From mid-December 1872 until he died four and half months later, Livingstone was to experience unremitting cold and wet, and the grey gnawing of almost continuous hunger. His dysentery and bleeding were to tighten their grip on his frail body. His illness and the dereliction of age were something over which even his will had no control.

With the gradual whittling away of his strength we were to see subtle changes in his character, as imperceptible as the lengthening of shadows towards evening. Perhaps it was the relaxation of a personality held rigid for so long by an unyielding will, or perhaps it was the realisation that his God may, after all, have had no more use for him on Earth. But slowly, slowly, over the next few months, the layers of his character were to fall away like the petals from a flower. When he was much closer to death, we were to be left with just the essence of the man Livingstone had once been.

20

In Mporokoso
by Aisling

Europe in Africa – it had all gone terribly wrong.
Shiva Naipaul, *North of South*

THE TOWN of Mporokoso is in the neglected quarters of Zambia, the sprawling rural wastes which the more affluent part of the country prefers to forget. Mporokoso is a dustbin for the country's ills, the place to which dishonest or incompetent civil servants are banished because sacking them is not permitted.

The town's government rest house seemed attractive from a distance, painted white and blue and with a deep veranda. But the place was in squalor. It had been built to run on electricity and piped water but had lost them both. The toilet was a bowl of sulphurous liquid around which mosquitoes hissed and cockroaches scuttled in the darkness. The bath had lost all its enamel and was brown from a combination of rust and filth of unknown proportions.

The other guest at the rest house was a short, pugnacious man from Lusaka, the capital, marooned in Mporokoso until an essential part could be found for his broken-down lorry. We shouted to each other on the veranda while a violent rainstorm emptied itself onto the mud beside us.

'But *why* are you going to these lengths for the sake of David Livingstone?' he kept asking, unsatisfied with my replies. 'Will you make money from it?'

'We might do, we may write an article.'

'Ah,' he said knowingly. 'I understand you now.'

Then he raised his voice against the pelting of the rain: 'You know, years ago I found a book on Livingstone. It was a small book and I don't think many people know about it. It told the truth about him and very few people know the truth.' He leant forward accusingly. 'He was an unpleasant man. He treated his family very badly. His wife and his children all suffered.'

'Yes, that's true,' I admitted. 'But he did repent before the end of his life. I mean, he wrote to his son apologising for the way he had treated him...

and I think his wife's death really altered him - he blamed himself for it.'

I thought the man would dismiss this but, to my surprise, he seemed to find these facts important. He questioned me in more detail about what exactly I meant by 'repented' and when Livingstone had done so. Then he said: 'You'll find that the religious people you meet on your way are *so* pleased about David Livingstone... he was the man who brought Christianity to Africa. They just don't realise that there were many others who brought Christianity as well. But the rest of us in Zambia, we are *not* interested in him. In fact, we have complaints about him. He brought cholera here by opening Africa up to outsiders.'

'But he was a humanitarian,' I argued. 'Forget about the religious side, there was more to him than that. He didn't trample on Africans, he cared about them.' There was no reply so I added: 'Everyone we've met so far – except you – has had good words to say about him.' I was surprising myself – a few weeks before I would have agreed with him unequivocally.

The man was dismissive: 'They're from the rural areas, they're not representative.'

We left him playing cards with some travelling civil servants who had drifted in for the night and seemed unconcerned about the lack of dinner. We hopped round the muddy pools left by the rain to get to the shanty part of town in search of food. We found it at Nelson's Café, a lively place squeezed between the shacks of the market and equipped with a deep freezer, a video and a stereo, none of which were working because the town had had no electricity for two weeks. Outside, a woman boiled rice for customers on a wood fire. Inside, young men lined the benches of the single room, drinking sweet black tea and speaking urgently of maize shortages, destructive exchange rates and how a nation of peasants had been tricked into voting for the incumbent president because he had distributed free tee-shirts emblazoned with his name. Frustration danced in the dim air.

*   *   *

Next morning, in the market, there was a feast of biscuits, nuts, rice and tins of pilchards and corned beef, as well as some evil-looking red mushrooms.

'They're poisonous unless you boil them with bicarbonate of soda for an hour.' The voice was unmistakably European. I spun round and was confronted by a white man: he wore a black tee-shirt and shorts, and looked in his late thirties, built like a rugby player. With him was a woman, fair-haired and fragile beside him. Dangling from a harness on her front was a kicking, complaining baby.

Jan was a Dutch doctor and we found his house that afternoon in the hospital grounds on a hill next to the town. Beside it was another large house where a second medical couple lived. We had stumbled on one of the remote towns inhabited by members of a Dutch aid scheme which distributes doctors around rural Zambia.

The hillside was bare. Jan led us round the back of the house to his garden. It was a bleak and windy place which I remember as chilly, although it cannot have been so. Much of it was unkempt: coarse African grass sprouting from a tough soil. In the middle of the garden Jan had sunk a forlorn swimming pool. I couldn't imagine ever wanting to bathe in it.

'We've just sacked our night watchman, who was also our gardener,' said Jan. I assumed it was an explanation for the desolate surroundings. 'We went away for two weeks and he never turned up to keep watch.'

'He made so many excuses afterwards,' said Natalie, his wife. 'He was sick; his radio needed mending; he had to do his farming. But really, he thought he could be paid for doing nothing while we were away.'

'And do you know,' added Jan incredulously, 'he was standing here when I sacked the previous night watchman for exactly the same reason. He heard it all. And yet he did the same thing. And then he can't understand it when we fire him.' Jan's handsome, slightly coarse face looked exasperated and, as he turned his back on the garden to lead us indoors, he said: 'I will never, ever understand these people'. Bitterness edged his voice.

The house was European and comfortable. Sunk into the sofa in the living room, and surrounded by books, was another man. At the sight of him, Jan cheered up:

'Hey, it will be quite a party tonight. Meet Thomas – one time health worker and wanderer, as far as I can make out. Heavens, we see no one for a year, and then three of you turn up almost together. Thomas, you seem to be driving from bleak outpost to bleak outpost, eh?'

'Wanderer' seemed an inappropriate term for Thomas, who was wearing a full expatriate uniform of pristine shorts and freshly ironed shirt. His bland face revealed little. He was in these parts 'looking for commercial opportunities', he said.

'I think I saw the other Dutch doctor earlier today,' I said, as Jan handed us each a glass. 'I thought I saw a white skin in the distance.' At that Jan stopped pouring the drinks and frowned. Natalie glanced up: 'I'm afraid we have very little to do with them'.

'Little to do with them?' Jan snorted as he left the room. 'We are not speaking to each other. In fact, we are virtually at war.' Natalie explained that the other doctor was older and had been an expatriate in Africa all his life.

'We differ over our methods, one might say. Jan had such great plans,' she sighed. 'He was going to change everything. He has a lot of energy...'

'Things have got so bad that I have applied for a transfer,' said Jan, returning to the room with another bottle. I watched him talk. He was a forceful man, given to explosiveness. Throughout the evening his wife bent like a willow to his orders. Thomas, by contrast, was quiet, but radiated a confidence and a calm strength that was magnetic, almost mesmerising. I found his presence deeply reassuring. Yet, by the end of the evening it was Thomas who would have shocked us, with the story of a betrayal which I still find hard to reconcile with the civilised man to whom we talked that night.

Natalie had dumped a big bowl of steaming spaghetti on the table and we began our dinner. Jan continued:

'In fact, I have decided since applying for the transfer to leave Africa altogether.'

'That's a shame,' said Thomas. 'There are so many adventures to be had in Africa. You've probably just spent too long in one place.'

'No, I never thought it would happen,' agreed Jan. He turned to Colum. 'I've spent my whole life training to come and work here as a doctor,' he said helplessly. 'But now I am going home. Africa has defeated me.'

'The staff are totally undisciplined,' said Natalie. 'Last week, there was an emergency here, but before we could do the operation the technician had to be found. He was drinking in town and would not come. We sent for him four times and he just went on drinking.'

'And what happened to the patient?' asked Thomas.

'He died.'

She went to pull the baby away from the dangers of an exploratory crawl in a corner of the room. 'They have no initiative,' she said over her shoulder. 'They always take an hour to sterilise the instruments, even if it is an emergency like a Caesarian where every minute counts - they just crawl, crawl, crawl, and people die because of it.'

The grievances tumbled from them for over an hour, as Colum and I ate steadily through several plates of spaghetti. Thomas ate quietly, strangely unanimated by Jan's stories.

'There's a man in Mporokoso who is doing well,' said Jan. 'He had a child which was horribly malnourished. A great distended stomach.' He moved a cupped hand to describe the familiar contour of children's bellies, which are filled only with cassava starch, once a day. 'Anyway, I told the man that his child was malnourished. I told him what to feed it. I told him several times. Later I told him his child would die if he didn't feed it better. And you know what happened... the child is dead. It died of malnutrition.'

There was silence, apart from the fat white baby's noisy progress around the sitting room floor.

Jan interrupted our thoughts: 'That's been one of my worst experiences. I knew what was wrong with that baby. I knew it could be cured easily. The money was there. The good food was there...'

Thomas was nodding his head as Jan continued: 'You just cannot educate these people.' That was his conclusion after two years' tumbling in a society whose laws he could not understand. Perhaps this was the first time in Jan's life that his clear formulae for the world had broken down.

'You have to understand,' said Thomas, turning to us, 'that in this part of the world there is no such thing as a natural death.' He stood up to help Natalie who was gathering a tray of table debris to take into the kitchen.

'Whenever there is a funeral *everyone* goes, everyone,' he called back to us. 'If you don't go you could be the witch that killed the man. The witchdoctor regularly accuses people of causing other people's deaths and, such is the psychology, they regularly admit to it. They say they did it.'

Invisible lines of force controlled these people's destinies. In the dark of a hut a man could create a secret spell and tomorrow his enemy would wake with the wasting disease. Sickness and death were tangible outcomes of powerful human forces of retribution, hatred, jealousy. A child died, a wife perished in childbirth. Their deaths were not part of the natural order, they were against it. They must have been caused by some unnatural force, some human dabbling in evil spirits. Yet Jan had arrived claiming that hearty adults could be sickened and killed by animals so tiny they could not be seen; by germs with no motives, no malevolence in their hearts. Try again, doctor.

'Those funerals,' I called. 'Do you go to them?'

'No, I don't get involved.' Thomas returned from the kitchen. 'You mustn't get involved.' His voice was commanding but mild. 'Once you are involved, you will never extricate yourself.'

'But that's ridiculous,' cried Jan. 'What are you here for if you're not involved?'

Thomas shrugged. 'I'm here for business and adventure. My days of being a hand-wringing do-gooder are over,' he said, a little patronisingly.

'You must do *some* good here, Jan,' I interrupted. 'Do you have any medical successes?'

'Yes, as it happens, we save many lives,' he said pointedly. He turned to me and continued more softly. 'Cerebral malaria we can often cure and most TB can be a hundred percent cured. But I think that in most other cases the people who manage to get up here to the hospital are the ones who are going to live anyway. And of course most of our beds are taken up with Aids patients - I would say eighty percent of our patients have Aids-related diseases.

'But to educate them about Aids is impossible.' He pushed his chair back and stood up, animated again. 'How can you tell a man to be less promiscuous when he believes he must empty himself every night for the sake of his health?' His voice was loud now with distress: 'Or when a new widow must be cleansed by the semen of her brother in law - even if her husband died of Aids?'

The cicadas rattled indifferently in the dense night outside. Somewhere in the valley a dog barked sharply and then was quiet. Through the window the bare garden was lit up by a ghostly, fluorescent glow.

'Well, ' Thomas said finally, 'I believe one does more for a country if one doesn't aim to help at all. I have my adventures, I set up business for my company – a farm, for example, which does of course create jobs – and then I move on.'

'And what else do you leave behind you – apart from a few jobs farming what was once their own land?' Jan's voice was still passionate.

Thomas's diagnosis was devastating. But he delivered it objectively as if he was little more than a professional observer.

'There is one town where I spent a lot of time a while ago. The hospital manager has Aids – it wasn't stopping her getting married though. The clinical worker has Aids. There is a health worker and a hospital assistant who both have Aids. They will all be dead within a year. All four.' He had counted them off on his fingers and now he presented his unfurled hand so there would be no mistake.

'And there is no one trained to replace them. So the health system will collapse, I should think.' His hand fell. 'You would have found it distressing, Jan, but really there is nothing one can do.'

Jan was restless. He put some music on, told the baby off, disappeared to make coffee while we examined his maps and discussed the routes we might take over the next few days.

Finally, Jan sat down again, announcing: 'It's time Niels went to bed'. His wife rose obediently from the table and we waved and cooed at the receding little face that peered over Natalie's shoulder, rewarded by the flexing of a chubby little hand.

'So you are leaving your beloved continent?' prompted Thomas.

'Yes, in fact we have just made the decision.' Natalie turned at the door. 'It will be better for Niels as well,' she said. 'After all, we chose to have a child. We owe him a proper education in Holland.'

'What will you do back there?' I asked Jan.

'I shall go into medical administration at a private hospital.'

'Aha! To occupy the new seat of power, wrested from the doctors and now in the hands of the managers!' Thomas sensed some sort of victory. Jan seemed to be a man whose prime need was to have power and to use it to make sweeping changes. That had been the real lure – and disappointment – of East Africa.

I took another draught of wine and there came to my mind an image of the young and impetuous Livingstone who in his early days had had his simple formula for improvement: medicine and a good sermon. He was lured from Britain on his first journey to Africa by adventure combined with the promise of a massive harvesting of souls. The work would be direct, at the cutting edge. And the achievement would be quick and visible, just as Jan had expected it to be. The resonance with Livingstone, setting off *'beyond every other man's line of things'*, was uncanny.

But Jan had been unexpectedly overwhelmed. He was drowning in a strange culture whose values were more alien than he had ever imagined. He was insulted by a land which, despite its obvious need, had turned its back on him. Livingstone had encountered this too. On the first of his three visits to Africa, when he was a missionary, the tribal machinery had clattered on with no need for the strange Christian parts that Livingstone had wanted to fit.

Jan uncorked another bottle, poured wine only for himself and said irritably: 'These people's way of life is simply incompatible with development. The whole culture needs to be dismantled if there is to be any progress'.

Livingstone had returned to Africa, on his Zambezi expedition, to embark on just such a dismantling programme. He armed himself with the weapon of international trade. But Jan? Although he evoked Livingstone more than anyone we had met on our journey – more than weary Hans or wavering Malcolm – his achievements would not be in Africa. There was something missing from his personality, something akin to an indefatigable optimism. Jan was too much of a realist.

'Well, well,' said Thomas, nursing his coffee cup without taking a sip. 'You are finally disillusioned. I must say it is not such a surprise. You have become too involved, Jan, you must skate over the surface.'

'Oh yes?' Jan was fierce. 'That's no way to live.'

'Believe me,' said Thomas. He was visibly nettled for the first time that evening, and a slight flush appeared at his neck. 'Nothing you do here will have any consequence.'

Jan said nothing. Thomas suddenly pushed his cup with both hands across the table and leaned forward.

'Let me tell you why I say this. Many years ago, when I was much younger, I took a medical post in an African town. I wanted to broaden my mind, see more than the western world.

'One day the police caught a criminal and they beat him up. They beat him up really badly. I mean... so badly that they killed him.'

We stared at him and at first he met our gaze but then his eyes dropped and his voice slowed and became even quieter.

'His family accused the police of murder and demanded an inquiry into his death.' Each word was deliberate, measured.

'The police came to my house, late one night. Five of them. They asked me to sign a form to say that the injuries they gave him did not lead to his death.'

We waited. Finally Thomas looked up, at Colum, his eyes narrow.

'I signed it,' he whispered.

There was a long pause.

'You signed it,' Colum said blankly.

'He was a known criminal.' Now the voice was urgent, angry. 'It was not for me to make the work of the police difficult. That was not my job.'

This time the silence seemed unbreakable. We were trapped, as if we had become a photograph of the moment when Thomas confessed, and our living counterparts were continuing the evening in another world. So this was what the adventurer had been reduced to. He had come here for new experiences, he had perhaps done much good, but without a purpose, he had been left rudderless in an African storm.

Eventually, Thomas sighed. His gaze had returned to his untouched coffee and he repeated with a soft venom:

'You mustn't get involved.'

Log Book Extracts

DAY 41 – Saturday 4th January

PHASE 3

REST DAY
   Staying in government rest house, Mporokoso.

DISTANCE TRAVELLED: None

BICYCLES: Disassembled both derailleur jockey wheels and cleaned.
   Checked tyres, chains, brakes. Aisling's bike has a clicking pedal.

WEATHER: Quite cloudy. Rainstorm at 3pm.

HEALTH: Aisling generally under the weather – head, stomach, throat
   all trouble her. Rash has spread down her back.

EQUIPMENT: Stitched and patched ripped clothing.

EXPENDITURE: Kw25,000 on provisions.

FOOD: During day: ground biscuits in milk.
         Lunch: fried mushrooms and onions with bread.
         Evening meal: spaghetti with fish sauce.

COMMENT: Changed $20 into Kw24,000.
   We have a sketch map of a short cut (the Zambians call it a 'shot
   cat') for the journey over the next four days. Tomorrow will be
   tough – 90km carrying 4 days' food supply. As usual, we have
   planned out each meal.

Note:
   Nshima (Bemba) = maize porridge

*   *   *

DAY 42 – Sunday 5th January

PHASE 3

FROM: Mporokoso

TO: Camp in forest

POSITION: 29°23'10" E
               9°32'29" S

TIME CYCLING: 9 hours 40 minutes

DISTANCE TRAVELLED: 90km (approx)

AVERAGE SPEED: 10km/hr (approx)

ROUTE: Take main Kalambe road out of Mporokoso

TRACK CONDITION: Good surface all day, some mud after rain.

BICYCLES – PERFORMANCE: Got muddy. Speedometer playing up for first 35km.

BICYCLES – MAINTENANCE: none

WEATHER: Sun and cloud until 1pm, when we endured 1 hour of heavy rain. Heavy showers on and off all afternoon, with thunder and lightning.

HEALTH: Aisling has swollen glands and a sore throat. Colum's stomach continues to be painful. Perhaps he ate too much fruit.

EQUIPMENT: We forgot to get replacement fuel in Mporokoso, so cooking continues to be an explosive operation.

LANDSCAPE: Low forest on gentle hills. Occasional small villages.

EXPENDITURE: Breakfast and provisions Kw5,000; 2 nights in Mporokoso rest house Kw9,000.

FLUID CONSUMPTION: 5 litres

FOOD: During day: biscuits, peanuts, avocado, bread
Evening meal: egg curry and rice with fried onions and tomato. Stewed mango and banana for desert. Cocoa.

COMMENT: This unsurfaced road from Mporokoso remains in good condition because no one uses it. We saw no vehicle all day. We normally try to camp within the confines of a village, but we've had no choice this evening. We were warned that the unrest in Zaire means that there are many refugees and mercenaries in this area. Hopefully the rain will keep them indoors. Tomorrow, over the Kalamboshi, we will turn south on the 'shot cat'.

LIVINGSTONE: Working along the Muchinga Escarpment parallel to us some 15km to our north.

21

From Mporokoso to Luwingu
by Aisling

Peel the mango with a paring knife; carefully slice the fruit off the pit in long sections, using the knife to feel the contours of the flat oval-shaped pit. Cut the sections lengthwise into quarter-inch slices...

From a recipe for mango and pineapple salad with citrus ginger vinaigrette, *Fields of Greens: New Vegetarian Recipes from the Celebrated Greens Restaurant* by Annie Somerville.

THE RAIN was sudden and ferocious and we dived into Nelson's Café for bread and fried eggs, and for advice on the next part of the journey.

'So do you think we can get there?'

Nelson's brother, Chisha, examined our map thoughtfully.

Livingstone had travelled west and then struck south, across a space on the map without contours and, even today, without tracks. It was an area latticed with rivers as numerous as the thin lines on an old man's face, and dotted with a symbol like a tuft of grass, endlessly repeating. At a place called Chibote, the cartographer had shown a lonely cluster of small rectangles huddled in the marshy wilderness. No slender road-lines held it stable on the map. Ever since I had first seen the maps one distant afternoon in summertime London, Chibote had seemed to be the epitome of all that was remote.

'Chibote,' said Chisha, 'Yes, I think you could pass through there.' And his brow furrowed as he sketched us a route, marking the crossing points on rivers. Finally he handed his sketch to Colum. 'The rains have started...' and he frowned. 'The ground may be wet in places...'.

He was right of course. Livingstone recorded how the rain was transforming the land:

Floods by these sporadic rainfalls have discoloured waters, as seen in Lopanza and Lolela today. The grass is all springing up quickly and the Maleza growing fast. The trees generally in full foliage. Different shades of green, the dark prevailing; especially along rivulets, and the hills in the distance are covered with dark blue haze.

Livingstone's impassive description masked a more sinister change: the full fury of the worst rainy season he had ever experienced was about to be unleashed, and was to dominate the last months of his life. His progress would be impeded by swollen rivers and the wet and cold would inexorably wear down his health. Continuous cloud cover would thwart his measurements, and as he moved farther away from familiar territory to the south-west of Lake Tanganyika, he would become less sure where he was and more dependent on local advice.

> *So cloudy and wet that no observations could be taken for latitude and longitude at this real geographical point. The Kalongwese is sixty or eighty yards wide and four yards deep, about a mile above the confluence of the Luena. We crossed it in very small canoes, and swamped one twice, but no one was lost... A wet bed at night, for it was in the canoe that was upset. It was so rainy that there was no drying it.*

At the end of a day's wet cycle from Mporokoso, we camped in the forest. The following morning we reached the Kalungwishi a few kilometres to the north-east of where Livingstone crossed. Where the track reached the river we loaded our bicycles into a small boat and were carried across the deep and slow-moving water. On the other bank we took a last, wistful glance at the track we had followed from Mporokoso, and turned south, into the empty lands.

> *A son of Chama tried to mislead us by setting out west, but the path being grass-covered I objected, and soon came on to the large clear path... Had we suffered the misleading, we should have come here tomorrow afternoon.*

Our guide was a young man of about twenty wearing a baseball cap. He was a tailor. No one could afford to pay for the clothes he made, he told us, except by barter. For a pair of trousers he charged two chickens.

He cycled with us for half an hour along a smooth path, complaining to Colum of the injustice of a world which had randomly allotted us the riches of Europe and him the cash-free backwaters of Zambia. He said nothing to me until I heard him remarking on my ability to ride a bicycle. I pedalled up behind him.

'Why do Zambian women not cycle?' I asked, wondering whether he would categorise it as a cultural difference or a gender imbalance that would one day be remedied.

'Because they are lazy and indolent,' he shouted back at me. 'They are totally dependent on their husbands.'

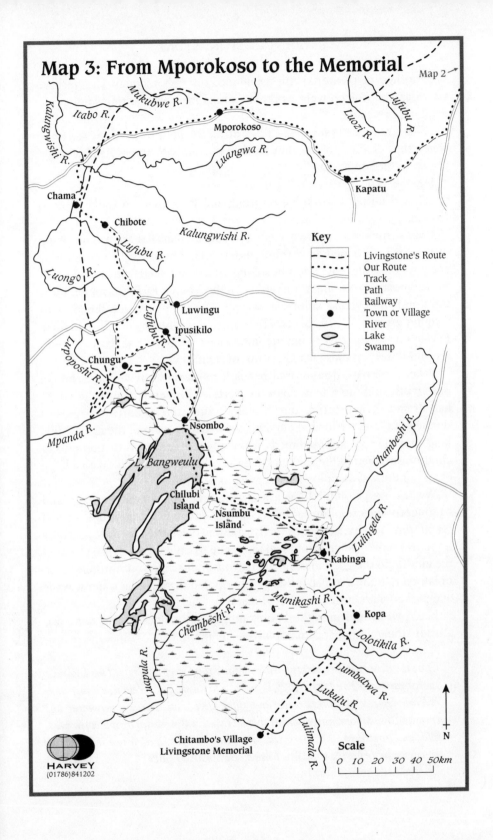

Map 3: From Mporokoso to the Memorial

Map 2

Mukubwe R.

Itabo R.

Kalungwishi R.

Luozi R.

Lufubu R.

Mporokoso

Luangwa R.

Kapatu

Chama

Chibote

Kalungwishi R.

Lufubu R.

Luongo R.

Lupoposhi R.

Lufubu R.

Luwingu

Ipusikilo

Chungu

Mpanda R.

Nsombo

Chambeshi R.

L. Bangweulu

Lulingela R.

Chilubi Island

Nsumbu Island

Kabinga

Munikashi R.

Kopa

Chambeshi R.

Lolotikila R.

Luapula R.

Lumbatwa R.

Lukulu R.

Lulimala R.

Chitambo's Village
Livingstone Memorial

Key

Livingstone's Route
Our Route
Track
Path
Railway
● Town or Village
River
Lake
Swamp

Scale

0   10   20   30   40   50km

N

HARVEY
(01786)841202

Snapshots of a hundred villages flooded through my mind. Everywhere we went, the women were working and the men were sitting smoking or drinking or talking.

'That's not true,' I snapped. 'They do all the hard work. They fetch the water, they do the cooking, they work in the fields. Whereas Zambian men just sit in the sun all day.'

He swerved slightly.

'That is all light work,' he retorted, and from then on spoke only to Colum.

I was surprised at my own anger. It made me realise there was one issue over which I retained an absolute moral certainty to rival Livingstone's, and it was an issue that underpinned the societies through which we moved: the subjugation of women. To put it simply, when it came to women I was right and the cycling tailor was wrong. Yet as my temper ebbed, mild disquiet grew in its place. Men's lives were so visible; women's so hidden. Perhaps it was too easy to impute indolence to those whose lives we could see and misery to those who kept out of sight.

Where the path disappeared beneath the water, our young Zambian misogynist drew to a halt. Soon we were knee-deep amongst the reeds, half-dragging, half-lifting our bicycles. After ten minutes the grasses thinned out, and we looked out across the main stream of the Luena. In a long, thin inlet amongst the reeds, leaky dug-out canoes were moored and children splashed in the shallows. On the other side a woman with a large cloth bundle was stepping into a canoe to be ferried across.

We balanced Colum's bicycle sideways across one of the dug-outs, and he gingerly lowered himself in behind it. For the first time since we had set off from Tabora, he looked really frightened. He tried to make his lanky frame as small as possible, but still the canoe wobbled. Grimly, he clamped the bicycle to the gunwales. As the narrow craft surged out into the river, I realised that the handlebar that gently rippled through the water was the one packed with our emergency dollars.

Later, we would miss the luxury of dug-out canoes. Livingstone was already doing without them in places.

Cross the River Lithabo, thirty yards wide and thigh deep… Crossed the Lopanza, twelve yards wide and waist deep, being now in flood. The Lolela was before us in half an hour, eight yards wide and thigh deep, both streams perennial and embowered in tall umbrageous trees that love wet… We crossed a rivulet ten yards wide and thigh deep, and afterwards in an hour and a half came to a sedgy stream which we could barely cross. We hauled a cow across bodily.

Now, with rain more or less every day, many rivers had burst their banks and extended across the surrounding flood plains. Our journey fell into a pattern: tramping through marshy grasslands; clambering into dug-outs to cross the main stream, and then floundering knee-deep in water to recover our bicycles and luggage to drier ground. Massing cloud and lightning often caused us to scamper along the paths until we found a hut. To the rolling of thunder and to the first heavy explosions of raindrops, we pleaded for shelter and were never turned away. But for Livingstone, the slave-traders had left fear and distrust in their wake.

> *Arrived at Chama's. Chama's brother ran before us to the chief's stockade, and made all the women flee, which they did leaving their chickens damless. We gave him two handsome cloths, one for himself and one for Chama, and said we wanted food only, and would buy it. They are accustomed to the bullying of half-castes, who take what they like for nothing. They are alarmed at our behaviour today, so we took quiet possession of the stockade, as the place that they put us in was on the open defenceless plain. Seventeen human skulls ornament the stockade.*

*   *   *

Near Chibote we argued. I don't remember what it was about. The rain was falling heavily, and the wind had a biting chill. Angry, I cycled on alone as Colum dawdled. Before long, worry overcame me and I returned for him.

The track was straight and gently inclined, so I was able to see some distance. The rain was a grey curtain, but I was still able to make out his shape hunched at the side of the track, his bicycle lying beside him. As I approached, I saw that he was shaking violently with the cold, every item of his clothing sodden. Spread out beside him on his waterproof were the toolkit and the bits of a brake. He looked up into my face as I drew up. There was a moment's silence.

'Come on, Colum, let's get on to Chibote.' He sighed deeply, and looked down in despair at the collection of parts. With a juddering hand he attempted to replace a tiny brake spring.

'Come on,' I said gently, 'you can do it later.'

The heavy rain continued as we arrived at Chibote. That name, which had become for me an icon of rural impenetrability, was in reality a peaceful scattering of buildings around a large mission occupied by a single priest. We spent two nights there, relieved to have a small, dry mission room in which our tent was necessary only as protection against the mosquitoes.

Christmas Day – I thank the good Lord for the good gift of His Son Jesus Christ our Lord. Slaughtered an ox, and gave a fundo and a half to each of the party. This is our great day, so we rest. It is cold and wet, day and night. The headman is gracious and generous, which is very pleasant compared with awe, awe and refusing to sell, or stop to speak, or show the way.

We collected as many mangoes as we could carry from beneath the heavily laden trees, and bought bread and eggs in the small village near the mission. On the first evening, we sat beneath the overhanging roof outside our room and cooked by the light of a candle. Colum drew out a pineapple which he had bought from a rain-drenched man on the path to the mission and we argued in low, vicious tones about how best to cut it up. In the end, I seized the fruit and threw it into the heavy darkness. Colum fell silent, and looked away.

The next day his silence continued. Soon after breakfast, he turned to the bicycles. I watched him surreptitiously for any moves towards reconciliation, but his preoccupation was total. He sat cross-legged among the assorted bits, and one-by-one, he worked through them, patiently polishing and oiling each.

By lunch time the ritual was coming to an end. Finally he twanged each spoke for tautness, and made tiny adjustments. Then he looked at me.

'We can't afford to waste food.' His voice was mild. I watched him uncertainly. He reached inside a pannier and pulled out the pineapple. Then he grinned.

'I got to it last night just before the dogs did...'

*   *   *

Early the next morning, when the shadows were still long, we left Chibote and swept through hills and miniature valleys until we came to high, flat ground, where rivers meandered through wide meadows. At the Lofubu there was a bridge made of a few trees which lay a metre below the clear, fast waters.

Along among the usual low tree-covered hills of red and yellow and green schists – paths wet and slippery. Came to the Lofubu, fifteen yards broad and very deep, water clear, flowing north-west to join the Luena... We crossed by a bridge, and the donkey swam with men on each side of him...

On the other side we crossed a plain of silvery grass that swished in the breeze, its whispers mingling with the peaceful call of the birds. Banks of cloud formed and chased each other around the horizon's edge, but it remained clear and hot. For Livingstone, the cold and damp continued, and gradually took its toll on his party.

'*A man, ill and unable to come on, was left all night in the rain, without fire. We sent men back to carry him. Wet and cold.*' By the following morning, the man was dead. '*Came on at 6am... as we have been unable to buy food, through the illness and death of Chipangawazi, I camp here.*'

At last our path, which had threatened on occasions to disappear altogether, became a track. Women in brightly coloured cloths straightened up from where they were working in the fields to watch us pass. Children chased us through settlements. Soon we were passing through larger villages. Here, the houses had drooping straw roofs with wisps that nearly touched the ground, like the long hair of an old woman. Behind the straw we glimpsed coloured bricks or patterns painted onto white plaster.

In one village, three smartly dressed men signalled us to stop.

'We are visitors too,' one of them said. 'We've come to this village to tell them the news.'

'What news?' asked Colum.

'The good news,' the man replied, and he reached into his briefcase and drew out a book. 'It is all in the Bible,' he said and thrust a leaflet into my hand.

'We are Jehovah's Witnesses...'

In the middle of the afternoon we reached the wide, metalled road which cuts across this empty quarter of Zambia. Fleeing before a gathering storm we turned east towards Luwingu on a small detour from Livingstone's route. We left him irrevocably weakened but still full of hope. We would return to him again in a couple of days and find him making impassive notes about the wet and cold, about the incessant clouds and the multiplicity of rivulets that were gradually dragging at his health. We knew, however, that his worst obstacles were still to come.

22

In Luwingu
by Aisling

Their story is not graven only on stone over their native earth, but lives on far away, without visible symbol, woven into the stuff of other men's lives.
Pericles, on the Athenian dead

LUWINGU was melting under the warm streams of an erupting storm. The ground flowed like a chocolate river down the hill, and the iron roof of the rest house boiled angrily, spilling violent currents onto the earth below. Inside we struggled through a plate of tough meat, which the cook said was fowl, while the rain voiced a fervent applause.

Sliding downhill in the exhausted aftermath of the storm, we reached a dim and crowded bar. Men steamed at its busy tables and crammed their mouths with fingerfuls of sticky *nshima* bathed in meat juice. We squeezed around them and into a corner, relaxing with the exuberance and ordering food and beer.

This was the final pause in our journey; soon we would leave for the swamp and the unmapped places, bent on understanding the macabre details of a dying man's struggle. At the end of the journey would be death and before it would be fear, born mainly of our empty ignorance of the land to the south.

Luwingu, I knew, also marked the end of our quest to understand the modern mentality of Europeans in East Africa. We would surely meet no foreigners beyond here. There had not been many on our journey, but those we had met were deeply idiosyncratic: cynical old Hans; introspective Malcolm; frustrated Jan. And then Fritz and Thomas, very different from each other but both little more than adventurers.

Today's crusaders quivered at the thought of doing inadvertent harm, or gave up in the face of an immutable society they did not understand, or were interested primarily in a character-building experience before continuing their lives back at home. To embody the soul of Livingstone required an unfashionable absolutism. Only the missionaries had dared to embrace such a thing and even they were now taught, however absurdly, to confine their views to the religious and leave the cultural alone.

Yet was East Africa really rid of Livingstone's spirit? Not quite. There is one iniquity there that the *mzungu* cannot tolerate, exemplified by my forceful reaction to the cycling tailor's story of the legendary laziness of Zambian women. Now, above the chatter of the *hoteli,* voices that had been no more than whispers during our journey filled my mind: the murmurs of women always bent low in the distant cassava fields, or tending smoking fires, or in remote clearings fetching water; the noise of men at ease in their open-sided huts where the women do not go, or eating heartily, or drunk.

The sadness of women and the laughter of men.

An engine sounded, a door slammed, and in the entrance there stood a white man dressed in the customary khaki shorts and tee-shirt. Everyone greeted him as he slipped, smiling and nodding, through the packed benches and squeezed into a tiny space beside us.

'Sorry to barge in,' he said as he sat down heavily. 'There wasn't anywhere else to sit.' His accent was Scottish. He was overweight and his neck was slippery with sweat. His shirt was newly pressed, hair cut cruelly short.

I ordered another chip omelette and listened to his tales of the road from Lusaka, terrifying in the chaos of the rain.

'But I always stop in Luwingu, I've got a soft spot for this *hoteli,*' he confided, surveying the lively room in satisfaction. 'Other places open and close but this one, somehow, manages to extract a tiny profit and stay popular.'

We talked above the noise of a newly erupting storm that promised to maroon us all in the café for the evening. I don't remember his name so afterwards I christened him Angus. He was a development worker who had just been promoted to be in charge of his charity's work in the region. It was the first day of a project to study all the rural schemes now under his control.

He had a lot to impart about his plans and we were willing listeners.

'Tell me something,' I shouted back eventually, leaning sideways as he was served his bright yellow omelette, glistening with fat. There was a question that had niggled me for a while and I wished I had asked it of others we had met. 'Do you ever ask local people what they want?'

He drained the last of his beer. 'Yes, of course we do. Although it's not a silly question – a lot of people don't.'

'So?'

'So... they want money.' He slid the empty bottle to the end of the table. 'But there's a trick to giving money.' He was intense. 'You've got to get it to the women rather than the men. Men spend money on beer and cigarettes; women spend money on health care and education.'

His eyes stared into mine with a sudden ferocity. Then he said, as if repeating a mantra: 'We *have* to get the power into the hands of the women.' And he shovelled in a few rubbery mouthfuls.

'Our charity now has women's representatives at all the villages we work in. In fact, we refuse to give the villages any help unless they put women on their committees. They treat women atrociously. I tell you…' he waved for more beer '… I tell you we're causing real upheaval.' There was satisfaction in his voice.

With a thump an inebriated man fell into a newly empty seat beside us and began to explain the country's problems from his own perspective. Our conversation with Angus was over. But it was enough. I could already feel the power behind what he said. He was part of a movement of enormous significance for rural Africa.

I knew first-hand the truth of his claims. We had witnessed our male guides drunk on their earnings while their wives longed for mosquito nets for their children. But I also realised that he articulated an idea that, back in Europe, could seem the merely obvious, the trivially true. In East Africa one could recognise that such agendas could indeed destroy the fabric of village society, just as Livingstone had wanted to do in order to plant Christianity. It was a potent feminism, though here it seemed empty of understanding of the male. It declared war on his offences but could not explain why he committed them.

Even Angus's certainty had significance. He was not troubled by relativism or introspection. He was too young to rue his impotence as Hans the White Father was doing in Mbala. He was too immersed in theory to be confused by the messy reality as Jan the doctor had been. And he was more thick-skinned than Malcolm who was burdened by every shadow he cast on village life.

Angus perceived a gross wrong and he was there to put it right. There would be many more like him. Across a century and a quarter Angus and his compatriot Livingstone could glimpse each other and recognise what they saw.

Log Book Extracts

DAY 47 – Friday 10th January

PHASE 3

REST DAY AT LUWINGU
   Staying in council rest house.

DISTANCE TRAVELLED: None

BICYCLES: Bought oil for chains. Stripped bicycle gears and cleaned.

WEATHER: Sun, cloud. Heavy rain with lightning pm.

HEALTH: Aisling has blocked nose, sore throat. Queasiness and then
   vomits after dinner. Forgot malaria tablets yesterday, so took today.

EXPENDITURE: Bicycle oil Kw1,000; Candles Kw800; Breakfast
   Kw1,500; Provisions for 3 days Kw31,500 (golden syrup, pilchards,
   corned beef, bananas, rice, nuts, tomatoes); Lunch Kw2,000; Dinner
   Kw3,500.

FOOD: Breakfast: tea and bread
        Lunch: chicken, egg, rice
        Evening meal: rice, chips, omelette and beef

COMMENT: Planning of Phase 4 of the journey. Over the next four
   days we will trace Livingstone's detour to the south-west. Maps we
   saw at Jan's house were a help, but by now, Livingstone's exact route
   is open to interpretation. We will again be going into an empty area,
   and will have to carry food to see us through. We have planned each
   meal, but will be very heavily laden. Due to the good track surfaces
   so far, we have gained some time, and have now revised our arrival
   at the Livingstone Memorial from 26/1 to 22/1. However, we
   forecast that we will be $90 short, so changed $90 for Kwacha with
   shopkeeper. We will have to make inroads into our emergency funds.

*   *   *

DAY 48 – Saturday 11th January

PHASE 3

FROM: Luwingu

TO: Chungu

CAMP: Tent in crumbling medical centre staff house.

POSITION: 29°38'18" E
                        10°35'42" S

TIME CYCLING: 7 hours 10 minutes

DISTANCE TRAVELLED: 70km

AVERAGE SPEED: 10km/hr

ROUTE: Took main road west from Luwingu. After 35km turned south along track towards Chungu.

TRACK CONDITION: Good, gritted surface on main road. Reasonable, though muddy, on track downhill to Chungu.

BICYCLES – PERFORMANCE: Got muddy in continuous rain

BICYCLES – MAINTENANCE: Checked tyres, chains

WEATHER: Rain, heavy and light, all day

HEALTH: OK

EQUIPMENT: Candles running low

LANDSCAPE: Forest

EXPENDITURE: Bread Kw5,500; Envelopes Kw2,200; Breakfast Kw1,500

FLUID CONSUMPTION: 4 litres

FOOD: Breakfast: bread, jam, tea
            During day: bread, golden syrup, bananas
            Evening meal: egg curry, bread, fruit salad

COMMENT: Livingstone was at this point on today's date, 1873.

LIVINGSTONE: We rejoin Livingstone's route at the turning south towards Chungu.

23

From Luwingu to Chilubi Island
by Colum

*The pugnacious spirit is one of the necessities of life. When people have
little or none of it, they are subjected to indignity and loss.*
David Livingstone, December 1872

TEN WEEKS from now, Livingstone was to begin a despatch to Earl
Granville, the Foreign Secretary.

*I have the pleasure of reporting to your Lordship that on the ___, I succeeded
at last in reaching your remarkable fountains, each of which, at no great distance
off, becomes a large river. They rise at the base of a swell of land or earthen
mound, which can scarcely be called a hill, for it seems only about ___ feet above
the general level... Possibly these four gushing fountains may be the very same
that were mentioned to Herodotus... The geographical position of the mound
or low earthen hill, may for the present be taken as latitude ____ and longitude
____. The altitude above the sea ____.*

As protocol demanded, his communiqué to a senior government minister
was formal and brief. Livingstone nevertheless allowed himself a modest
note of triumph that his theory concerning the source of the Nile had, after
all, been correct.

But it was pure fantasy. The source of the Nile was to be discovered half
a continent away, and the latitude and longitude of that elusive prize were
to be furnished by another. Livingstone's despatch would remain forever
uncompleted, its carefully arranged blank spaces a testimony to the
dreams of a man for whom the line between hope and reality had become
blurred.

In the ten weeks since he had passed near modern Luwingu, terrible
changes had been wrought in the man. He had been ravaged by illness, he
was emaciated by sustained under-eating and he had become a beggar at
the mercy of others' generosity. By the time he wrote his despatch he was
child-like in his acceptance of the problems that beset him, and although

his grand purpose remained unwavering, his day-to-day activities had become vague and unfocussed.

After Luwingu, we were to watch these changes coming about. We were to see how hardship slowly unravelled and subtly modified the essential strands of his character – his fortitude, his obsession and his relationship with his God. In a rain-lashed hut on an island in Lake Bangweulu, we would at last be confronted with what was left of the man, a man for whom writing a fanciful despatch afforded some bittersweet comfort. In his mind's eye at least, he could walk the sunny uplands where the Nile rose.

*   *   *

I stretched the map out on the bed. Here at Luwingu we had to draw our own conclusions about where he went before he sat down to write his despatch. We could no longer rely on his journal alone, because David Livingstone was lost.

It was entitled *A Map of a Portion of Central Africa by Dr Livingstone, from his own Surveys, Drawings and Observations* and represented the Western World's total knowledge of Central Africa in 1874. This was the chart drawn up by cartographers in Britain after Livingstone's death. Their task had been to unravel his notes and observations, and to reconcile the measurements of latitude and longitude which the explorer had taken over the last seven years of his life.

Livingstone's record contained only one significant inaccuracy – an error which he was about to confront, and which would contribute to his decline towards death. On his arrival in Africa for the third and last time in 1866, he had set off inland across what is now northern Mozambique, and skirted around the southern end of Lake Malawi. He then headed north-west to investigate a large body of water of which he had heard. In July 1868, Livingstone at last stood on the shores of Lake Bangweulu, the first European ever to do so.

The rainy season had recently finished, and much of what he assumed was lake was no more than flooded swamp. Damaged survey equipment gave him erroneous readings and compounded his misjudgment of the lake's extent: he estimated it to be 230 kilometres from east to west. In fact, it is barely more than thirty.

Now, five years later, Livingstone was again approaching Lake Bangweulu, this time from the north. But his flawed perception of the geography was to have disastrous consequences – he was to spend the next four weeks wandering hopelessly in the swampy ground north of the lake, trying to find his way round to the southern shore, to the place where he believed he would find the Fountains of Herodotus.

*   *   *

We sped back west on the metalled road from Luwingu to rejoin Livingstone at his melancholy campsite. It rained heavily. Livingstone noted hopefully that the new moon was imminent, and that '*people assert that it will bring drier weather*'. But when we sheltered in a roadside church, the priest was adamant that tomorrow's new moon meant nothing but continued rain: 'After all, how can the moon's face ever become full again unless it is given a good wash?'

Later, we lunched on bread and syrup in the dripping forest and Livingstone's last cow died. '*People buy it for food, so it is not an entire loss.*' He was sanguine, although this must have been a terrible blow. His dysentery could be controlled to some extent by milk, but now he was deprived of his own source.

Deep in the damp forest we came to Chief Chungu's village. Livingstone's friendly overtures towards the chief were not, at first, successful.

'*When we prepared to visit Chungu we received a message that he had gone to his plantations to get millet. He then sent for us at 1pm to come, but on reaching the stockade, we found it being shut from terror. Chungu says that we should put his head on a pole... the terror that guns have inspired is extreme.*'

At last, however, Chief Chungu mastered his fear, and sent Livingstone a goat and a big basket of flour – a welcome present, for food was scarce. But despite the chief's cordiality, Livingstone did not seek advice about the best way round the lake. It was to prove a costly oversight: Livingstone began a pointless and debilitating detour to the south-west, floundering for two weeks across the flood plains. Finally he was thwarted by swollen rivers and forced to return once more to Chungu's village.

Early one morning we set out to trace Livingstone's detour, following a small path which led through the reeds of the Lopopussi flood plain where, knee-deep in the still water, we waited. The sun had just risen and the river glittered between the rushes. In the distance, tufty islands of forest floated on a bright cushion of mist. Beside us, each reed was encrusted with dew which shone like diamond dust. The spiders' webs were nets of silver thread.

After a short time, two slim dug-out canoes appeared, punted by sinewy men the colour of carved mahogany. With some misgiving we laid the bicycles across the narrow gunwales of one canoe and cautiously lowered ourselves into the second. It was extremely narrow – too narrow, in fact, to accommodate even the most economically built of buttocks. Our boatman hung his weight on the pole at an alarming angle, and the little craft thrust forward, ripples trailing from the bow, and an appreciable amount of water seeping through the hull.

We glided through a silent world of whispering reeds, and gradually I became aware of quiet, gurgling eddies as we approached the main stream. We came to a weir made of thin branches where, with movements of his hand, our boatman indicated that it was to trap the fish. When I slipped into the stream to help the canoe through, the clear warm water felt little different from the heavy warm air.

Over the weir and into a fast moving current. The canoes lurched, and the boatmen bobbed from side to side to keep them level. Here we passed another canoe – a volley of shouted greetings across the rapids – and back into a slow, deep-flowing section with water the colour of dark honey, where white and pink lilies ducked their heads.

On a slate-grey day of cloud and freezing rain, Livingstone crossed the main stream by a rickety bridge: '… *the bridge was 45 feet long, and showed the deep water; then 100 yards of flood thigh deep, and 200 or 300 yards of sponge. After this we crossed two rills called Linkanda and their sponges, the rills in flood 10 or 12 feet broad and thigh deep.'*

Even in these bleak and watery surroundings, he found reason for optimism: '*Cold and rainy weather, never saw the like; but this is amongst the sponges of the Nile and near the northern shores of Lake Bangweolu.'*

For us the day stayed bright and dry and we flew along winding paths splashed with the light that filtered through the forest canopy. We came to the Kalomboshi river – '*never was in such a spell of cold and rainy weather since Loanda in 1853'* – and crossed in a leaky rowing boat with a mother and her wide-eyed children. At the junction of the Kasie and the Mozinga, Livingstone recorded swollen rivers and extensive 'sponge'. Nowadays, a small bridge leads over the gently flowing river and a steep track leads up to the village of Katuta. It was Sunday. People dressed for church lazed in the shade of mango trees. The school headmaster shepherded us into his office and cross-examined us. We left him gasping with excitement that the great Christian and explorer had come to this, his own humble village.

The following day a local chief finally persuaded Livingstone that he would never reach the lake's southern shore by this route. So he began the long trudge back towards the Lopopussi, angry with himself, but reserving his venom for Chungu who, he was convinced, had knowingly let him set off on this time-wasting detour. He wrote in his journal that he had been… '*treated scurvily by Chungu… a worthless, terrified headman.'*

*　　　*　　　*

In a palace like a detached suburban house erected incongruously in the bush, the modern Chief Chungu was in residence. He is the grandson of the chief who played uneasy host to Livingstone 125 years before and, obligingly, he granted us an audience.

We waited at the palace gate and watched as preparations were made in the reception hut. The thatch swept down so that it almost touched the ground, but through the low gap we could see furniture being arranged and an old pair of feet, in an older pair of slippers, shuffling into place.

At last we were invited in, stooping so low under the thatch as to be almost kneeling. We emerged in a large circular hut supported by a ring of sturdy branches. Low stools were arranged between them to form a rough circle, open at one end, and opposite the opening sat a little old man on a faded deckchair. On his head was an embroidered fez. He wore a beige anorak and worn beige trousers covered by a piece of coloured, patterned cloth, like an apron. His knobbly hands were closed around a short, polished stick which lay across his knees.

We knelt and clapped, as the Bemba do. The chief acknowledged our traditional greeting with a brief nod, and a young man showed us to stools on the chief's right. Two other men, old and shrivelled, eyed us from stools on his left.

'I am the Chief Chungu's son. I speak some English.' The man, who wore a faded red tee-shirt and worn trousers, settled himself on a stool between us and the chief, who looked us up and down with lively, searching eyes. Then he spoke.

'What brings you to Chief Chungu's village?' the son asked.

'We're doing research on David Livingstone and on the last journey he made.' The man nodded and relayed my answer.

'And are you relatives of Dr Livingstone?'

'No, not relatives, just… just interested.'

The man translated and the chief nodded, readjusting his grip on the knobbled stick. There was a pause, and the chief spoke quietly to the two old men beside him. I turned to the interpreter again:

'Does the chief know that one of his ancestors met Livingstone?'

'Yes,' he replied, 'the chief has told me many times that he remembers his grandfather telling him the story… Livingstone was looking for the source of the Nile.'

'That's right,' I replied. 'It was his last wish, to find the source of the Nile.'

He gave a start as Chief Chungu administered an indignant prod with his stick and then hurriedly relayed our conversation. Then the Chief frowned and uttered a few words.

'Livingstone was sick... he died soon after. Chief Chungu wants to know what was the cause of his death?' the interpreter asked.

'In his journal he wrote that he was bleeding... he was an old man. He wore out really – nature took its toll...'

The man translated, but this time Chungu shook his head.

'My father does not understand this death. Nature does not make people die.'

I was perplexed. 'Yes it does – natural causes, you know, not because of an accident or anything...'

Again the man conferred with the chief, and the chief spoke with the two old men, who tutted and pursed their lips.

'Chief Chungu says that there is no such thing as a natural death...' I looked across at the two old men. They stared back, unblinking.

Soon after, we got up to leave. As we walked clumsily backwards towards the low fringe of the roof, I heard the chief's voice again.

'Chief Chungu wants to know if Livingstone mentions the chief's grandfather in the journal?' his son asked.

'Just his name,' I said, and I turned and ducked out into the night. It did not seem fair, somehow, to expose the petulance of an ailing old man.

Livingstone's outburst over Chungu was uncharacteristic, charged with the impotent rage of a man who had always been able to rely on his own resources, for the final word on his exact whereabouts. But now he was thwarted when he tried to use his sextant. Time and time again, his complaint was the same: '*No observations because of clouds and rain... Tried to observe lunars in vain; clouded over all, thick and muggy.*'

So Livingstone was thrown back on his memory of the geography and on the erroneous records of his previous visit. Day by day, his confusion mounted, as his references to being '*near the Chambeze*' demonstrated. He knew that this large river flowed into Lake Bangweulu from the north-east, but he was to wander for another eight weeks before he reached its banks.

In days gone by Livingstone had been infallible but now the thread of his reasoning had been broken and he had become rudderless. Though his will remained strong, he had started to wander with the vagueness of a failing old man.

*   *   *

On returning from his detour through Chungu's village Livingstone's irritation with the chief meant that he again omitted to ask him for his advice. This was unfortunate, because it meant that he struck out in the wrong direction once again, describing a second long detour to the south-east. This, at least, was more consistent with his vague understanding of the local geography, but within two days he was confronted with a new and desperately serious problem: '*Population all gone from the war of Chitoka with this Chitunkubwe.*'

There were few people to give him directions or to trade food for his beads and cotton, and his anger and uncertainty bubbled to the surface again. The old paranoia and distrust, hitherto reserved for unfortunate Europeans, was now focussed on the terrified natives whom he did find: '*It is trying beyond measure to be baffled by the natives lying and misleading us wherever they can. Their unfriendliness is made more trying by our being totally unable to observe for our position.*' They were strong words from a man whom posterity has credited with an unusual affinity with Africans.

A few days later, with a candidness that suggests the old man knew his infallibility was cracking, Livingstone made an extraordinary admission: '*I don't know where we are, and the people are deceitful in their statements,*' and, plaintively, '*unaccountably so, though we deal fairly and kindly*'. The next day, his confusion was pathetically apparent: '*The rivers are so numerous that there has been a scarcity of names. Here we have Loou, and Luena. We have had two Loous before, and another Luena.*'

To make matters worse, he was running out of food. At first, he sent back to the previous villages, only to be sent '*a wretched present of bad flour and a fowl, evidently meant to be rejected*'. Meanwhile, his men were combing the surrounding swamp for game with no success.

At the end of January he was compelled to slaughter his last two calves '*to give each a mouthful*'. Now he was totally dependent on others and the search for people became tinged with a new desperation: '*I resolved to send out scouts South, South-East and South-West*'. In a flash of optimism or self-delusion he added: '*The music of the singing birds, the music of the turtle doves, and the screaming of the francolin proclaim man to be near.*'

In fact he was wandering in what, even today, is an empty area. His guides returned with talk of nothing but endless, lonely swamp, and the sombre lake at the end of a day's march. It was too far and his resources were exhausted. For the second time he turned back, making for Chitunkubwe's village, near Chief Chungu's stockade.

As he retraced his steps the cold and wet persisted. '*Rain, rain, rain, as if it never tired on this watershed. The showers show little in the gauge, but keep every place wet and sloppy.*' But by now, the unrelenting hardship was more than just an irritation: '*I lose much blood, but it is a safety-valve for me, and I have no fever or other ailments...*' Day by day he was growing weaker. He no longer even had the strength to wade the rivers:

Carrying me across one of the broad sedgy rivers is really a very difficult task. One we crossed was at least 2000 feet broad, or more than 300 yards. The first part, the main stream, came up to Susi's mouth, and wetted my seat and legs. One held up my pistol behind, then one after another took a turn, and when he sank into a deep elephant's footprint, he required two to lift him, so as to gain a footing on the level... Susi had the first spell, then Farijala, then a tall, Arab-looking man, then Amoda... and each time I was lifted off bodily and put on another pair of stout willing shoulders, and fifty yards more put them out of breath: no wonder!

Soon the leader's failing health began to wear away his charisma: '*I arranged to go to our next River Luena... but another plan was formed by night... Not wishing to appear overbearing, I consented...*' For the first time in his life, Livingstone had surrendered his authority. It was Chuma and Susi, his two faithful lieutenants, who gently suggested 'the alternative plan' which Livingstone meekly accepted. His old inflexibility, the intolerance that had always precluded any voice of reason except his own, was gradually slipping away.

The last part of the march back to Chitunkubwe's village was completed on empty stomachs. They arrived in the rain on 5th February – a handful of travellers straggling in, skinny, wretched and filthy. Livingstone must have been pale by now, his dark eyes more sunken than ever. He was in no doubt now about the vulnerability of his situation. In his journal, he wrote: '*We are at Chitunkubwe's mercy.*'

At the chief's village Livingstone rested and obtained food. He also found time to brood on the '*half month lost in this wandering*'. It was only in passing that he remarked: '*I got lunars, for a wonder*'. But his sextant measurements must have horrified him; they showed him to be more than one hundred and forty kilometres west of where he thought he was. If he felt any dismay, however, he did not record it in his journal. It is almost as if the issue had become too big to contemplate and, like a child, he put away his most frightening problem for consideration another day.

With Chitunkubwe's guides Livingstone made quicker progress. He had resolved to make for Matipa, a chief whom he understood to be at the northern tip of the lake. He retraced some of his previous route east, but then took a more northerly path which skirted the worst of the 'sponges'. Nowadays, a modern track leads north from near the site of old Chitunkubwe's village. After some kilometres, you can turn east on a rocky path which roughly corresponds to Livingstone's route. By lunchtime, we had emerged on the main track leading south to Nsombo. It was just to the east of this fishing village that Livingstone caught his first glimpse of Lake Bangweulu since 1868.

*   *   *

We reached Nsombo in the late afternoon, fleeing before a gun-metal sky. At the edge of the village we heard the roaring of the rain working up behind us through the bush. Within a minute the deluge had engulfed us, and we struggled forward in a new medium, a turbulent mixture of air and water.

The gently inclined track was soon a river axle-deep. Night came abruptly with the storm, and through the thundering darkness we shouted warnings to each other about rapids which threatened to sweep us off our feet, and about potholes transformed into gushing waterfalls.

A dark form careered past me. I paused in mid-stream, dumbfounded. In the next flash of lightning I saw a man on a bicycle coasting down the main torrent, a miracle of perseverance and balance, with the black water surging and bubbling just below his wheel axles. His sodden clothes were clinging to his stark form and his glistening face was puckered with a mixture of terror and intense concentration.

We stumbled on the government rest house and were installed in a small clean rondavel. I dragged the bicycles in from the rain, and unpacked the last of our food. Everything was sodden. Outside the rain abated, and a star shone in the washed-down sky. I crossed the mud to where a light flickered on a dark veranda. From inside came comforting noises of a meal being prepared, and in the gloomy dining room Aisling was asleep, her head on the table.

*   *   *

Chief Chaluba sat with his knees apart, his hands resting on his stick. His plump face was unshaven, and he wore a soft felt hat. The man who had announced himself to be 'the private secretary to the chief' smiled ingratiatingly. He was thin, arrayed on his chair like a bundle of dry sticks.

The young woman who served us dinner the previous evening had summoned us to the veranda of the rest house for this audience with the chief at 7am. We were muzzy with sleep and had pulled on clothes that were still uncomfortably wet. The chief eyed us and then spoke to his private secretary.

'So what brings you to these parts?' the private secretary asked, his grin widening. We explained our project, the private secretary translated and the chief nodded, his eyes slipping past us. How long were we staying, he wanted to know, and could he have our addresses?

There was a pause as the private secretary laboured over a note-book, and then the chief spoke again, addressing his question to the grey horizon. The secretary hesitated before translating, and his smile wavered. 'The chief wants to know what gift you will give him as a remembrance of your visit?' The chief listened as our excuses were translated. Then with a curt nod, he got up and left. We watched as he and his secretary picked their cautious way amongst the puddles on the muddy track.

'It is a shameful thing. He always comes here when he hears that there are visitors.' The young woman's voice was quiet but trembled with feeling. 'It is a truly shameful thing that he should come and ask you for money.' With short, angry strokes she swept around our chairs. 'After all, it is not as if he is going to do anything for you.'

After breakfast we went into the village. A large, battered lorry dominated the main street, one back wheel deep in the mud. A small knot of people were deliberating about what could be done, their fitful conversation progressing in low, resigned tones. A little apart from the group stood the chief in a scruffy hat and worn jacket, its collar turned up against the cold.

*   *   *

'We can't pay that much for fish and rice...'

Aisling was exasperated. The restaurant-keeper was crestfallen. We were his only customers.

'But the season is finished – fish are difficult to get...'

It was true that the season was finished, but in the market the rickety tables were piled high with fish. We turned to go.

'No wait... How much will you pay then?' We returned to our seats. 'It's just that times are so hard...' We nodded. 'And in this town, well, it's...' He shook his head and carried on setting the table.

Nsombo was a desolate place, where hope seemed to have dissipated into the marshes that lay beyond. Amongst the people on the grey, dusty main street there was an unfocussed, self-destructive energy. Young men loafed around the shop fronts and watched us coldly; sullen women gathered in knots and fell silent as we passed. In the market a drunk man followed us with a group of jeering boys in his wake.

The restaurant-keeper brought us our meal. Now that our quarrel was over he seemed keen to chat. 'Living here is tough nowadays,' he continued. 'The fish are smaller and there are far fewer than there used to be.' In colonial days, Nsombo had been a thriving port. There were colonial buildings set discreetly back from the main street, and there was even a canal linking the village to the lake, about a kilometre away. But now the buildings were derelict and the canal had silted up. Nsombo was a shadow of its former self.

His work complete, the restaurant-keeper sat down at the table.

'In season it's not so bad. But when the fishing is finished, there's nothing to do. The people here live by fish, so for three months they have to fish outside the law, or go hungry.'

'So people go on fishing?'

He shrugged. 'Well… they have to survive.' He gazed out through the window. 'It is harder, of course. But the police have only got two boats to cover the entire lake, and they never have any petrol… And there are other ways of not starving…'

I looked at him.

'They rob. They fight. Last week they beat up a policeman, and there was a gun battle here in the street.' He rose and started clearing our plates.

From where I was sitting I could see out through the door, past the broken buildings, past the rusting wreck of a car, as far as the grey police station, with its gaping windows and tumbledown fencing. A few trees still held on there. Beyond, there was unspeakable flatness and the howling stillness of the marshes.

The restaurant-keeper was absently wiping a plate as he, too, stared out at the wasteland. 'Yes, the police got him in the end. The man died out there in the marshes, from a bullet wound.' It was a fitting end for the random violence: a spreading numbness and a life draining out across the cold grey mud.

*   *   *

'*Public punishment to Chirango for stealing beads, fifteen cuts…*'

Livingstone's brutality would have surprised his party: as a rule, he did not resort to corporal punishment unless severely provoked. But he was changing: his charisma was fading and that goaded him into a desolate and savage anger. The following day was Sunday. His small party must have formed a dispirited and cowed congregation at the service he conducted beneath a grey sky in the endless marsh. Afterwards, they killed a goat. It was their last. More than one of them must have wondered what they were going to eat after that. Livingstone had further problems of his own: '*I remain because of an excessive haemorrhagic discharge…*'

This time there was no talk of 'safety-valves'. He was in a fatalistic frame of mind, a circumstance which afforded him a rare moment of detachment: '*If the good Lord gives me favour, and permits me to finish my work, I shall thank and bless Him, though it has cost me untold toil, pain and travel; this trip has made my hair all grey.*'

For almost two weeks he loitered on the bleak shoreline. '*We wait hungry and cold for the return of the men who have gone to Matipa, and hope that the good Lord will grant us influence with this man.*' The chief, Livingstone hoped, would be persuaded to send him canoes from the island where he had his stockade.

In the meantime Livingstone filled his journal with the day-to-day difficulties he was facing: '*A cold wet morning keeps us in this uncomfortable spot. When it clears up we go to an old stockade, to be near an islet to buy food. The people, knowing our need, are extortionate.*' Later, he wrote: '*The people bring food, but hold out for cloth, which is unfortunate.*'

When his messengers finally trailed in, he greeted their excuses with scorn: '*Our men have returned today, having obeyed the native who told them to sleep instead of going to Matipa…*' At last, on 26th February, there was a note of triumph:

'*Susi returned this morning with good news from Matipa, who declares his willingness to carry us… for the five bundles of copper wire I offered.*'

*   *   *

'So how much will it cost?'

'We will talk about that later. Let me arrange matters first.' Chief Chaluba's private secretary smiled a slow, lazy smile. His nose was sharp and his eyes were narrow.

'OK. You come and find me when you have your canoes. We will need at least two.' And I turned, and walked back through the curious crowd that had gathered around us.

Later I sat on the steps of our hut and worked on the bicycles. A watery sun had broken through and the ground steamed. The private secretary approached silently and I gave a start when he spoke.

'Fine bicycles.'

'Yes.' I returned to oiling a chain.

'I have found some men who will take you to Chilubi.'

I looked up. Chilubi Island lay adjacent to Matipa's Isle, separated by a channel only a few metres wide. The private secretary's mouth smiled, but his eyes remained level and steady. 'We can go tomorrow.'

'And how long will it take?'

'Very quick – just a few hours.'

'How much?'

'We discuss that tomorrow.' And then he walked away and I was staring at his back. I got up and wiped my hands on my trousers. 'Wait…'

He half turned and looked at me enquiringly.

'What time tomorrow?'

'Sunrise.'

I never saw the private secretary again. The following day, we set out in a small motor boat with a priest. He was returning to his parish on Chilubi Island.

We nosed down the canal from Nsombo, our bicycles and panniers piled in the bow. In places, I got out to manhandle the small boat over bars of sand. Before long, we had emerged from the canal mouth and were on the lake.

The flatness was mesmerising. The lake felt like a high place. No mountains broke the horizon: the water and sky were the same endless, unbroken grey. As the land receded behind us we seemed to be locked motionless at the focus of a colourless, concentric world, the water slipping silently underneath us.

We passed lone fishermen punting their boats across the shallow water – sharp, upright silhouettes against the low, grey perspectives. They had been camping on distant slivers of island. It was on one of these reedy strips of mud that Livingstone and his group passed an uncomfortable night. '*We are on a miserable dirty fishy island called Motovinza; all are damp.*' It was not until the following day that he arrived at Matipa's Isle – '*the miserable weather rained constantly on our landing...*'

On his previous visit to Lake Bangweulu, Livingstone had been close to this point, and had even recorded the position of Chilubi Island. But now, blighted by the errors in his measurements, he believed himself to be far away from anywhere he might have known. It was probably for this reason that he failed to recognise Chilubi, separated from Matipa's Isle by that channel, so narrow that you can step across it.

During his time at Matipa's encampment perhaps he did hear of the island that was only a few kilometres away. Perhaps the name of Chilubi even triggered unease in his mind, the faint but uncomfortable recollection that things somehow didn't fit. But if that was the case, he was quick to dismiss his reservations and absorb himself in the organisation of the next leg of his journey.

Log Book Extracts

DAY 53 – Thursday 16th January

PHASE 4

REST DAY ON CHILUBI ISLAND
  Staying at Santa Maria Mission.

DISTANCE TRAVELLED: None

BICYCLES: Oiled chains (bicycles not used since Nsombo).

WEATHER: Sunny.

HEALTH: Colum's shoulder is troubling him – he thinks he strained it getting the bikes out of the boat. Took weekly malaria tablets.

EQUIPMENT: Repacking of panniers. Sharpened machete.

EXPENDITURE: Guides Kw55,000; Boat fuel Kw100,000; Boat hire Kw30,000; Santa Maria Mission board and food Kw20,000

FOOD: Lunch: maize, bread, mango jam
        Evening meal: beans, rice, *nshima*, meat, cabbage

COMMENT: The cost of chartering a boat is wildly expensive. The cost of the two guides is also astronomically high because they insist on being paid the grossly inflated government rate, including huge charges for being away overnight. This has further depleted our dwindling money.

*   *   *

DAY 54 – Friday 17th January

PHASE 4

FROM: Chilubi Island

TO: Kasenga (a small settlement on the east bank of the Chambeshi)

CAMP: By a hut, under a mango tree.

POSITION: 30°40'57" E
            11°20'00" S

TIME TRAVELLING: 11 hours 30 minutes (by boat)

DISTANCE TRAVELLED: difficult to assess.

ROUTE: Boat from Chilubi Island past Nsumbu Island (Livingstone's 'Matipa's Isle'), through extensive swamps to the mouth of Lake Chaya, then up River Chambeshi.

BICYCLES: Sat in the front of the boat.

WEATHER: Rain, alternately light and heavy, until mid-afternoon, when the cloud broke up.

HEALTH: Both of us have sore backsides after a day in the boat. Colum has recurring indigestion.

EQUIPMENT: Had to use foam mattress as an additional waterproof. Changed torch batteries.

LANDSCAPE: Tall papyrus and thick grasses for much of the day, with stretches of open water as we approached the river.

EXPENDITURE: None

FLUID CONSUMPTION: None

FOOD: Breakfast: bread and mango jam at Santa Maria Mission
During day: bread, mangoes, some peanuts
Evening meal: rice, pilchards, corned beef, cocoa

COMMENT: Our guides got lost, and have left us on the river bank still some way from Kabinga.

LIVINGSTONE: Livingstone also stayed in this village (Kasenga). One of his canoes sank in the Chambeshi; a woman was lost, and his donkey saddle.

24

From Chilubi Island to Kopa
by Colum

These are people come to look for Livingstone, wherever he may be. By this paper they have freedom to roam in Kopa's chiefdom.
Document handed to Aisling and Colum by Chief Kopa's Chancellor, January 1997

THE RIGOURS of the last months had weakened Livingstone and left their mark on his character. Unfamiliar emotions moved across his personality like patches of shadow and light across a landscape. He had known impatience, detachment and meekness, and his mental acuity had begun to peel away. By 12th March, when he sat down to write his despatch to Earl Granville, Livingstone was an altered man.

A softer man was emerging. 19th March was Livingstone's birthday: '*Thanks to the Almighty Preserver of men for sparing me thus far on the journey of life. Can I hope for ultimate success? So many obstacles have arisen. Let not Satan prevail over me, Oh! my good Lord Jesus.*'

Livingstone's prayer echoed with a new self-doubt, a nagging unease: he was invoking an altogether gentler God than the one who had inspired him to take his young family across the arid wastes of the Kalahari many years before. Then, he had written: '... *who that believes in Jesus would refuse to make a venture for such a Captain?* But on this last birthday his bleeding was profuse. In his relationship with his God, as well as in his dealings with men, Livingstone felt a new tentativeness. He had six weeks to live.

*   *   *

By the end of March Livingstone was attempting to rent canoes from Matipa to head south across the lake. '*He says that the five coils (which brought us here) will do to take us...*' But during negotiations with the chief, Livingstone was prevailed upon to go instead to visit Matipa's brother Kabinga, across the mouth of the River Chambeshi, on Bangweulu's eastern shore: '*... I am rather in a difficulty, as I fear I must give the five coils for a much shorter task; but it is best not to appear unfair...*'

Carefully, I unpicked the lining of my travel-stained shirt. The material was threadbare now, and ripped.

'A single, long day should get you to Kabinga, assuming you don't get lost,' the Zambian priest said. We were sitting on the balcony outside the old Santa Maria mission on Chilubi Island.

'Of course, you may have trouble getting through – the water is very low this year...'

Through the cloth I could feel the small, tightly wrapped package. I hoped vehemently that it had not leaked.

'You should employ Justin. He is the village headman, and knows the waterways well.'

Slowly, I eased the package out.

'And Quinchino. He should be your coxswain. He always travels with us when we go through the swamps. Of course, it normally takes a lot of fuel...' The priest's brow wrinkled briefly, and he threw me a questioning glance.

I pulled the tape from the package, and made a small incision with my knife. 'Will you accept dollars?'

'Oh yes, we're very happy with dollars.' I wasn't surprised. The value of the Zambian kwacha was sinking by the day, and life was expensive. This would use up the last of our hard currency, but it was the only way.

'*I gave Matipa a coil of thick brass wire and his wife a string of large neck beads, and explained my hurry to be off. He is now all fair, and promises largely...*'

Early on a grey, still morning we loaded the bicycles into the bow of a long narrow boat with an outboard engine. We glided out of the inlet, and were soon clear of the reeds and heading down a wide channel. The outline of the trees around the mission dissolved in the drizzle and we were alone, the dull whine of the engine swallowed by the vast emptiness around us.

Before long we entered a narrower channel and the rain became countless small explosions flickering on the surface of the water. We sought out ever smaller channels until the papyrus rushes were standing tall over the boat – huge banks of green and grey vegetation hemming us in. Once a tall, awkward bird with an orange beak a foot long peered at us, puzzled, through the reeds. The heavy rain continued and Aisling huddled under a waterproof. Justin, Quinchino and I were drenched, our muscles shuddering. We moved, reluctantly, only when we had to bale.

We punted for six hours to a little islet without a tree, and no sooner did we land than a pitiless pelting rain came on. We turned up a canoe to get shelter. We shall reach the Chambeze tomorrow. The wind tore the tent out of our hands, and damaged it too; the loads are all soaked, and with the cold it is bitterly uncomfortable... the wind on the rushes makes a sound like the waves of the sea.

The rain continued. Often, the grasses brushed our faces and through the thick vegetation we could hardly see the water under the hull. Towards mid-afternoon the waterways opened out – *'a grassy sea on all sides, with a few islets in the far distance'*. Now we passed through small lakes where crocodiles lay like logs amongst the reeds. Justin followed my gaze. 'People believe that old folk can turn into crocodiles at will.'

I nodded, too cold to answer.

'When someone is taken by a crocodile, the people will often beat to death an old person they suspect.'

I watched the crocodile until it slipped quietly beneath the surface and I was left watching widening grey ripples. All colour seemed to have drained from this place – the desolation was enough to provoke in Livingstone's mind the spectre of failure: *'Nothing earthly will make me give up my work in despair...'* And, as he had done on his birthday not many days before, he banished his fears by the invocation of his God: *'I encourage myself in the Lord my God and go forward.'*

*   *   *

We started at 7.30am and got into a large stream out of the Chambeze called Mabziwa. One canoe sank in it, and we lost a slave girl... Fished up three boxes and two guns, but the boxes being full of cartridges were much injured; we lost the donkey's saddle too. After this mishap, we crossed the Lubanseunsi, near its confluence with the Chambeze, 300 yards wide and three fathoms deep, and a slow current. We crossed the Chambeze. It is about 400 yards wide, with a quick, clear current of two knots, and three fathoms deep... The volume of water is enormous. We punted five hours, and then camped.

The Chambeshi is a wide, meandering river between steep, forested banks. Small settlements cling to the shore, and heavily laden canoes ply the shallows, bringing firewood downstream to the fishermen on the lake. At last the sun came out and for the first time that day my shivering abated.

We were lost. Justin's and Quinchino's continuous glancing at the bank, and the muttered conversation between them made it clear that they had missed a vital landmark. Our global positioning system confirmed that we were too far north-east. The sun was sinking and the river banks were now empty. We began the return down the river scanning the banks for signs of life and soon we saw a small canoe drawn up on a muddy shore.

In the last of the light we unloaded our bicycles, and an escort of children led us up a muddy slope. This was the village of Kasenga. There were a few mud buildings, some plots of maize, a heavily laden mango tree.

> *... we heard the merry voices of children. It was a large village, on a flat, which seems flooded at times, but much cassava is planted on mounds, made to protect the plants from the water, which stood in places in the village, but we got a dry spot for the tent. The people offered us huts. We had as usual a smart shower on the way to Kasenga...*

As we prepared our camp beside an old man's hut the sky turned red and then black. Slow, heavy rain began to fall. Inside the tent, we boiled mangoes and drank the last of the cocoa, our meagre meal illuminated by stutters of lightning.

*   *   *

As we struck camp the following morning, there was another downpour. Sodden, we slipped away through the trees towards Kabinga. The rain eased and the sky lightened, and for two hours, we cycled along a dyke path over a floodplain. It was perfectly still and we were alone in a wide, open, silent place, and we were elated. A long way off sedate trees lined the horizon. Near at hand, exotic black birds with tails that hung like kites hovered and swooped. Clusters of lemon yellow butterflies burst apart as we approached them. After two hours we reached the trees and came to Kabinga.

Chief Kabinga was dead. Protocol demanded that no new chief could be appointed until harvest time, when the old chief would be buried. We could not afford to wait.

'*Kabinga keeps his distance from us, and food is scarce; at noon he sent a man to salute me in his name.*'

Because some of his men had to return to Matipa to pay for a damaged canoe, Livingstone was delayed for a week at Kabinga. He used the time attempting to replenish his provisions. But, as before, he was subject to the whim of the chief –

> *... Kabinga attempts to sell a sheep at an exorbitant price, and says that he is weeping over his dead child... I bought a sheep for 100 strings of beads. I wished*

to begin the exchange by being generous, and told his messenger so; then a small quantity of maize was brought... The man said that Kabinga would send more when he had collected it.'

But Livingstone no longer had the stomach for hard bargaining: '*Sent Kabinga a cloth, and a message, but he is evidently a niggard, like Matipa: we must take him as we find him, there is no use in growling.'*

*   *   *

By 5th April, the party was again ready to move off. '*March from Kabinga's on the Chambeze, our luggage in canoes, and our men on land. We punted on a flood six feet deep, with many anthills all about, covered with trees. Course S.S.E. for five miles, across the River Lobingela, sluggish and about 300 yards wide.'*

Since Livingstone's day the water in Lake Bangweulu has drawn back. Even with the wet season well under way we found no more than a meandering river where Livingstone had encountered the swollen Lobingela estuary. Nowadays, not far from where he must have crossed, a track leads over a rough bridge.

On the bridge we paused a little, the rain falling steadily around us. In my mind's eye, I watched Livingstone's men sorting out the luggage, and saw the land party heading off into the waterlogged bush. And then I looked back to where he remained in his canoe, a pale, shrunken old man, crouched beside his baggage. For the best part of a week, Livingstone's anal bleeding had plagued him continuously and with a new intensity. Finally, the proud explorer had elected to continue by canoe because it had become too painful for him to continue by foot.

'*The fish eagle utters his weird voice in the morning, as if he lifted it up to a friend at a great distance, in a sort of falsetto key.'*

We turned our bicycles southwards down a narrow path that skirted the swamps. All day, we travelled through torrential rain. The path often disappeared, and we floundered in the swaying reeds, knee-deep in mud and water. Somewhere out to our right, Livingstone wandered in his canoe in the desolation of the swamp:

'*... and we pulled and punted six or seven hours S.W. in great difficulty, as the fishermen we saw refused to show us where the deep water lay... at a broad bank in shallow water near the river, we had to unload and haul...'*

For several days Livingstone and his land party lost contact with each other. But he showed no sign now of irritation at being lost; no impatience at the slowness of progress. Neither was there any railing at the watery wilderness in which he found himself. Perhaps it was because of his continued bleeding, and the gradual draining away of his strength that his writing was imbued with a simple matter-of-factness, and a quiet marvelling.

> *The whole country south of the Lake was covered with water, thickly dotted over with lotus leaves and rushes. It has a greenish appearance, and it might be well on a map to show spaces annually flooded by a broad wavy band, twenty, thirty and even forty miles from the permanent banks of the Lake; it might be coloured light green. The broad estuaries fifty or more miles, into which the rivers form themselves, might be coloured blue, but it is quite impossible at present to tell where the land ends and the Lake begins... The amount of water spread out over the country constantly excites my wonder; it is prodigious...*

Once, he touched on his old obsession: '*...it is all water, water everywhere... It is the Nile apparently enacting its inundations, even at its source...*' But now his mind glided easily over it, and it was soon forgotten.

'*A species of wild rice grows, but the people neither need it nor know it. A party of fishermen fled from us, but by coaxing them, we got them to show us deep water. They then showed us an islet, about thirty yards square, without wood, and desired us to sleep there. We went on, and then they decamped.*'

At the Muanakazi, we passed a grass lean-to on a low mound. A fire was smouldering beneath a rack of rubbery brown fish, and fine nets were stretched out between stout poles. Silent fishermen watched us as we pushed our bicycles past where their dug-out was tethered. The water was up to the top of my wheels. It was time to borrow canoes.

'*Pitiless, pelting showers wet everything, but near sunset we saw two fishermen paddling quickly off from an anthill, where we found a hut, plenty of fish, and some firewood... There we spent the night... Heavy rain. One canoe sank wetting everything in her.*'

Extract from Aisling's journal: Sunday 19th January

Crossed the Muanakazi in fishermen's canoes and arrived at Kopa at dusk. We are sitting under a mango tree and Colum is trying to coax the cooker into life. It is almost dark, and the rain is about to begin again. The tent and the other soaking contents of our panniers are beginning to mould. The bicycles are barely working. There is not enough food to last us, even on meagre rations, and it looks like there is not enough kerosene either. I am watching for wild dogs – Chief Kopa's minister warned that they prowl the area at night. The cooker has just burst into a smoky flame and Colum has put mangoes and the last of our milk powder and rice into a pot. We must leave at least half of what we cook for breakfast. The rain has started.

By 10th April, Livingstone was able to hide the truth from himself no longer. '*I am pale, bloodless and weak from bleeding profusely ever since the 31st March last: an artery gives off a copious stream, and takes away my strength. Oh, how I long to be permitted by the Over Power to finish my work.*' In his new candidness was the melancholy acknowledgement that he was dying.

25

Livingstone:
The Final Journal Entries

Whilst his servants were busy completing the hut for the night's encampment, the Doctor, who was lying in a shady place on the kitanda, ordered them to fetch one of the villagers. The chief of the place had disappeared, but the rest of his people seemed quite at their ease, and drew near to hear what was going to be said. They were asked if they knew of a hill on which four rivers took their rise...
Horace Waller's description of Susi's and Chuma's account of 25th April 1873, five days before Livingstone's death

ACCEPTANCE of the truth liberated Livingstone. In the last three weeks of his life he became a man with serenity of spirit. He wrote with fresh lucidity, as if he was seeing the world with new eyes. As he confronted death, he rejoiced in the detail of nature, the manifestation of God.

The rains were over, and he saw the sun break through. It was a time of rebirth, and he watched new life swarming in the receding waters. Between rivers, he passed through sunny prairies, where silvery grasses rippled in the breeze.

Now he could write freely of his declining health, his words resonating with the peaceful acceptance that the end was close. Once more he heard the haunting cry of the fish eagle and, gradually, his journal entries became shorter as his strength ebbed. Finally, near the very end, he managed only to write the date. Shorn of his physical strength, Livingstone found a new detachment, and at last saw himself for what he really was: a frail human being about to return to the arms of his God.

*   *   *

12th April: Cross the Muanakazi. It is about 100 or 130 yards broad, and deep. Great loss of αιμα made me so weak I could hardly walk, but tottered along nearly two hours, and then lay down quite done. Cooked coffee – our last – and went on, but in an hour I was compelled to lie down. Very unwilling to be carried, but on being pressed I allowed the men to help me along by relays to Chinama, where there is much cultivation. We camped in a garden of dura.

13th April: Found that we had slept on the right bank of the Lolotikila, a sluggish, marshy-looking river, very winding, but here going about south-west. The country is so very flat that the rivers down here are of necessity tortuous. Fish and other food are abundant, and the people civil and reasonable. They usually partake largely of the character of the chief, and this one, Gondochité, is polite. The sky is clearing and the SE wind is the lower stratum now. It is the dry season well begun. Seventy three inches is a higher rainfall than has been observed anywhere else, even in northern Manyuema; It was lower by inches than here far south on the watershed. In fact, this is the very heaviest rainfall known in these latitudes; between fifty and sixty is the maximum.

One sees interminable grassy prairies with lines of trees, occupying quarters of miles in breadth, and these give way to bouga or prairie again. The bouga is flooded annually, but its vegetation consists of dry land grasses. Other bouga extend out from the Lake up to forty miles, and are known by aquatic vegetation, such as lotus, papyrus, arums, rushes of different species, and many kinds of purely aquatic subaqueous plants which send up their flowers only to fructify in the sun, and then sink to ripen one bunch after another. Others, with great cabbage-looking leaves, seem to remain always at the bottom. The young of fish swarm, and bob in and out from the leaves. A species of soft moss grows on most plants, and seems to be good fodder for fishes, fitted by hooked or turned-up noses to guide it into their maws.

One species of fish has the lower jaw turned down into a hook, which enables the animal to hold its mouth close to the plant as it glides up or down, sucking in all the soft pulpy food.

The superabundance of gelatinous nutriment makes these swarmers increase in bulk with extraordinary rapidity, and the food supply of the people is plenteous in consequence. The number of fish caught by weirs, baskets and nets now, as the waters decline, is prodigious. The fish feel their element becoming insufficient for comfort, and retire from one bouga to another towards the Lake; the narrower parts are duly prepared by weirs to take advantage of their necessities; the sun heat seems to oppress them and force them to flee. With the south-east aerial current comes heat and sultriness.

A blanket is scarcely needed till the early hours of the morning, and here, after the turtle doves and cocks give out their warning calls to the watchful, the fish eagle lifts up his remarkable voice. It is pitched in a high, falsetto key, very loud, and seems as if he were calling to someone in the other world. Once heard, his weird unearthly voice can never be forgotten – it sticks to one through life.

We were four hours in being ferried over the Loitikila, or Lolotikila, in four small canoes, and then two hours south-west down its left bank to another river, where our camp has been formed…

I sent over a present to the headman, and a man returned with the information that he was ill at another village, but his wife would send canoes tomorrow to transport us over and set us on our way to Muanazambamba, south-west, and over Lolotikila again.

14th April: at a branch of the Lolotikila

15th April: Cross Lolotikila again (where it is only fifty yards) by canoes, and went south-west an hour. I, being very weak, had to be carried part of the way. Am glad of resting; αιμα flow copiously last night. A woman, the wife of the chief, gave a present of a goat and maize.

16th April: Went south-west two and a half hours, and crossed the Lombatwa River of 100 yards in width, rush deep, and flowing fast in aquatic vegetation, papyrus etc., into the Loitikila. In all about three hours south-west.

17th April: A tremendous rain after dark burst all our now rotten tents to shreds. Went on at 6.35am for three hours and I, who was suffering severely all night, had to rest. We got water near the surface by digging in yellow sand. Three hills now appear in the distance. Our course, SW three and three quarter hours to a village on the Kazya River. A Nyassa man declared that his father had brought the heavy rain of the 16th on us. We crossed three sponges.

18th April: On leaving the village on the Kazya we forded it and found it seventy yards broad, waist to breast deep all over. A large weir spanned it, and we went on the lower side of that. Much papyrus and other aquatic plants in it. Fish are returning now with the falling waters, and are guided into the rush-cones set for them. Crossed two large sponges, and I was forced to stop at a village after travelling SW for two hours: very ill all night, but remembered that the bleeding and most other ailments in this land are forms of fever. Took two scruple doses of quinine, and stopped it quite.

19th April: A fine bracing SE breeze kept me on the donkey across a broad sponge and over flats of white sandy soil and much cultivation for an hour and a half, when we stopped at a large village on the right bank of _____ , and men went over to the chief Muanzambamba to ask canoes to cross tomorrow. I am excessively weak, and but for the donkey could not move a hundred yards. It is not all pleasure this exploration. The Lavusi hills are a relief to the eye in this flat upland. Their forms show an igneous origin. The river Kazya comes from them and goes direct into the Lake. No observations now, owing to great weakness; I can scarcely hold the pencil, and my stick is a burden. Tent gone; the men build a good hut for me and the luggage. SW one and a half hour.

20th April, Sunday: Service. Cross over the sponge, Moenda, for food and to be near the headman of these parts, Moanzambamba. I am excessively weak. Village on Moenda sponge, 7am. Cross Lokulu in a canoe. The river is about thirty yards broad, very deep, and flowing in marshes two knots from SSE to NNW into Lake.

21st April: Tried to ride, but was forced to lie down, and they carried me back to vil. exhausted.

22nd April: Carried on kitanda over Buga SW 2¹/₄

23rd April

24th April

25th April

26th April

27th April: Knocked up quite, and remain — recover — sent to buy milch goats. We are on the banks of the Molilamo.

I turned the page in our tattered copy of Livingstone's journal. The next was blank. At some point during the night of 30th April, David Livingstone died.

26

The Four Fountains:
End of a Dream
by Aisling

DURING the last three weeks of his life Livingstone travelled less than five kilometres a day, around the marshy fringes of the lake. Since his day, Bangweulu has shrunk and we were able to follow his route on dry forest paths. The weather stayed bright and warm, and our progress was rapid. We crossed some rivers by canoe, and waded chest-deep through others, carrying our equipment and bicycles piece by piece above our heads. On the morning of the second day after we had left Kopa, we emerged at last on a track. We had come to the edge of our final map, and were unsure exactly where we were.

We cycled past it the first time. Only after the second look at the small turning did we realise that we had reached Livingstone's memorial. We laid our bicycles at the edge of the clearing, approached the monument and read the commemorative plaque. It was a quiet place, surrounded by tall trees like the pillars of a cathedral. The gentlest breeze stirred and patterns of light and shadow slid across the monument's smooth, grey surface. I sat down with my back against a tree and watched Colum, tanned, filthy, skinny, but now at last with his dream fulfilled. He was silent, inaccessible as usual. But for once, I did not resent it. Deep inside, I felt only a great emptiness.

We loitered there for some time, not quite ready to leave, but not really sure why we were staying. At last Colum drew the stump of a cigar from a dented case. I recognised it as Malcolm's. It must have been a gift, and Colum had kept it, like Malcolm, for a special occasion.

The noise of an engine sounded in the distance. A minibus drew up, and people spilled out: a handful of adults, children. Bantering English voices, and a shrill child shouting: 'We've found Livingstone, we've found Livingstone…'

Like animals woken from a slumber, we stirred. I picked myself up from the dusty ground and Colum drifted away from the monument towards a small knoll overlooking the clearing. He clambered 'up amongst the saplings and lay down amongst the tall grasses. A thin twist of smoke from his cigar was the only indication that he was there at all. I joined him, sitting down where I could survey the monument and our bicycles a little below us.

Time drifted by. Colum's eyes were half closed. The tourists below us had taken their photographs; the women and children had finished their biscuits; the men had emptied their cans of beer. They were restless now, ready to leave. At last they scrambled back into the minibus and the engine started.

Slowly, the bus reversed into the clearing. There was a dull crunching and the ecstatic screech of metal on metal. At first, I did not associate the noises with the crushing of Colum's bicycle. It was only absently that I observed it jerking as if in spasm as the vehicle rolled over its frame.

Colum's eyes snapped open and he sat upright. Instantly he was on his feet and bounding down the knoll. The special cigar had been crushed in his fist and then dropped, still smouldering. I put my heel on it and ground it into the dust before following him.

The minibus door sprang open and people spilled out. Now everyone was talking without listening. Arms waved, people gesticulated, children milled around. The men shouted instructions over the revving of the engine, and the bicycle continued to twitch as the minibus wheels rocked over it. Two women were talking at Colum, consoling hands moving to touch his arm, his shoulder. He remained an island of stillness, his face white. At last I heard him speak. His voice was far away, hollow: 'No, no, it really doesn't matter. We're going home now anyway...'

Colum sat in the minibus and I supervised as my bicycle was wheeled over, lifted up and secured on the roof rack. Then I turned my attention back to the ruin that had been Colum's bike. Piece by piece, I stripped the panniers from it, and finally, with the toolkit, I set about removing undamaged parts. At last, all that remained was the mangled frame and a buckled wheel: there was no point in taking them. I moved them to the edge of the clearing and laid them against a tree. In the minibus, I laid the salvaged bicycle chain across Colum's knee. He did not seem to notice. The engine started, and we pulled away.

*   *   *

The minibus was hot and full of noise.

'So where have you come from?' asked one of the women over the din.

'From Tabora.' Colum's voice was lifeless. Then, like a mantra: 'Following Livingstone... by bicycle.'

'That's nice... and is Tabora near here?' But then she turned away to quell a squabble between two of the children. When she turned back, she found that Colum's gaze was fixed steadfastly at the forest beyond the window. She addressed her next question to me.

'So why did he die here?'

'His obsession killed him. It wasn't a natural death.' I had answered without thinking.

'Oh...' She was quiet for a bit. Then: 'And why here, exactly?'

'He was looking for the source of the Nile...'

'He was a bit out, wasn't he?' There was a beery guffaw from the front seat. The children bickered and whined.

'Mummy, I want the toilet. Duncan hit me...'

'Well you'll just have to wait. Duncan, stop it.'

'Well, they didn't know in those days...' I said.

The adults fell silent and the minibus laboured on along the track, through the hottest part of the day. Then the driver belched, and said, half to himself: 'Blimey, what a place to die...'

Colum's eyes were shut, his head knocking gently against the window with every jolt. The other woman leant across and I was enveloped in the sickly smell of after-sun lotion. 'Is he still upset about his bike?' she hissed in my ear. 'We'll pay for a new one...'

'No, no, that really doesn't matter...' She nodded comfortably.

'It's just that...'

Reproachfully, she searched my face. I wanted to say that a small part of my husband had died when the bike was crushed, that we were leaving a small part of him at Livingstone's memorial.

'... well, he's not been very well.'

The woman smiled sympathetically and settled back in her seat.

*   *   *

'Well, did you find him then?'

'Who?'

'Livingstone... you said you were following him, didn't you?' The tourist winked mischievously at me as he handed down a pannier from the minibus roof.

'Well, I'm not really very sure...' My voice trailed off.

If we didn't find him, I wondered what we had to show for our efforts. He passed me the salvaged remains of Colum's bike.

We had certainly come to know Livingstone, intimately, through this journey. But what of his spirit, what of the absolutism that was his hallmark?

In my head, the moral certainty of Angus the development worker rang out like a clarion call: 'Empower the women of rural Africa.' I looked up as the tourist scrambled down.

'Yes… yes. I suppose we did find him in the end…' He nodded absently, wiping his hands on an oily rag. But I felt uneasy. Over the last few months we had also seen the misgivings and frustration of other Europeans in Africa. Angus's moral certainty was surrounded by a sea of confusion, of frustration. Amongst the disillusionment there seemed little with which Livingstone would have identified.

I leaned through the minibus door. Colum was where I had left him, sitting alone.

'Colum, come on. It's time to go. We're going to see Chitambo.' Slowly, he climbed out of the minibus and straightened up in the sunlight. In one hand he still clutched the chain.

Now the other tourists had arrived back from the small shop by the side of the track and were scrambling into the minibus. The man grinned and regarded us both: 'Shouldn't think there was much trace after… how long did you say?'

'125 years.'

'125 years,' he repeated.

'Well, actually there was…' but he had clambered into the vehicle and had started up the engine.

Livingstone had left footprints – of that I was certain: we had found them in abundance. His legacy lived on in the walls of the mission at Karema, and in a thousand vibrant mud churches up and down the land. It lived on, most spectacularly of all, in the monastery at Mvimwa.

But Livingstone's legacy went further than that. Prompted by the differences he saw between the life of the African and that of the European, he had established the precedent of active intervention in Africa. Many followed in his wake, some to address the needs of the natives, others to exploit the opportunities that Africa afforded. Today the tradition continues: missionaries and development workers still flock to remote areas to improve the people's lot.

There are other Europeans as well, who have come to exploit the uniqueness of Africa. They include the adventurers on bicycles. I looked at Colum's haggard face: we had travelled for two months searching for Livingstone's legacy and only now did I see where we fitted in. Really we were ourselves a tiny part of Livingstone's legacy – here so that we could be '*beyond every other man's line of things*'.

With a crunching of gears the minibus drew away, engulfing us in a cloud of dust. Now we were just two again, with a pile of battered panniers and a single bicycle. Colum had drifted into the shade of a tree and was standing with his arms limp, staring at the wheel that I had salvaged.

We had come as a camera, looking for the ripples that Livingstone had made. But in Africa, you have to get involved. I moved over to my husband and prised his fingers open to release the chain. He frowned slightly as I gently laid it in the grass by the side of the track.

THE END

Epilogue
by Aisling

HIS ROYAL Highness Chief Chitambo IV, in denim jeans and a trilby, sat behind his desk and surveyed his latest visitors. They were, as always, European tourists. They had come hoping for an audience with the man whose great grandfather met David Livingstone.

Chitambo told his guests a little about Livingstone and then something of the Chief Chitambo of 1873 who hosted Livingstone's death. He finished his performance with stories about life as a chief: of land disputes and the ancient rules by which he settles them; of the cases of sorcery he judges on Thursday afternoons. In return for this he asked his visitors for a present. It is a major infringement of tribal etiquette not to give a present to a chief, he explained.

In the hierarchy of chiefs, Chitambo is of middle rank. But while his betters across the lake dress in decaying raincoats and flip flops and sit in state under eaves of straw, Chitambo lives on a wealthy ranch where every building has been newly painted. Lorries load farm produce on his private road. Bodyguards lurk in doorways. For the ordinary visitor on a bicycle, instructions are painted on the dazzling gateposts:

HATS OUT
OFF THE BICYCLES

Chitambo is known around the Western world. He flies to Britain as the guest of environmental charities; he opens exhibitions. He has imbibed the European business way yet his appeal lies in his authenticity as an African chief – and in the legacy of Livingstone.

Livingstone would have approved of the incumbent Chief Chitambo. He had always wanted Africans to grow wealthy by selling their resources on the international market. But he would have been a little taken aback that the enterprising chief's resource was Livingstone himself.

'So,' said Chief Chitambo, 'you have come from the memorial?'

'Yes,' murmured Colum, 'from the memorial.' I gazed at him in surprise. He was staring at the floor. Chitambo nodded.

'Actually,' I said, 'we've come from a lot farther than that.' I smoothed our rumpled map onto the chief's desk. Overlying Livingstone's meandering black lines were now our own marks: coordinates, dates, names, question marks. The white expanses of ignorance that had appeared so large a few months ago seemed smaller now, criss-crossed with creases and stains. Chitambo looked at the map briefly, thanked us and then showed us to the door. He was not interested but then – why should he have been?

A lorry snorted into life outside. I ran and scrambled into the back – Chitambo had offered us a lift with his men who were driving to Lusaka. Colum followed slowly, walking beside the chief and abstractedly rummaging in his pockets and handing over something. Obviously our present had not been sufficient.

Colum climbed in beside me and sank inertly onto the hard bags of maize. The lorry jolted away.

'What are you thinking?' I asked.

'About Chief Chitambo. He told me it's only a few days' drive from Tabora. He wondered why we came the long way round.'

Appendix

Note: This table has been compiled from Livingstone's notes and from modern maps.

Livingstone's route	Date he passed through	Comparative itineraries, with modern names
Chapter 3: From Tabora to Ipole (25–27/11/96)		
Kwihara	24/8/72	Livingstone lived at Kwihara, 10km from modern Tabora.
Manga village	25/8/72	
Boma of Mayonda	26/8/72	
Ebulua village	27/8/72	
Kasekera village	27/8/72	Kasegera village. Livingstone headed SSW from Kasekera, passing a few kilometres to the W of the modern village of Tutuo.
Mayole village	28/8/72	Mkolye hill is approximately 5km SE of Tutuo, and probably took its name from Livingstone's Mayole.
Gunda		Modern Ugunda forest is in the vicinity of the modern village of Ipole.
Kasira village	31/8/72	Livingstone also referred to this village as Kisari's.
Pinta village	31/8/72	On old maps, Pantula village is shown 10km WSW of modern Sikonge and WNW of modern Ipole.
Chapter 5: From Ipole to Inyonga (29–30/11/96)		
Chikulu village	1/9/72	
Liwane village	4/9/72	
Manyara's village	5/9/72	
Ngombe nullah	8/9/72	On old maps, Gombe is shown on the Msima, a tributary of the Ugalla. However, using Livingstone's estimation of his own speed, he could not have reached the Msima by this stage. It is concluded that the Ngombe nullah (river) is the Ugalla, which he must have crossed NW of modern Koga.
Mwera's village	10/9/72	No direction is given, but it is likely that Livingstone struck W at this point. Modern Inyonga is approximately 30km S of his route.

Livingstone's route	Date he passed through	Comparative itineraries, with modern names

Chapter 6: From Inyonga to Mpanda (2–4/12/96)

'hills'	15/9/72	Livingstone passed through hills that are identifiable as the Kanono Escarpment and directly crossed the Metambo. He made no mention of the Urawira Escarpment, which suggests he was heading due W approximately 15km S of modern Urawira and Mpanda.
Metambo river	17/9/72	He crossed both the Mtambo and the Katuma, which confirms his position relative to modern Mpanda.

Chapter 8: From Mpanda to Sibwesa (7–8/12/96)

Merera's village	17/9/72	
Simba's village	20/9/72	
Boma Misonghi	24/9/72	The *Boma*, or fort, possibly took its name from the nearby Msaginia river.
Mpokwa river	29/9/72	
Katuma river	3/10/72	The Katuma runs across the flood plain to the E of modern Sibwesa.

Chapter 9: From Sibwesa (9–10/12/96)

Usowa district	10/10/72	Usowa district is to the N of Karema.
Kalema stockade	11/10/72	Karema village and mission

Chapter 12: To Kipili (13–14/12/96)

Fipa	14/10/72	Ufipa region
Mukembe	14/10/72	Mkombe village. Livingstone also referred to this village, at which he reached Lake Tanganyika, as Ukombe and Mokaria's. It is not modern Kabusa.
Mpimbwe mountain	17/10/72	Cape Mpimbwe is beside the modern village of Utinta. The modern village of Isaba is on the shoreline further S.
Kilando village	18/10/72	Kirando village
Kalenge Island	19/10/72	This is probably Manda Island. Kalungu is the name of the modern village on the shoreline opposite.
Kafungia inlet	21/10/72	Kafunje river
Pillar mountain		This is probably an island opposite modern Kipili. We walked from Kipili to Msamba.

Chapter 14: From Kipili to Mvimwa (16–20/12/96)

Motoshi district	23/10/72	Mtosi village
Linde village	24/10/72	Ninde village
Mesamba's village		Msamba village. We canoed from here to Kizumbi.

Livingstone's route	*Date he passed through*	*Comparative itineraries, with modern names*
Uringa river		Ulinga river
Kitanda Island	26/10/72	This is probably the island offshore of Kizumbi.
Chisumbe's village		Kizumbi village
Mpembe village		Wampembe village. We struck away from Livingstone's route here to avoid mountains impassable by bicycle, ultimately reaching Mvimwa. Livingstone persevered as far as modern Kasanga.
Thembwa river	29/10/72	Ntembwe river
Burungu region	29/10/72	
Kirila Island	30/10/72	This is probably Isinga Island.
Winelao	31/10/72	
Mulu river	1/11/72	
Liemba village	3/11/72	This is probably Kirambo village.
Luazi river	3/11/72	Loasi river

Chapter 16: From Mvimwa to Kasanga (23–26/12/96)

Kawa river		We rejoined Livingstone's route at the Kawa river, near modern Kasanga.

Chapter 17: From Kasanga to Mbala (27/12/96–1/1/97)

Kalambo river	11/11/72	The Kalambo river today marks the Tanzanian–Zambian border.
Mosapasi village	11/11/72	Musipazi river
Halocheche river	13/11/72	Lucheche river
Zombe's village	13/11/72	Modern Zombe is 25km NE of the position it occupied in Livingstone's day.
Lonzua river		From the Lunzua Livingstone headed SW. Our route was parallel to his and approximately 25km to his SE, through the modern town of Mbala.

Chapter 18: From Mbala (1–2/1/97)

Aeezy river	17/11/72	Chikana river
Mbette's village	18/11/72	Mbeta bay
Muanani river	24/11/72	
Mosingese river	24/11/72	Msengesi river
Molulwe river	24/11/72	Mululwe river
Loela river	26/11/72	Luela river
N'dari's village	27/11/72	
Lofu river	28/11/72	Lufubu river
Loozi river	29/11/72	Luozi river
Malembe hill	29/11/72	Malimbi-Muchinga Escarpment. Livingstone headed

Livingstone's route	*Date he passed through*	*Comparative itineraries, with modern names*
		W and NW as far as the Lupere, which he crossed on 14/12/72. Our route was parallel to his, through Senga Hill and Kapatu mission. We were approximately 25km to his S, on the other side of the watershed.

Chapter 19: To Mporokoso (2–3/1/97)

Chiwe's village	29/11/72	
Lovu Katanta river	1/12/72	
Kanomba river	3/12/72	Kangomba river
Lampussi river	3/12/72	This is probably a tributary of the Malunda river.
'mountain'	6/12/72	This is probably part of the Muchinga Escarpment, near the modern town of Mporokoso.

Chapter 21: From Mporokoso to Luwingu (5–8/1/97)

Sintilla village	6/12/72	
Motosi river	8/12/72	Mototoshi river. We crossed this river just outside Mporokoso.
Kafimbe's village	8/12/72	
Mukubwe river	11/12/72	Mukubwe river. Livingstone crossed this river twice more in the following two days.
Mokoe river	12/12/72	Mukubwe river
Mokobwe river	13/12/72	Mukubwe river
Mekanda river	13/12/72	
Menoba river	13/12/72	Mingomba river
Lupere river	14/12/72	Lupere river. Livingstone turned due S at about this point.
Lithabo river	15/12/72	Itabo river
Chikatula river	15/12/72	
Chipala village	15/12/72	
Lopanza river	16/12/72	Lupanga river
Lolela river	16/12/72	
Kasiane village	16/12/72	
Kisinga district	17/12/72	
Kalongwezi river	18/12/72	Livingstone reached the Kalungwishi about 1km E (upstream) of the Luena confluence, but W (downstream) of the Luangwa confluence. We crossed downstream of the Luena confluence.
Chama's village	21/12/72	We passed near modern Chama which is within a few kilometres of the position it occupied in Livingstone's day.
Misangwa river	23/12/72	Misangwa river

Livingstone's route	*Date he passed through*	*Comparative itineraries, with modern names*
Lopupussi river	24/12/72	This is the Mopoposhi, which Livingstone also called the Liposhoshi. It runs past Chibote village.
Lofubu river	26/12/72	Lofubu river
Luongo river	29/12/72	Luongo river
Kitila river		Chitila river
Situngula river	3/1/73	
Lopopozi river	4/1/73	Lupoposhi river. We took a detour E to the modern town of Luwingu.

Chapter 23: From Luwingu to Chilubi island (11–15/1/97)

Kizima river	4/1/73	
Kamolopa river	7/1/73	
Moenje village	8/1/73	
Nkulumuna river	9/1/73	Nkulumina river
Lopopozi river	9/1/73	Livingstone had crossed the Lupoposhi further upstream on 4/1/73.
Chungu's village	9/1/73	The modern village of Chungu is N of the Lupoposhi. From Chungu, Livingstone embarked on a detour to the SW.
Pinda river	12/1/73	Lipinda river
Kalambosi river	13/1/73	Kalamboshi river
Mozinga river	14/1/73	Moshinga river. The modern village of Katuta is at the junction of Moshinga and Kashie rivers.
Kasie river	14/1/73	Kashie river
Mpanda river	14/1/73	Mwampanda river
Monsinga river	15/1/73	Moshinga river
Lopopussi river	16/1/73	Livingstone returned to the Lupoposhi, but arrived downstream of the bridge he had used on 9/1/73, and so had to head upstream.
Mononse river	19/1/73	Munshishi river
Lovu river	20/1/73	This is probably the Kafinsa river. Having returned from his detour to the SW, Livingstone headed E. We avoided the empty lands in which Livingstone now wandered by taking a route further N, through modern Ipusikilo.
Malalanzi river	21/1/73	Mulalashi river
'another rivulet, possibly Lofu river'	22/1/73	This is probably the river Livingstone later called the Kwale.
'large river'	24/1/73	This is probably the Mufili river.
Loou river	25/1/73	Lufubu river. Livingstone repaired a bridge to get his party across.
	26–29/1/73	Livingstone headed S down the Lufubu but was clearly lost and did not record any names. He

Livingstone's route	Date he passed through	Comparative itineraries, with modern names
		probably crossed the Muchishe or its tributaries.
	1–2/2/73	Livingstone began to retrace his steps to Chitunkubwe's village, staying in the camp he had used on 28/1/73.
Lovu river	3/2/73	Lufubu river. Livingstone reached the bridge that he had repaired on 25/1/73. In error he believed himself to be 'on the Luena'.
Kwale river	4/2/73	This is possibly the river he crossed on 22/1/73.
Chitunkubwe's village	5/2/73	
Malalenzi river	5/2/73	Mulalashi river. This is the same river that Livingstone had crossed on 21/1/73. After resting at Chitunkubwe's, he set out E again.
Miwale river	9/2/73	This is probably the river Livingstone called the Kwale on 4/2/73.
Mofiri river	9/2/73	Mufili river
Methonua river	9/2/73	
Lofu river	10/2/73	Lufubu river. Livingstone crossed by the bridge he had used on 25/1/73 and 3/2/73.
Kachibwe stream	11/2/73	Livingstone 'reached old camp'.
Kasoso river	12/2/73	Chifunso river. Livingstone noted that it 'joins the Mokisya river'.
Mokisya river	12/2/73	Muchishe river
Mofungwe river	12/2/73	Fungwe river
'In site of Luena and Lake'	13/2/73	Livingstone was NW of modern Nsombo and could see Lake Bangweulu.
Luena river	19/2/73	From Nsombo we travelled by boat across the mouth of the Luena estuary to Chilubi Island.
Motovinza island	1/3/73	This unidentifiable islet is one of many at the edge of the lake.
Matipa's Isle	2/3/73	This is Nsumbu Island, which Livingstone also called Masumbo Island. It is separated from Chilubi by a channel a few metres wide.

Chapter 24: From Chilubi Island to Kopa (16–19/1/97)

Luangwa island	25/3/73	Luangwa island
Kasenga village	25/3/73	Kasenga, a tiny village on the banks of the Chambeshi.
Chambeze river	26/3/73	Chambeshi river
Mabziwa river	26/3/73	Mashiba river
Lubansensi river	26/3/73	Lubansenshi river
Kabinga's village	27/3/73	Kabinga's village
Lobingela river	5/4/73	Lulingela river
Muanakazi river	7/4/73	Munikashi river. The modern village of Kopa is between the Munikashi and Luitikila rivers.

Livingstone's route	*Date he passed through*	*Comparative itineraries, with modern names*

Chapter 25: Livingstone: The Final Journal Entries

Lolotikila river	13/4/73	Luitikila river
Muanzambamba's	15/4/73	Mwansabamba
Lombatwa river	16/4/73	Lumbatwa river
Kazya river	17/4/73	Kashia river
Lokulu river	20/4/73	Lukulu river
Kalunganjovu's village	26/4/73	
Molilamo river	26/4/73	Lulimala river
Chitambo's village	29/4/73	The modern village of Chitambo is approximately 25km E of the position it occupied in Livingstone's day. The Livingstone Memorial marks the spot where Livingstone died.

About the Authors

Colum Wilson spent his childhood in Scotland and Ireland, and was educated at Shrewsbury School. After a short army commission he studied at Durham University. He trained initially as a journalist and then took a master's degree before becoming a civil engineer, specialising in water and in development issues. He has worked in Sudan, Kyrgyzstan and Tanzania.

Aisling Irwin was educated at King Edward VI Camphill School and Wycliffe College, reading chemistry at Durham University, and the history and philosophy of science at London University. She has been a journalist for eight years, working for the *Times Higher Education Supplement* and as science correspondent for the *Daily Telegraph*.

Colum and Aisling are husband and wife. They enjoy exploring remote regions together. This is their second book.